Cherish the Challenge

TOM O'CONNELL

ISBN 979-8-88685-639-2 (paperback)
ISBN 979-8-88685-640-8 (digital)

Christian Faith Publishing
832 Park Avenue
Meadville, PA 16335
www.christianfaithpublishing.com

Printed in the United States of America

1

The Contest

I was fourteen years old and a nincompoop; the fact that I was six feet, two inches tall and had been shaving for the prior two or three years did not seem to matter. I would remain a nincompoop for a good many years, as would most boys of my age. The girls were light-years beyond us in maturity. At sixty-nine, I've closed the gap, but to be honest, I still scratch my bald head at some of the antics I continue to do.

When I was six years old, I was enrolled at St. Patrick School in East St. Louis. I don't know whether any of my classmates attended kindergarten, but since it was not required, my parents didn't send me. My first structured learning environment was first grade with Sister Thomas Ann. Before I began school, my mom had a long talk with Sister. I don't know what they said: whether it was that Tommy or TJ, as my mom called me then, was a good little boy and that she

1

should have no trouble with the lad, or a terse "good luck, Sister, I am only a phone call away." Knowing my relationship with Mom at that time, I assume they were cooking up a strategy should events with TJ go awry.

I hadn't the foggiest notion of what a C was or what a vowel meant. I figured Sister Thomas Ann reviewed all that stuff from scratch with her forty-five or fifty students. Unfortunately, before she could do any teaching, she had to convince about a quarter of us that she was not a demon in her black dress that hung to the floor, or that Mommy really would return for us at the end of school, and that she would not give us away to the black dress people. Ten or twelve of my classmates cried their eyes out for the first week or two. The first-grade teacher needed extreme patience to put up with the daily grind of teaching all of us children.

It's easy to understand why Sister was upset with me in December. She had convinced all of us that she was going to release us at three o'clock. She had time to ascertain our abilities in reading, writing and arithmetic and had placed us in groups to learn at our own pace. Moreover, she had convinced most of us that learning was fun, so when I disturbed the equilibrium that day, causing half the class to cry their eyes out, one could see why she was upset.

It all started at recess following lunch. I lived about a block from St. Patrick, so each day I ran home, gobbled down my lunch, and headed back quickly to school so I could have the maximum amount of playtime before the bell. A few of us were discussing what gifts we were hoping to receive at Christmas. My classmates were wondering if they'd get what they asked for from Santa.

Now when I entered the first grade, I had four brothers and four sisters. Financially, times were tight for Mom and Dad. My siblings and I did not receive many presents, but my parents provided enough food to eat, a place to rest our heads, and a sense of security and love. About a year prior, I had pinned down my father to a yes or a no regarding the existence of Santa Claus. I deduced, since I didn't see how he could deliver all those presents in one night, and moreover, why he was so stingy with the O'Connell clan, that he was a made-up character. I could have believed in him if I were the only one to get gifts, or to be penalized with a chunk of coal. I was constantly mean to my younger brothers and knew I did not deserve much of anything. I also considered my four sisters and four brothers; a couple of them didn't quite meet the standard for a good little boy or girl. But all of them, naughty little children? It didn't make sense.

Although he could stretch the truth as much as the next man, my father was not a liar. If you asked him a direct question, he told the truth. He confirmed my suspicion about Santa Claus and watched for my reaction. My father had believed in the mythical man until the third grade.

I said, "Well, Dad, I didn't figure there was a real Santa. I just wanted to verify it with someone who would tell me the truth."

He said, "Are you okay with this, Tommy?"

"Yeah, Dad, I'm okay with it. It clears up a lot of stuff. You would have had to answer a whole lot more questions if you'd said Santa was real."

So when I went to recess that day, it was my moral duty to tell my classmates the truth. "There is no Santa

Claus, Buddy. Your parents buy all those presents and just say they're from Santa Claus."

"You're crazy, Tommy, there certainly is a Santa Claus!" exclaimed one of the guys.

"No, there isn't," I said. "My dad told me so before last Christmas."

"Well, then your dad is crazy too!" said the boy.

Now, I could have continued with a "No, he's not, yes he is" discussion for about an hour on the topic as I did with my brothers on occasion, but when a person tells you your father is crazy, those are fighting words! I popped the kid a few times until he started crying and the fight was finished. It's the rule; when somebody cries, the fight's over, or when you knock a guy down, you don't jump on him and knock the snot out of him (except if he's your brother). Marquess of Queensbury rules.

Now I do not know whether the boy told Sister Thomas Ann, or if someone else spilled the beans, but I was placed in the hot seat, having to explain why I made this boy cry.

"He called my father crazy, Sister. That's why I had to hit him."

"He said his father told him that there isn't any Santa Claus," the boy retorted.

As I attempted to rebut, the room filled with cries of "What? There isn't any Santa Claus?" followed by banshee wails from the mouths of babes as their lives lay shattered.

"Out, Tommy! You have completely upset the class! Do you hear all the crying?" It was worse than ever. "Haul your desk out into the hall. You're banished! Do you hear all the crying you've caused, Tommy?" she demanded for a second time. "Out, out into the hall until I can control my temper."

"I'm sorry, Sister! I didn't mean to cause all this commotion."

"Well, you did, Tommy. Get out into the hall until I can get the class calmed down."

During my first few minutes in the hall, banishment didn't seem all that bad. I did not have to listen to Sister, just sit and relax. As time progressed, another ten minutes, I got bored. I wondered if I should just chuck it and go home for the day. Will Sister let me back into the classroom? Just then, Sister Mary Margaret, the principal, came by and noticed me sitting there. She had taught two of my older sisters who were excellent students and never caused any commotion, which was good for me.

"Tommy," she said, "what did you do to merit sitting in the hall like this?"

"I beat up a kid at recess, Sister."

"Why did you hit the boy, Tommy?"

"Well, we were having this discussion and he called my dad crazy. I can't let anybody call my father crazy and get away with it."

"Why did he say your dad was crazy?"

"Well, I told him my dad said there isn't any Santa Claus."

"Oh, so here is the crux of the matter, Tommy. You ruined his Christmas by telling him there wasn't any Santa Claus."

"I didn't mean to, Sister. It didn't matter too much to me when my dad told me. I had it figured out anyway.

Then, when somebody told Sister Thomas Ann that I made this guy cry, I told her he said my dad was crazy. In front of the class, I said what my dad told me—no real Santa Claus. Our teacher did not like what happened next."

"I see," said the principal, "so you ruined Christmas for everybody who still believes in Santa Claus. I can see why you are out in the hall, Tommy. Do you understand why your teacher is upset? Her class must be in a shambles. Didn't your father tell you never to tell anybody who still believes in Santa Claus that he doesn't exist?"

"Well, he did mention not to tell any of my younger brothers and sisters, but I didn't think that counted with anybody else."

"That doesn't make a whole lot of sense, does it, Tommy?"

"No, I guess not."

"Now I can see standing up for your father, but you should not have told the boy there wasn't any Santa Claus! Just think about it, Tommy, until Sister lets you into the classroom again."

As Sister Mary Margaret was walking away, out walked my sister Anne from the fourth grade to get a drink of water. She was a little bit more than two years older than me, but we were separated by three years in school. I thought, even though she liked me, she might snitch on me simply to derive pleasure from putting me in hot water with my mom.

To cut expenses, my dad cut the boys' hair. Depending on the timing of the last crew cut from my dad, I could resemble my mom's dad who was absolutely bald (devoid of hair down to his ears), or possibly the character Alfalfa in the *Little Rascals* film shorts made in the 1930s, with a spike of hair rising for some unknown reason three to four inches smack in the middle of my head.

Out in the hall, I tried to cover my head and face, but I guess the shabby O'Connell clothes, plus the zeroing in from all the fourth-grade girls, did not give me much of a shot at being an unknown naughty boy sitting outside the first-grade classroom.

As soon as I got home after school that day, my mom gave a shout "TJ! I want to talk to you."

Anne must have been hauling to get home before I arrived so she could spill the beans. I told Mom the whole story and she ripped me up, not so much about the fight, but about having to sit in the hall all afternoon. Furthermore, she said she was going to tell my father of the incident and that he would have a good talk with me.

I cannot remember getting into too much trouble with my father. It was his honor I was defending. But I remember him stressing vehemently not to tell anyone who still believes in the mythical man, about his true status.

From this episode, Anne telling on her favorite brother, I deduced that girls were never to be trusted with information that had even a remote chance of getting you into trouble. I followed this credo for the next five or six years, and if not for the fact that when I got to the sixth grade, girls suddenly seemed not particularly bad, I would still be following it to this day.

I was excited during the last month of grade school in 1967. In addition to looking forward to three months of summer vacation, I was planning a trip to Washington, DC, as the representative of East St. Louis for the Patrol Boy Parade. (I guess it would be called the Patrol Person Parade now if it still exists.) A couple of months prior, I'd been elected to represent our school. I do not understand why; there were many boys far more deserving of the honor.

I was well liked as I remember. I was quiet, at least after the event of my stroke in the third grade. Maybe, had the stroke not occurred and I still had the speaking ability I was born with, I would have been the last guy to represent St. Patrick's. I was not the most popular boy in the room. I campaigned hard for the honor of representing our school. Many schools in East St. Louis were represented. I figured if just one person were to represent the city, I would have to be luckier than I was to be picked, so I just forgot about it.

I do not know whether it was two weeks or two months to the day of the announcement, but I remember vividly the moment I learned I was going to Washington.

It was one of those gorgeous springtime days. The temperature was perfect, the flowers beginning to bloom, and the air had that pleasant springtime aroma. Everything was bursting forth from winter. The trees were losing their buds, replaced by brilliant new green leaves…and then the noontime bell rang. Recess was over, and we lined up to return to the drab, old schoolhouse to study geography, or take a spelling test, or worse yet—suffer through English class.

I wished this were Saturday instead of a school day. I wondered if I could convince Sister Michael Mary that I was sick and needed to go home. I would take the long way home. I might go up Thirty-Fourth Street, cross St. Clair Avenue, and tromp through the woods on the way to Jones' Park. On the tracks, there might be a freight train moving slow enough so that I could hop aboard, hang onto one of the boxcar ladders, and ride the train for a mile or two. Oh, never mind. I would not get away with it. One of my classmates would say, "He didn't seem that sick a couple of minutes ago on the playground, Sister." Maybe Sister would know intuitively. I mean, it doesn't take a genius to know how pretty a day it is today.

"Hey, Tom, come on!" someone yelled, breaking into my daydream. "You're making us wait, you clown."

As I walked up to get in line, an excitement arose from the kids in line ahead of me. It was as if I'd arrived too late. I had dillydallied too long, and now everyone except me knew a secret. All heck broke lose a second later, and everyone was slapping me on the back saying, "You won, you won!"

"I won what?" I asked.

"You won the contest, you won the contest, Tom!" everyone shouted.

Now I was totally confused. *Maybe I am sick and should go home via the direct way of a block and a half and go to bed,* I thought.

"Which contest are you talking about?" I asked.

"You're going to Washington! You know, the Patrol Boy thing," someone said.

Then it dawned on me. I was ecstatic for the rest of the day.

My uncle was pastor of St. Patrick Parish at that time. He had attended the drawing where they asked if he wanted to pull the lucky name. Fortunately, he told them his nephew was up for the prize. I can imagine there were many looks that went his way when the winner was his very nephew, Tom O'Connell. If he had drawn my name? Oh, what looks and sneers he would have endured.

The parade was to take place on the second weekend in May. My parents took me across the Mississippi River to St. Louis on Wednesday to meet the other Patrol Boy reps. We were going to take a two-day bus ride to Washington, DC, which excited me for several reasons. First and most important was that I would legitimately miss four days of school.

Second, it was going to be a bus ride for two days without anyone to boss me around. I had been on a bus a few times. We were bussed once a summer to the St. Patrick Parish Altar Boys' picnic. We rode a bus to St. Louis a few times in the seventh grade to attend the St. Louis Symphony orchestra concert in the afternoon. This may have been an attempt by Sister Mary Daniel to civilize us through the symphony. For me, listening to the orchestra was interesting, but the bus ride to St. Louis and missing our afternoon studies was much more appealing.

Finally, it was going to be an adventure. We would travel to see sights I thought I never would see. I would eat breakfast with our US Representative Melvin Price and walk in the nationwide parade. Pretty heady stuff for a kid who had been in only four states until then.

My mom and dad took me to the appointed place in St. Louis and told me to behave. I was good enough on the trip so that I did not become the actual reason there were no more patrol boy contests in our city. Mom gave me $20 for unexpected expenses. Twenty dollars doesn't seem like much today, but it was a hefty sum to my parents—almost 20 percent of my father's weekly pay. If I had thought about what it meant to the family, I would have returned the money, but as a fourteen-year-old scatterbrained boy, I took the money and thanked my mom. I only used around three dollars to buy Mom a knickknack replica of the Washington Monument, and I returned the remainder. There was only one other souvenir—one that was free of charge. While we stood in line for the tour of the White House, I leaned over the fence and plucked some blades of grass from the White House lawn and put them in my pocket. I gave them to John, my closest brother, and he put them in a bottle. He was quite impressed and still has them, although they're gnarly and brown by now. Hopefully, the statute of limitations has passed regarding my brazen theft of grass from the president's house.

The bus left at noon. I was not gregarious, especially with people I didn't know, so I looked out the window and thought about things for a long time. Daydreaming was one of my favorite pastimes. I know there are people who consider daydreaming a waste of time, but I do not, especially when there was nothing better to do from a fourteen-year-old's perspective. Where would I be in six months or a year? Would I like the all-boys high school? I would miss all the young women from my class, even though I was scared of them. All my classmates except one or two were nice to me. Why did they all like me? Why did they elect me Patrol Boy representative? Darkness began to settle in. (I had been thinking for a while.) We stopped at a little place in Eastern Ohio for dinner. It reminded me of a *Twilight Zone* episode "Will the Real Martian Please Stand Up?" In the episode, there was a little diner called the "Hi-Way Café" and the story ended with this Martian and a guy from Venus talking about who was going to take over the earth.

I do not know whether the prices compared with the Hi-Way Café's—fifteen cents for a hunk of apple pie and thirty cents for a hamburger—but it was only the second time in my life I ever went out to eat. Mom would go to Henry's Hamburgers in East St. Louis when they had a special—twenty hamburgers for a dollar—but I'm not counting the burgers. Mom and Dad took the family once for a professional photo. Perhaps my mom's parents had given them the money; I can't imagine they ever had enough extra cash to afford it. I don't remember the name of the place where we stopped after a painful experience for the photographer, but I recall that I ordered meatballs and spaghetti. The meatballs and spaghetti did not compare to my mom's, but I consumed every bit down to the last noodle. Although I'd had better meals at home, this one was special. My family all breaking bread together and enjoying the evening meal someplace special, somewhere my parents could not afford—a wonderful experience! That's why I recall the little diner in Eastern Ohio.

Each segment of the trip seemed long. I don't know how many chaperones were with us, but they all were men—ancient men, I thought; they must have been at least thirty to forty years old. There were forty or fifty very young men who could get into deep trouble if the old guys were not vigilant. They were careful not to let any of us get stranded in western Pennsylvania.

It must have been past midnight when the bus left the little diner. As we wound through the cat ear of West Virginia and into Pennsylvania, I grew weary and dozed off until we arrived at Gettysburg.

At Gettysburg National Park, we watched a presentation of the horrendous battle that took place in that small Pennsylvania town. We entered a room and sat on what best can be described as high school bleachers about eight or ten levels high. Our seats surrounded a square. Within the square was a map representing Gettysburg and the area that encircled the town. The lights dimmed and the electric map presentation began. I know this may sound silly fifty years later, but I was fascinated with the green flashing lights that represented the Union holding the high ground, and the blue, yellow or red lights for Robert E. Lee and the Confederate forces stationed at a certain point after the first day of battle. You have to remember the times. My older brothers used slide rules for calculators in high school a couple of years back; there was no such thing as the internet.

In the three days of battle at Gettysburg there were fifty thousand casualties. On the third day, 12,500 Confederates charged across an open field in hopes of breaking the Union line. In the scant time of an hour, only half of those men lived to fight another day. Pickett's Charge was what it was called. A sad, sad three days for America.

We headed south into Maryland and east to Washington, DC, stopping at a place where we were separated into groups of four and assigned rooms to spend the next three nights. There were two bunk beds in our room. I was six feet two and 125 pounds on a good day, so I was assigned to three bigger guys, three or four years older than me. After the three older guys chose their bunks, I was left with a bottom bunk—a bunk suited for an average ten- or twelve-year-old or a leprechaun, not anyone taller than six feet, I thought, as I laid down for the first time that night.

As I lay crumpled up in the bed, I could not help but wonder what the next three days would bring. I am not sure I slept well that night, partly because of the miniature elflike bed, but also the excitement of what was to come.

I can't remember the order of events, but I do remember all that we did: going to see the White House and borrowing several blades of grass while we waited our turn to see the three or four rooms where they allowed us in, seeing where the laws were made at the Capitol, checking in at a Congressional meeting and hearing the leaders of Congress talk, blah, blah, blah, or so it sounded to me.

We visited Arlington National Cemetery, saw the eternal flame, and went to George Washington's place at Mount Vernon. We got to see where dollar bills were made (unfortunately, we got no samples) saw part of the Smithsonian Institute one evening and ate breakfast with US Representative Melvin Price of East St. Louis on the weekend.

The parade took place on Sunday. The chaperones were peeved with us because we didn't measure our steps and march perfectly in line as soldiers do. I thought the old guys in charge should have made us practice the soldier march at least once before the parade—to bone up a little, so we did not look like slobs. I place the onus on them. Since the age of nine, my right leg does not fare well. The yeoman's work for me to walk is about 90 percent left leg and 10 percent right leg. So I was glad that the chaperones did not make us practice. They surely would have focused their disgruntlement on yours truly when we messed up!

Between other activities, we saw the Lincoln Memorial and the Washington Monument, the best part of our trip.

The Lincoln Memorial was impressive, with the many steps leading to the chamber where Abe Lincoln is seated. He looks tired and sad, I thought as I gazed at the statue. At age fourteen, I did not understand all that he had on his mind, just that he looked weary. I luckily have never had to weigh the consequences of an action that could affect as many people as a war. While growing up in Kentucky and Indiana, and later in Illinois, I'm sure young Abe never thought about the decisions he would have to make in later life.

After leaving the Lincoln Memorial, we walked along the reflecting pool toward the towering Washington Monument. Once arrived, we all lined up to take the elevator to the top. As we waited, I noticed the stairs, which I assumed were an alternate way of getting to the top of the monument.

"Sir, can I go up the steps instead of waiting for the elevator?" I asked one of the chaperones.

"Are you nuts?" he said. "I'm sure not going up there with you, Tom, and I'm not letting you go alone."

"I'll go up there with him," echoed about a dozen of my colleagues.

"Forget about it, guys, we're going up the lazy man's way. In about twenty-five years, you can climb the stairs with your kids. I'll give you my address and you can write to tell me how it went." As we grumbled silently enough that the grouchy old chaperone couldn't hear, it was our turn for the elevator to the observation deck. As I recall, there were about thirty steps up from the elevator to the observation point.

We looked through the tiny observation windows at the city below. Impressive. It was amazing that in 1908, Gabby Street caught a baseball dropped from this height, even if it took him thirteen tries, I thought. After five or ten minutes of observing, we descended the steps and headed to the elevators.

"Hey, Tom," said the grouchy chaperone, "You can go down the steps if you want. I'm sure I'll beat you down on the elevator. But you'd better make it all the way down, Tom. I'm going to be angry if I have to go up and fetch you."

Some version of "We'll make sure he makes it" came from the mouths of about three-fourths of the boys as they rushed to the stairs and began bolting down the nine hundred steps. As I reached the stairs, I thought if I have trouble traversing these steps the grouchy chaperone will have to come to my rescue. The guys who said they would help had a thirty- or forty-step lead as I started my descent.

I grabbed the banister and took the steps slowly at first. As I quickened my pace, I settled into a cadence, a sort of rhythm broken only by the decision to take two steps instead of one or jumping to the landing from three or four steps up.

It took me five minutes (maybe a little more) to arrive at ground level; I was breathing only slightly heavier than normal. The grouchy chaperone had anxiously waited a couple of minutes, wondering whether it was a good decision to let me walk the steps. When I arrived, he was amazed when he saw that I was barely winded. It was evident I had a bum leg, although he did not know why. He could surmise I'd had a stroke because of the atrophied right arm and hand. *How could a guy run down nine hundred steps with a bum leg and hardly be winded?* he must have wondered.

2

The Project

Now at over sixty-nine years old, I have a better perspective as to why the grouchy chaperone was amazed. It has been fifteen years since I've attempted to run. I chucked the idea of running when I could not catch my own four-teen-year-old son, who (let us be nice about this) does not have world-class speed. To be frank about it, I fell in three or four inches of snow. But I still have this haunting, sick feeling that on a beautiful late-spring day, I could not have caught him.

My wife and I have a tidy two-story house. When I attempt the feat of descending from the second floor to the first, I take it easy with the thirteen steps. With my left hand, I grab the handrail with a viselike grip and gingerly count the steps as I proceed. For some reason, it appears that either my feet have grown four or five inches, or the steps have shrunk by that much since I was fourteen. I must turn my feet sideways as I descend. I doubt my feet have grown that much since I was fourteen. I was six feet two inches then, and since I am currently six-five (closer to six-four without my hair) the steps must have shrunk. I'd have to be eight feet tall to have sixteen-inch feet. I cannot feel really well with either foot, so to successfully descend the thirteen steps, I place my entire sole securely on each of them, rather than bouncing down on my toes, as when I was younger.

Most people gain a little bit of weight as they age. I was 125 pounds at age fourteen, and I weigh a mite more at sixty-nine. At 210 pounds on a good day, my weight could make a difference going up or down the steps, especially considering the sneaky extra eighty-five pounds. Considering the muscular contrast between my right and left sides, one would have to conclude if both sides were equal in girth that the 125 or 210 pounds would have to be multiplied by a factor of more than one to arrive at a true picture of my weight. I do not know, nor do I want to know what this factor is. Please do not be mean to me.

Since I relearned to walk after the stroke, I drag my right foot and sometimes toppled off-balance and begin to fall. Usually, this was not a problem. I would simply begin to trot, do a spin move if I were going to charge into someone (like running backs do to spin from tackles), then regain my balance beautifully and go on my merry way. Unfortunately, the process of catching my balance does not work as well now and has not for the last fifteen years. I continue to strive for perfection, at least in catching my balance, but realize that a more prudent way of walking, henceforth, is to measure each step carefully or bear the consequences.

Years ago, my son was in the midst of his Eagle Scout project, which was to clear a bike path in the woods, make a couple of bridges over small gullies, install a bench overlooking a creek, and restore an existing path back to nature as best he could. Since he did not yet have his driver's license, I agreed to take him to run through the planned project one last time with the park supervisor who was to assist him.

It was exciting, as this was the first time, I would see the location of his project. We arrived at the park and waited a few minutes for the supervisor. When he arrived, we started toward the woods to the site of his project.

"Let's go the short way," Tommy said to Mr. Renner.

"Your dad might prefer the long way, Tommy. If we go down the short way, there's that hill, remember?"

"I think I can handle a hill, if my son can, Mr. Renner," I answered, not knowing what was in store for me.

"Tommy and I will go down first, Mr. O'Connell, but please be careful on your way down."

The descent was a watershed runoff down the hill to parts unknown. I held several disadvantages to making a successful descent. First, I was in desperate need of some new shoes. There might have been some tread left on the soles, if you looked hard, but my shoes were better classified as skis. Also, due to either my diabetes or the fact that I underwent a back operation several years prior, the toes and the underside of my feet were numb, which did not help. Lastly, it had heavily rained the night before, so I had to be extra careful, or I would have fallen several times in the mud before I made it down.

I started carefully, spotting a tree, approaching it gingerly. After successfully grasping its trunk, I looked for another safety point, either high weeds (hopefully not poison ivy) or another tree. At times, there were no safety points, so I had to go for it, ten or fifteen feet on my skis with numb toes bearing down on them, as I suppose monkeys do to avoid falling.

I wondered if there were picnics at the bottom of the hill. Would some smart-aleck teenager be cheering for the old man to make it down the hill, or hoping that he would not? There would be side betting on whether or not I would make it. I would not have bet on my own success unless the odds were at least two to one in my favor.

As I made it to the bottom of the hill without falling once, mind you, I rested on one of the picnic tables for a spell, basking in the glory of a successful run. As I rested, a sickly feeling came over me. I did not know where in the heck Tommy or Mr. Renner had gone. I could see the woods, but I didn't have the foggiest notion of where they were.

There were several options. I could stay sitting on this comfortable table and wait for them to return. Momentarily, this sounded like a good option. After waiting a bit, I asked myself if I had made it all the way down the hill to just sit here and wait for those jokers to return? Not a happy prospect.

One of my gifts is a good set of lungs. I might have been an opera singer if only I could carry a tune. I stood up, cleared my throat a little, while gazing out at the vast expanse of the woods and yelled, "Tommmmyyyyy!" I didn't know how far away they were, might have been a mile. If they were a mile away, it would take about five seconds for my yell to reach them, I thought. So I listened for about thirty seconds, hoping they were not that far away. I knew they could hear me, but would I hear their response?

I yelled again and waited. In about five seconds, I barely heard, "Dad, we're over here!" I walked in the general direction of the voice.

I crossed a nice-sized bridge over a creek and continued about a quarter mile toward the general direction of my son's faint response. Well, I must be a lot closer to them than I was at the picnic tables, I thought. Time for another good yell, and one of them will come out of the woods. I yelled again, this time, with the volume turned toward the direction of Tommy's response.

In about thirty seconds, out popped my son from the forest about 150 yards away, with a terse "Dad, we're over here." I thought, you know, *Tommy, if you had waited for me to get down the hill to at least see the general direction you were headed, this could have been avoided.*

As I peered into the forest where Tommy had disappeared, there was nothing that looked like a path. I was able to see the two of them in a discussion about one hundred yards into the woods. To make any headway, I would need to traverse several three- to four-foot-high old fallen trees and avoid numerous thornbushes while maintaining my balance on very uneven terrain. There are probably some snakes in there, I thought, and it would be my luck that at least one or two of them would bite me while I was trying not to fall.

"Mr. Renner, I don't think it would be wise for me to attempt to catch up to you. Is there a path where I could see what you're doing and be reasonably assured that you won't have to call the paramedics to pull me out of here?"

With a smile on his face, he replied, "Yes, Mr. O'Connell, there's one about forty or fifty feet back toward the bridge. Just be careful, okay?"

"Thanks, Mr. Renner," I said as I walked slowly down the forest line, trying to find the path. Sure enough, there it was. I moved toward their conversation.

I wonder why they're not converting this one to the bike path. Well, they want the path close to the creek, I thought, as I followed them, listening carefully along the way. About six hundred yards into the forest, we converged.

"Is that about it for Tommy's project?" I asked Mr. Renner. My son responded with such an angry face that had I been closer to him, he might have tried to poke me one to silence me.

"Mr. O'Connell, there's quite a bit of work to do," he said. "Remember, Tommy has to clear the forest for the bike path, pat the earth down so it's reasonably flat, bank the turns, build the bridges over the gullies, and let us not forget, install the bench. That's quite a bit of work, don't you think?"

"I think it's more than adequate, Mr. Renner," I said.

"Let's go back to the cars on this path. How about it, Mr. O'Connell?"

"Sounds good to me, guys. I'm going to take it easy on the way back, so you don't have to wait for me. I'll catch up," I said.

As I was admiring the trees and the deep blue sky, I did not pick up my right foot high enough to clear the small root of a diminutive tree which threw me off-balance. Off I careened to catch myself as I had successfully done hundreds, maybe thousands of times. There was no one for me to dodge, make my patented spin move to avoid crashing into ladies, or catching a cabinet or two with my off-center body.

As I tried to regain my balance, my trot rapidly turned into a run without any semblance of balance. Unfortunately, the path took a slight downgrade which I failed to realize while listening to Tommy and Mr. Renner on the ascent. I wonder when I'll fall, I thought, as the trees zipped past me at an alarmingly quickened pace.

Why don't I grab one of these trees to break my speed a little? I thought. It might wrench my left arm a little, but at least that option is better than somersaulting down the hill, only to be stopped by a tree or a thornbush. As I reached for the next available tree, I snagged it, only to have it ripped out by the roots, barely stopping my acceleration, and now I was running down the hill carrying, conservatively speaking, a twelve-foot-long spear.

Things get hazy from here. I do not know how long I hung onto the spear, possibly longer than an Olympian before he chucks it as far as he can. (I know it's the javelin, but it's spear-chucking to me.) My spear was held long enough for my son to about have a heart attack, for as I fast approached him, the spear was aimed at his right kneecap. I am not a doctor, and I make no claims about this matter, but if I'd popped off his kneecap, we would still be looking for it in the forest.

As I raced past Tommy, he half-heartedly attempted to slow me down. I can't say I blame him for not trying too hard. Passing Tommy, I was like a 230-pound locomotive bearing down on everything in my path.

As I passed Mr. Renner, I looked toward the right side of the path for a place to bail out and not hit a tree. I had already destroyed one. Ahead was a clearing where I had a halfway decent chance of landing without being hospitalized. I sprung off my left leg, did a 180 and landed in a thornbush, barely missing a tree. Mr. Renner and Tommy raced up to see if I was hurt. When I told them that only my pride was wounded and I would have to extract about fifty thorns from my backside, I couldn't blame them for their loud and long laughter at my expense.

Mr. Renner asked if he could help me up. He realized I was in my late fifties and since my walking was slightly impaired, maybe I was hurt.

"No, Mr. Renner, I landed on the seat of my pants and this thornbush broke my fall. Besides, if you tried to help me, both of us might get hurt. I'm not a small man, you know, but thanks for the offer." As I rolled over to my knees and stood up, I realized I had escaped from my misadventure barely marred.

I took the long way to the car, knowing my son could not go home without me. Since then, there have been other mishaps. Some happened at work when I would lose my balance from failing to lift my right foot off the carpeted floor. I would almost fall but save myself by grabbing the nearest desk or wall. At inventory time on one occasion, I fell flat on my face, barely missing a four-inch-high angle iron that ran along the side of the building. This incident turned out well for me, as after that, I no longer had to take inventory. If I had hit the angle iron square in the face, I think it would have killed me. Sometimes I fell on the grass, not realizing that I was not twenty-five years old anymore and not lifting my right foot high enough as I walked. After a number of these incidents, it dawned on me that I should be more careful while walking.

Long past were the times when my brothers and I played chase around our block in E. St. Louis or tore up the remaining patches of grass by hacking a plastic golf ball around the house. It had been twenty years since I had made a half-hearted attempt at sprinting, and at least ten years since I'd walked a mile. My occupation was accounting, a sedentary job. I was aging and could not expect to be in optimum shape my whole life. But still I could walk without falling.

My goal was that at age seventy, I'd be able to walk at least a mile. I cannot say I tried walking every day, but when I walked, I tried to walk at least as far as the last attempt. My wife and I started by walking up to the end of our street and down Sentry Lane a ways and back again. It could not have been much more than a quarter of a mile, but it was all I could do at first. My back hurt when we arrived home, and my feet felt heavy as iron. My shirt was drenched with sweat; it felt so good to get back and sit on my recliner. As I inhaled huge gulps of air, I wondered what had happened to the old Tom. *I know you're out of shape*, I thought to myself, but that distance is only a little bit more than around the block of the house where you grew up.

As I tried to get into better shape, I realized I would never regain my youthful fitness and speed, nor indeed the energy to walk as far as I wished. In my late fifties, there were mitigating circumstances besides age: my dead leg from the stroke, and the fact that I had no feeling in either of my feet. Growing old gracefully is a challenge for everyone. There is only so much a person can do, I guess, but being able to walk only a paltry quarter mile at fifty-seven years of age is preposterous. I vowed not to let age thumb its nose at me.

There are sidewalks on every street in our neighborhood, which is nice if you hanker to walk several miles without risking your life on the street. I started by hanging a right from our house on Knollmont Drive, walking three blocks and turning left on Oakbrook. The sidewalk continued down a little hill; I crossed a street and went up a slight rise that ended at Pleasant Valley Road at a stoplight. The total circuit, from my house to Pleasant Valley and back again, was 1.2 miles.

In the beginning of my exercise routine, I was unable to complete the journey to the stoplight. The first few times, I wrenched my back while navigating Oakbrook. I called that hill many uncomplimentary names as I hobbled to a level place to lick my wounds. I know it was not the hill's fault; it was only sitting there minding its business when this clown came along. I hold no grudge against the hill. However. You do have to take a stand sometimes, like when your little brother has the audacity to steal the basketball from you and you retaliate by hip checking him into the bleachers when he thinks he has a step on you to the basket the next time he has the ball.

After a few attempts to conquer Oakbrook, I made it to a bench where I rested on my laurels, and after five or ten minutes, returned home the sneaky way, so I did not have to climb Oakbrook's steep hill. I traveled around four-fifths of a mile on those occasions, but it was a cheating distance because I rested halfway. After a few more attempts, I went the additional two tenths of a mile up to Pleasant Valley Rd and two tenths to the bench where I rested before going home. I had accomplished my goal, albeit after two rests, but I had walked 1.2 miles total. It was two or three months before I completed this walk without resting; I was proud.

Now more than ten years later, I walk about two and a half miles three times a week. It's a lonely task that I do not like. And it is a walk I take by myself since my wife works full-time. These days, I have a touch of arthritis. When I start, my right hip hurts, as does my right knee and ankle. After I walk for a mile or so, all or most of the pain disappears and I can finish fairly pain-free. Walking is the best exercise for me, which is why I get out and walk the streets.

I meet neighbors on the various routes. Some of them I see often, and we exchange pleasantries as we pass. Then off we go. Some slow down and I walk with them awhile, listening to stories of their lives past or present, making the walk go by quicker and taking my mind off the pain if I'm at the start. I do not know whether or not this makes me strange, but I am genuinely interested in the twists and turns of people's lives. What makes a person who they are? If they hurt deep inside, what I can do to ease their pain, or at least give them a unique way of perceiving it? If someone does not want to share or thinks I'm nosy, that's okay. I know many people prefer to keep things inside.

I am unique; everyone can see that I experienced a profound event. I walk with a limp and my right hand is rolled into a neat little ball due to the atrophy of the right arm and hand muscles through inactivity. I hope I make a positive contribution by listening and understanding folks as I walk my path through life.

3

Unbridled Stallion

Regardless of whether you believe the Earth started four and a half billion years ago or several thousand years ago, if you think about it, you will realize you're a very fortunate person. My dad was drafted into the army in 1941, a few months before the bombing of Pearl Harbor. He was stationed at Camp Polk, Louisiana, where he met my mother in Jasper, Texas. After a courtship of several months, they were married, and my mother followed him to various camps until he was sent to Europe in July of 1944. My mom gave birth to their second child, Maureen, while Dad was traveling to England by ship.

He had a firm belief that he'd never again see his wife, nor his children Maureen and Kathleen. He was certain there was a bullet with his name emblazoned on it: William James O'Connell—a bullet meant for him before the end of the war. As a staff sergeant responsible for the implements of war, he was not in battle, yet he was close enough to gunfire that any day could be his last. Fortunately for Dad, his belief in his own death was in error. If he had been killed, my mother would never have given birth to the nine other children born of her union with my father after World War II, the fourth of those being yours truly, Thomas John. I'm grateful that my dad was not a good prognosticator.

My grandfather, David, was born in 1880, in a small town called Cahersiveen on the southwest coast of Ireland. He was raised in a family of eighteen children. Life was hard; only about half his siblings survived past age three. Pop was strong and lived until he was seventy-seven, fortunate for me. At about age twenty, he left for America, the land where the streets were paved with gold, never again to see his mother and father. He arrived in St. Louis, Missouri, where he fell in love with Annie Stokes, whose family had moved from Ireland to near Dodge City, Kansas, in 1881. Annie was born there in 1884; her family moved to St. Louis, where she fell in love with Dave O'Connell— another lucky break for my father and me.

Things could have been much different. One accident to my mother or father, and I would not have been born. If the United States had made a policy decision that all men twenty-seven or older would not be drafted in 1941, or if my father were sent to another camp for basic training, they would never have met.

If we assume that human beings started seven thousand years ago, not that life started 3.5 billion years ago, the number of generations to date would still be 250, if we count a generation as twenty-eight years. That's 125 times longer than the scenario of my parents and grandparents. One can see the astronomically high probability of me not being here to share the story of my life!

God has a purpose for me and all human beings. Had I not been an O'Connell, God would surely have found a place sometime, somewhere for me—to test me, to say, "Here you go, I am going to create you, Tom. Let's see if you can make a small positive difference in the world. Your life will be all your doing, you'll make all the decisions, and you determine what you do. To keep you on your toes, I'll throw in an occasional monkey wrench, Tom. But never will I give you too much. If you try, you'll succeed. Your life might not be the same as yesterday, but you will attain true peace with whatever comes your way. If ever you think life is too much, call on me, Tom, and I'll help you."

I was born in 1953. I was not born feral. The psychotic part of me might have developed during my formative years. I am not a direct descendant of Romulus or Remus, nor do I yearn to be raised by a she-wolf in the Lupercal or any other cave. I was born with ample will, and Katie bar the door, if I really want something, I will go to all lengths to achieve my goal. Call that stubbornness or drive if you like but I have it.

My mom might have wished God had given me a little less drive—stubbornness, as she called it—at least to start. I was the sixth child born of her union with my father, so she had a lot on her plate at the time, even if I had been a good baby like my sister Anne. It all started turning sour when I began to walk at nine months, the earliest of any of my siblings. I have a younger brother, Larry, who is less than a year younger than me. When Mom wasn't feeling well, and shortly after I learned to walk, she had her hands full contending with my high energy. Like most babies, I was inquisitive, and I put everything in my mouth. Her sewing machine fascinated me. I liked the whirring sound that emanated from deep within the contraption while a giant (Mom), sat next to it playing with little ingots. (She called them bobbins.) As soon as she put them down, I wanted to play with them too. I'd grab one of the ingots, examine it, and stick it into my mouth to see how it tasted.

This infuriated the giant, for she stood up, saying something like "Take that bobbin out of your mouth, you little stinker!" as she simultaneously pried open my mouth and removed the bobbin. Then she would give me a ride; a whee is what I called it. Higher and higher she lifted me (must have been hundreds of feet in the air) and brought me down quite securely on the other side of the room. She swatted me a couple of times while shouting, "You do not put my bobbins in your mouth, Tommy! You might choke!" Depending on how hard she swatted me (I might have had to dust off my britches a bit as I got to my feet), I would run over to the sewing machine and look Mom square in the eye.

The battle was on. My mother, not a passive or demure thirty-two-year-old woman, but a person with enough drive to break almost any stallion and a nine-month-old, twenty-five-pound child who should have known not to put bobbins in his mouth. You could tell she was serious. "You better not, Tommy, you better not." She must have seen that I was serious too. Although I could not yet talk like a Philadelphia lawyer, she knew what my eyes were saying.

Yeah, giant, I know that you can catch me now, pry open my mouth and retrieve the ingots. Take me for another whee hundreds of feet in the air, set me safely on the other side of the room, pop my butt a little bit harder, but you are not fast enough to make it over here before I stick this in my mouth. After a brief eye-to-eye showdown, enough time to let the giant know who was really in charge, I'd pop it in again. Mom would charge over, retrieve the bobbin, haul me to the other side of the room, and pop me a little harder. In response, I would charge over to the sewing machine and look her square in the eye, ready to do battle once more.

After four or five rounds of trying to break me, Mom must have either grown weary or realized that there would be plenty of other days to do battle. I was not the winner that day, ladies and gentlemen. I mean there are just so many chances before you're deemed incorrigible and must be incarcerated in the penal system of the playpen. Mom said on many occasions, that had it not been for Larry and the fact that our playpen was not equipped with a segregated area (some people call it the hole or solitary confinement, designed especially for the protection of other inmates, i.e., my brother, Larry) that I would have been imprisoned for much longer. I got no reprieves for good behavior.

I don't know whether I was farmed out to my older sisters, Kathie and Maureen, or if my crib was conveniently located in the same room where they slept. They were responsible for my care in the early morning hours. I know that they argued over who would get up to attend to my necessities when I awoke. My dearest sisters would pretend to be asleep by doing some poor imitations of snoring—i.e., kornwheeelll…kornwheeelll—until one of them, usually Maureen, would come over and see what damage I'd done to the crib and to myself, her sweet baby brother. Maureen was a pragmatist. First, she didn't know if Kathie was awake, or if this was just another one of those Saturdays that she'd sleep well into the afternoon. The situation with her baby brother, Tommy, and the crib would worsen by some geometric equation if the situation were not promptly addressed. I will not tell you what I was doing during the war of wills between my sisters, but only mention that Maureen knew without a doubt I was either born wild or, had she not known my parents, was actually the Prince of Darkness.

I only vaguely remember these events, as it was just after my first birthday. Over time, family stories become exaggerated. But I do have confirmation from outside sources that I was a devil child. When my mom was delivering her seventh baby, Larry, I was farmed out to my Aunt Helen and her husband, Dave. I was slightly under the age of one, and Dad was busy selling life insurance and collecting the premiums. My sisters were in school, so Aunt Helen was generous enough to watch me for the ten days my mother was in the hospital.

I must have made a negative impression on Aunt Helen because she decided that she could not return me to Evelyn. I'd be the coup de grace for the poor woman just after having given birth. She kept me for an additional week, God bless her soul. I'm sure my mom would readily canonize her soul for sainthood for that little kindness. My Aunt Helen died on November 22, 1997. I told her son, Dave, how much her generosity had meant to my mom. Dave is three and a half years older than me, which would put him at about four and a half years of age when I was thrust upon his parents for a little more than a fortnight. As I told him of the kindness his mother did for mine, you could see horror grow in his eyes. After I finished the story, he couldn't form the words: "Tom, you were really Tom, Tom, Tom, Tom." The man was approaching fifty years old and could not even finish the sentence. "Tom, Tom, Tom, Tom" was all he could say. I had made an impression on my cousin. For this, I am a little bit proud.

My mom and I not only battled over the bobbins when I was a tyke, but she also had to endure the daily fights over whether I was going to wear long or short pants or shoes versus no shoes each time the seasons changed. Each day for about two weeks, the battle was on. When we had finally reached an accord, the seasons would change again, and we'd resume battle. When I was refusing to wear shoes, my technique would be to curl my toes, similar to a cat spreading out its legs to make it incredibly difficult to put it in a carrier. I made it impossible for her to put the mugs on my feet.

One day, probably when she was in a grouchy mood, at least from a one-year-old's perspective, my mom was having the usual difficulty putting on my shoes. Aggravated and determined to get the shoe on my right foot, she secured it and quickly pulled the shoelaces as tight as she could, quadrupling or quintupling the bow.

I was grouchy too, pulling at the right shoe and crying more than usual. My mom was busy that day, as every day. With a brood of seven, all her work was done manually. Every day, there was the peeling, cutting into chunks, and boiling of endless pounds of potatoes for dinner. She washed our clothes with an old wringer washer, hung them outside to dry and ironed the shirts, pants, and dresses (no permanent press when I was a child). She was too busy to fight with an obstinate baby.

I can't imagine how guilty she must have felt when she took off the right shoe and found that my toes were black as night. No one could have consoled the woman who bore this child with the excuse that he was obstinate.

My parents hauled me to the family physician who had always treated us, mostly with shots when they were due. My father immediately lost respect for the man's medical credentials when he mentioned that he might have to amputate my five little guys—just when I'd become rather fond of them. When the doctor mistakenly took a chunk of good red meat off one of my toes, my father called off the fight. "No mas, no mas, that's enough for you, Doctor, I'm taking my boy to somebody who knows more about his predicament than I do."

The new doc administered ultraviolet treatments, which must have worked because I still have a set of five toes on each foot, although on my right foot, the toenails look gnarly, perhaps because of this incident, but probably due to walking on them after the stroke. I cannot tell you if they were in the current state before then, mostly because I can't remember checking them in my formative years. I would never take a bath until Mom threatened me with several trips to the woodshed. While cleanliness is next to godliness, my thoughts on the matter were an aberration in those days.

I'm told I was interested in travel when I first learned to walk. After my first few attempts at running away, my older brothers and sisters were told to be sure to secure the door or they would be indirectly linked to the disappearance of their younger brother. They were all diligent, at least for a while, as they did not wish to be responsible for decreasing the size of the family from nine to eight.

Inevitably, when I was on release from Mother's penal system, I would spot a weakness in the fort and away I'd sail into the great beyond. It did not matter to me which way I headed; I didn't pause to think of my best option. I ran as fast as I could, as I knew that Mom, the wily old warden, would soon notice I was missing and order her forces to scour the wilderness for me. One time I was running toward State Street, and I was captured by a neighbor who knew I was a member of the O'Connell clan. I yelled and cried. She let go since she didn't want to look like a kidnapper! Running at breakneck speed to Evelyn's house, she quickly arrived and told Mom where her baby had last been seen. Kathie, the oldest of mom's forces, headed out and caught me just in time before I ran into the traffic of one of East St. Louis's busiest streets.

Another time, I headed out our back door. I don't know how I escaped the warden's clutches that time; she was probably washing clothes. I passed the barrel where we burned our trash (remember, this was 1954) ran across our alley and onto College Avenue and headed toward the Mississippi River when Charley Loyet caught me. He was a boy in my oldest brother Bill's class who knew who I was and took me home. I tried the yelling and crying bit again but all he said was "Nice try, Tommy, but you're going home, buddy."

I know there must have been other times when I tested Mom's patience. To get laughs from my older siblings, when I finished a meal, I'd dump the remaining plate of food on my head. Certainly, Mom was tested by each of my ten brothers and sisters as well. While the two of us may have waged many a war, there was never any doubt as to whom I would run when I was hurt.

Once, Mommy had to fix up my tummy, which had been sliced open by a bedpost. I don't know whether I was assigned to sleep in my older brothers' room or whether I was visiting them. I began jumping from a five-foot-high chest of drawers onto either my bed or one of my brother's. Exhilarated, I would land on the bed and propel my body about eighteen inches up from the springs. Seeing their kid brother bounce around on the bed springs after leaping amused Billy and Danny.

I don't know how many times I jumped. I only remember the last time I tried it. Everything was working perfectly when I came up a bit shy of the mark and slit my chest wide open on the post of the iron bed. I found out the cruel, yet effective way—through experience—that you had to make sure you didn't hit the top edge of the posts that were perched at a dangerous right angle.

I was bleeding badly from the error of my miscalculation, plus I did not know the collateral damage of my wound. An intense pain erupted from my chest and tummy area, and I wailed, followed quickly by cries and tears that I did not know that I could even summon up at age three. The one I ran to was Mom. I knew she was my best shot at stopping the bleeding, having the pain subside and fixing me so I might see another sunrise. My older brothers would not have had as much expertise to fix chest wounds as my mother. They were discussing how to get out of trouble with my mom for allowing me to get hurt. That's what I would have done in their place.

Mom's words were soothing: "It'll be okay, Tommy. Let's take a look, and we'll fix it. I know it hurts, Tommy. It'll be okay, Tommy—let Mommy look at it." I knew that, at least on the front end, there wouldn't be any "Why were you jumping off the dresser, Tommy? Bill, Dan! Why would you let him jump on your bed like a wild man?" which I know would have negative repercussions all around.

My mom was exceedingly calm, as if she did this every day, although I know that her insides must have been churning as much as they were during the blackened-toe incident. She did eventually stop the bleeding and applied adhesive tape horizontally down my chest and tummy. The worst part was the methylate she swabbed over the entire area, which burned like fire. I do not remember if it was then that she scolded me for jumping off the chest of drawers, but I remember her taking a slice of bread, spreading it with butter and grape jelly and shipping me outside. I went to the backyard, climbed onto the hood of a purple car that had seen its better days, awaiting the day of disposal at my dad's discretion. What a horrible day it would be if my luck did not change, I thought.

There would be many more battles of will with my mom, and many occasions when I deemed her the meanest woman ever to walk the Earth. But I knew, in the heat of our deepest battle, that she'd do anything for me. There never was any doubt that she loved me and the ten other people she had borne into the world. She had the heart of a lion for her children and became instantly incensed if she thought any of them got a raw deal. On most occasions, my parents agreed with the school authorities. After we were punished at school, my brothers, sisters, and I had to deal with Mom.

When she died in May of 2007, Father Hitpas gave the eulogy at her last Mass at St. Stephens. She had worked for religious education of the Belleville Diocese until she was seventy-five and served Father Hitpas for many years during her tenure there.

During his eulogy, Father mentioned that my mom had a cut-and-dried opinion of people in general. To Evelyn, you were either a lamb or a goat, with most folks falling into the category of lamb. Father said he had always been a lamb in her eyes and was grateful never to have landed on the side of the goat.

4

Backing Me Up

The stroke happened in March of my third-grade year, paralyzing my entire right side. Unfortunately, I was born right-handed and was not ambidextrous. The good thing about the stroke, as I saw it, was that I missed the rest of the school year. Then came the summer, and I was off for an additional three months.

After spending six months free from school and recovering, I figured when September came, my siblings would return to school, but that I'd get to retire. I knew how to read, add, subtract, multiply, and divide; wasn't that all a person needed to learn? My grandfather had only three years of formal education, and he did all right. I had about three years. Seemed fair.

My mom said that wouldn't cut it. Monsignor O'Connell, my dad's brother and pastor of St. Patrick was gracious enough to let me proceed to the fourth grade with my classmates in September of 1962. I don't remember when my mom gave out the unwelcome news, but I remember Maureen trying with little success to teach me to write with my left hand. I had other more important things to do, like trying to walk and then run and trying to balance the basketball on my left hand and somehow get it up to the basket. Besides, I had retired from school, right?

I guess I'm not the only kid who got bored on hot days when there was nothing to do, who longed for friends and wished that school would start again, only to be followed in two or three weeks by the stark realization that I should have kicked myself in the backside for wanting school to start in the first place.

My classmates greeted me like a long-lost friend at first, which amazed me because in the prior three years, I had created some fierce enemies who now were my friends. After a while, most of them buckled down and did their best. Well, not their best but definitely more than me. All through the fourth grade, I went to Parks Elementary School for physical therapy on Mondays, Wednesdays, and Fridays. The bonus was that my mom picked me up at school at about a quarter to three, a good twenty-five minutes before the last bell. Yes, I was a slob; anything to leave school was my motto. I didn't care much about the rehab of my right hand; I had a spare one, didn't I?

Especially in grade four, I struggled with penmanship as I converted from my right hand to the left. I should have tried harder with Maureen that summer in handwriting practice. Unfortunately, my left side has never since been as adept as my right. I was born right-handed, and I am right-handed now, although there seems to be a slight problem with the mechanics of the brain telling the right side what to do. Through about sixty years and counting, I can do anything with my left side; it's stronger than my right side would have been if not for the stroke. It's the little niceties that never returned, like the ability to scoop up those final few peas on your plate or knowing where the ball will land after you release it, that have me stymied. Oh, mind you, I really like my left side, would have one heck of a time without it, but it was clumsy when I was born and it's clumsy now, albeit much less clumsy of late.

So you can see the problems I had with the left hand, especially since I had little, if any, experience as I walked into the first day of the fourth grade. As if my predicament were not bad enough, we were switching to the fountain pen from the pencil. My speech was affected by the stroke, and I was slowly but surely recovering the ability to talk. I would skip words or syllables due to my mind going faster than its connection to speech, or to writing with my left hand.

I'm not begging your sympathy; I tell this so you can envision how horrible my handwriting was. Had I been any other child who did his best and turned in a penmanship paper that looked like mine, I should have gotten a sound whopping at the nearest woodshed. I gave it the good old college try with my left hand (well, not college) but what with the torn paper from the fountain pen, the unknown language with the missing syllables and skipped words due to the lack of cooperation between my mind and left hand, clearly the penmanship paper was unacceptable.

For the first quarter at St. Patrick, one of our parents routinely met with the teacher to learn how well we were doing scholastically, and to find out if anything needed to be addressed before expulsion of said student from the private school. I was not a problem to any of my teachers or classmates.

Now I know my mom was prepared for the meeting with my teacher, and she hoped it would not be too bad. She had asked me on several occasions why I was not doing my written homework for the night or studying the spelling words before my test the next day. I'm not sure how I answered those questions. I might have said that my teacher did not believe in written homework, or in spelling, that I had it squared away. But I know my excuse was not I'm angry about having to go back to school, Mom, or "I am too lazy, Mom." I know she wanted to haul me to the woodshed for some of my ridiculous answers, but she was stymied.

"Mr. And Mrs. O'Connell, we don't know what caused the stroke; we can guess that it was a congenitally weak blood vessel that clotted," said the neurologists at Cardinal Glennon Hospital.

"Don't put any pressure on him. If he wants to study and make good marks, good for him. If he does not, do not push him. Try to convince him gently because we just don't know what caused the accident."

When Mom saw my report card, I know it was worse than she'd imagined. There were several Ds. Clearly unacceptable, but it was the one E that upset her. My teacher became a goat in Mom's eyes that day. This was not because of the Ds. I'm sure she talked with Dad about ignoring the neurologist's advice and taking me to the woodshed for those grades. She was a teacher too, and if you merited an F, she was more than happy to give it.

It was the mark on handwriting that infuriated her, and I imagine she told the teacher exactly what was on her mind, without any buffer. My teacher gave me an E in handwriting. Objectively, if they gave Gs and Hs instead of Es for failure and called it imprisonment for a G and you're going to the box, son, for an H, I'm sure that my work merited an H, a G if I'd been the teacher's pet, so it wasn't that big a deal to me. I'm glad the teacher gave me an E in handwriting because it lessened the impact from Mom on the other marks.

"She knows what happened to you!" Mom raved. "She knew this was your first crack at trying to write with your left hand, and here she gave you a failing mark!" I could have tried to convince her that my teacher was just trying to be fair and objective, that I deserved an E, although she might have given me a break and changed it to a D.

Hold on, hold on, my good fellow, I thought. *Are you being prudent? Do not let her forget about the handwriting, my good man, or she will zero in on the rest of the report card.* "Yeah, Mom, I tried my best, but you know I'm not ambi-dextrous. Maybe after more practice, I'll do better."

My mom supported me on dozens of times as she had for my other brothers and sisters through the years. I don't know what she said to my teacher, but it must have made a huge impression because for the next three quarters, I received Ds in handwriting. And let me tell you that the quality of my work merited a G for imprisonment, surely not a D for poor work. It was not that her children could do no wrong in Mom's eyes; I took trips to the woodshed two, three times a night before the stroke, as she highly regarded the old axiom "Spare the rod and spoil the child." But whenever an injustice was done, you could count on Mom to step up and fight the good fight on your behalf. In this instance, she thought I needed some support since she, like most people, thought that the loss of a side of one's body is traumatic. She would darn well not let anyone make me feel I was a failure because of what I couldn't control.

5

The Paper Route

That is not to say my mom looked at me as her fair-haired boy. She knew I was sneaky, and I am sure she often wondered how much I'd gotten away with without a proper reprimand from her. Sister Tarsella, my fifth-grade teacher, caught me in the hall one day and asked me to do her a favor. I said, "Sure, Sister, what do you want?"

"Your younger brother Larry is neglecting his homework, and I want you to tell your mother about this and get him into trouble at home."

"Sure, Sister, I'll tell my mother." Now Larry and I were not on the best of terms, but you would have to torture and kill me before I would rat on my brother, and I assumed he would have extended the same courtesy to me.

We got into enough trouble with Mom without the threat of spies reporting on us for doing something a little sketchy.

I reasoned that my mom was a girl who at some point became a mom, deducing that moms had forgotten the joys of telling on boys since they now had to focus on raising their children as respectful citizens. Still, though, hidden deep within each mom, there must be that little girl waiting to let the cat out of the bag to get some unsuspecting boy into trouble. Oh, I know I deserved every bit of trouble I got myself into, but had it been my dad as a kid who knew a secret about his brother, Laur—say that he didn't do his homework—he certainly would not have blabbed it to his mother or, more importantly, to either of his two sisters.

I made it to the sixth grade, having been promoted on the first go-round from the fourth and fifth. I was earning slightly better grades then and was more studious but still not trying my best. Three weeks or so into the year, my teacher took me aside after school. I had no idea what she wanted to say, but I bet it wasn't "Tom, you're doing wonderfully in school, and I just want to congratulate you on your work. I wish that all my boys would do as fantastic a job as you!"

As I cautiously approached the desk, I said, "Ms. Lawrence, you said you wanted to see me. Have I done something wrong?"

"No, it's nothing about your behavior. I have no problem with your manner in class. But, Tom, you never complete your written homework—this is the problem. I've spoken to you on several occasions about the necessity of getting your homework turned in, and I'll bet you never complete any of the reading assignments either. Is that correct?"

"Well, I don't know about never, Ms. Lawrence. That's kind of hard to say."

"The point is, I've warned you on several occasions, and now you'll have to stay after school to catch up, Tom."

"Ms. Lawrence, I can't. I have a paper route, and my family depends on every little amount I can make."

That was the truth. My younger brothers and I were delivering papers six days a week. We each received one dollar for this, and Larry and I received twenty-five cents extra for collecting the money that was due. The remainder of the money went to my family.

"Well, Tom, that really places me in a bind," Ms. Lawrence said. "Listen, please do your written homework. It is inexcusable for you not to do it, but I'm not going to make your family suffer because of your laziness."

I have to admit, upon long contemplation of this episode, that Ms. Lawrence was quite a person. She could have said, "That's not my problem. You're the one whose making your family suffer." Instead, she considered the human side of the equation.

"Thank you, Ms. Lawrence, I will do my written homework." At the moment of the promise, I was determined to follow through for Ms. Lawrence. She was giving me a break.

I kept my word for three, four days. Then the lazy side of me cut in and asked what I was doing. The sun was shining, it was beautiful outside, and there I sat with my nose in homework. I'm sure Ms. Lawrence was disappointed; I had her snookered. She could not keep me after school because I would lose the paper route job and my family would suffer, but neither could she convince me that homework was a necessary part of school.

On Saturdays, I had the unenviable task of going to each of my paper route customers to collect the remuneration due. Half of them were never at home, and I was not about to return three or four times a week just to suit their convenience. Also, everyone had an unchained, unfenced outside dog, so that too often, I'd have to run and jump on the hood of the nearest car to save my hind end from severe injury.

My parents decided to drop the paper route about two weeks after I made the homework deal with my teacher. It could have been that the money we collected was not offsetting the cost of papers.

I rarely did my homework, so one might conclude that I would be busy keeping Ms. Lawrence company on most school nights—had she known my paper route duties had ceased. I thought briefly about telling her, followed in short order by the thought, "Are you some type of idiot? Oh, I know a noble man would do it, maybe George Washington or Abraham Lincoln." I'm certain my sister Anne would run like a gazelle to tell Ms. Lawrence. But Anne or those noble men would have done their homework. They would have escaped any repercussions.

Suppose I was in the midst of a heated basketball game and purposely just hacked a guy, which the refs did not see. Would it be my responsibility to tell the referees that I just deliberately plastered this guy and to please kick me out of the game before I really hurt somebody? Certainly not. I escaped getting caught, and I would not expect any reasonable player to inform on themselves either. That's the breaks of the game and if Ms. Lawrence learns that I do not have a paper route anymore, well, I'll deal with her. I wondered whether she might be angry if she knew. I liked her. She never blew her top, although she seemed to be more than happy to hand out writing assignments, particularly to the boys, like, "I will keep order and pay attention in class" a hundred times. When she returned after stepping out for a minute to find us acting like feral animals, a hefty writing assignment would follow, maybe 150 sentences. As these assignments were nonnegotiable, I'm sure I owe her a heap of sentences.

As handwriting punishments went, the stroke was a bonus. My writing had improved a little, to a D if I'd go slowly. Ms. Lawrence was always lenient on my penmanship. She might have given me a C one term, although I may have dreamed that. She knew I wasn't a natural southpaw, so she compensated by handing me a break. On those assignments, I'd start slowly and, before I knew it, pick up speed to the point where I would scribble as if I'd recently discovered writing implements with no idea of what to do. However, I always accurately listed the numbers. I was no fool who'd skip a sentence.

Once she stopped me: "It looks like you scribbled the last eighty-five sentences, Tommy," she said. "I know you're trying to get them done as fast as you can, but slow down."

It was the beginning of November, and the first quarter had ended. My mom talked to all our teachers at St. Patrick, saving the meeting with my teacher for last. If she could have had her druthers and avoided the meeting with my teacher, she would've gone home and thanked the Man upstairs for giving the duty to someone else.

I don't know what they said in there, but afterward, my mom had a rascally grin on her face that scared the heck out of me. At home, she went over the report cards with my two younger brothers and younger sister, Eileen. After threatening Larry and John with nightly trips to the woodshed if she saw anything less than a B on their next report cards, and complimenting Eileen for getting all *A*s and *B*s, she turned her attention to me.

Mom commended me on the two *A*s in arithmetic, computation, and reasoning. You may wonder why I was always studious only about arithmetic, as math is difficult for many folks, but I always had a knack for numbers. When I was three or four, Dad would work with me using the coins he collected for John Hancock Life Insurance. Fascinated by how quickly I caught on to making change, he started formulating story problems:

"You have on your list two loaves of bread at nineteen cents apiece, five pounds of potatoes at twenty-three cents a bag, a quart of milk at fourteen cents, and a couple of pieces of candy for a total of two cents. You have a dollar, Tom. How much change should you get back?"

After thinking for a while, I said "Twenty-three cents, Dad, I should get twenty-three cents back."

After a number of these solved problems, Mom began sending me to the corner confectionary store at Thirty-First Street and Summit Avenue. I remember more than once or twice correcting the clerk on his errors.

Once, Mom must have needed a few more purchases than usual because she handed me her coin purse and told me to guard the money and not lose the purse. As I was walking the sidewalk between our house and the corner store, I hoped that no one would see me with a girl's coin purse. The confectionary was about a hundred yards from our house, so I thought I might have a better than even shot at concealing the purse. I noticed a few boys outside the store. I must have looked guilty as sin.

"What's that behind your back, kid?"

I knew that I needed to answer this ten- or eleven-year-old boy because I was only four and a half at tops. Slowly, I revealed the quaint little pink purse from behind my back.

"Is this cute thing what you use to carry your little coins to the store, you panty-waisted sissy?" he asked. Hmmm, I had been called a panty-waisted sissy. I do not know all those words, but I know what a *sissy* is.

"Heck no," I answered quickly, "I wouldn't be caught dead with a girl's purse. I found it a little ways back! I'm taking it to the store up there so they can give it back to the little girl, mister."

"Hand it over, punk, I'll see that it gets to the right person."

"Sure." I handed it to the boy who I was positive would beat me up. "I was getting girl cooties even holding it," I said as I spun around and ran home as fast as I could. I think I might have heard, "Hey, punk, I'm not through with you," as I quickly rounded the corner and into the house.

"Mom, Mom! This big kid robbed me up at the store!" I shouted out. Poor mom, thirty-six years old with nine children, but the minute she heard that someone had copped her change purse, she bolted from the house and ran to the confectionary flying like a night-spooked deer. (Well, not a deer, but she was running about as fast as I was.) "There's the robber, Mom," I shouted, pointing at the boy with the pink purse.

Mom lit into him as she snatched it back. "How dare you take money from a four-year-old! Without waiting for an answer, she smacked the robber with a right to his left cheek, a backhand to his right cheek and another right to his left cheek with the purse and the boy took off toward the Mississippi River at a clip closer to a deer's pace than Mom's. *I'm almost five, Mom!* I thought. Man, those right clips to the jaw with that sissy purse must have hurt. It was bigger than Dad's wallet!

Mom didn't entrust me with her precious funds after that little debacle, at least not for a while. She did resume handing me a set amount of money and sending me to the store, but never again with her sissy pink coin purse.

After her compliments for the good grades in arithmetic for the first quarter, she told me I should never receive a grade lower than a B on anything except handwriting and art, and "That D in English? I'd better not see it again, Tom." I took Mom at her word and tried not to repeat bad grades in two consecutive terms, if they were lower than a C.

"Mom, did you like Ms. Lawrence? She's a nice teacher, isn't she?" I said.

"Oh, she seems nice, and she had a lot of good things to say about you, Tom. She said you are quiet and do not disrupt class. All of your classmates like you, but she knows you could do much better in scholastics."

"Mrs. O'Connell, most of the time he does not complete his written homework," she reported to Mom. "I've tried talking to him, even threatening to keep him after school. But with the importance of the paper route, I'm stymied, Mrs. O'Connell."

Hmmm, I had been meaning to tell Ms. Lawrence I didn't have the route anymore. "Was that about the end of your meeting with my teacher, Mom?" I asked.

"Do you think that should have been the end of the discussion with your teacher, Tom?" Mom asked.

I wasn't sure if that was a rhetorical question, so I asked, "What did you say when she brought up the paper route, Mom?"

"What do you think I said, Tom?"

"Was she mad when you told her there isn't a paper route anymore?"

"Yes, Tom, I think I'd call her a bit perturbed, son. I'm certain that you and she will have a discussion tomorrow. I don't know whether a *discussion* is the proper word, I think it might be rather one-sided, if you know what I mean, son."

I mean, what could I think, except, "You fool, you should have done your written homework for the first term and then relaxed and enjoyed the rest of the year, knowing that Mom wouldn't see Ms. Lawrence after the first quarter." Of course, then I would have had to lie, say that I had a paper route when I didn't. That's worse, isn't it? I did tell Ms. Lawrence the truth; I had a paper route then, didn't I? I just didn't keep her updated is all. I'm not a noble man like George or Abraham.

Before school started in the mornings, we attended Mass each day at St. Patrick Church. After Mass, I usually walked to school slowly, absorbing my last few seconds of freedom. As I climbed the steps to the second floor and was about to enter the sixth-grade room, I felt this hard tug on my left arm, causing me to turn about 180 degrees with my back to the wall. I felt a finger poke me in the stomach and this gruff, mean-sounding voice: "I want to see you after school, buddy!" Now I didn't usually get into much trouble with the boys in my room, but I surmised there would be a butt kicking that day, and it was my butt that'd be kicked, judging from the sound of that voice.

As I raised my eyes from the poking finger, I saw Ms. Lawrence's fiery eyes with a mean grimace, a look I never imagined could come from her. "You got it, Thomas?"

"Yes, Ms. Lawrence," I answered, terrified of getting the tar beat out of me come three fifteen. She's never called me Thomas. She was more than a wee bit angry after her meeting with Mom. She took her finger away from my belly and let me pass into class. I quickened my pace in case she had a mind to kick me in the seat of the pants as a preview of what would happen at three fifteen. *You're not tricking me, Ms. Lawrence*, I thought, as I scuttled into the room.

There was a 180-degree turn in her demeanor as she opened the door, smiling. Once more, she was the nice, sweet teacher, the calm, levelheaded person who never lost control. A little heavy on the writing assignments as punishments, but I really liked her as a teacher. I had seen her darker side a moment ago, which put the fear of God into me. I might have made a mistake not updating her on the paper route. She had given me a break.

I began assessing my options. I could run away after class, which would bring temporary relief, but still I would have to attend the next day, and boy, she'd really be angry then. If she started to hit me with haymakers, I could retreat and run around the outer edges of the room, as I was faster than she. No, that would not work either. Retreating and taking cover would only cause more discomfort when she caught me.

I decided my best option would be to let it happen. If she wanted to slap me around a bit, maybe a few closed-fisted punches, take it as a man, maybe cover-up, but let Ms. Lawrence tire herself out. I deserved it, or that's how my eleven-year-old mind worked.

At three-fifteen, my classmates exited, and I approached Ms. Lawrence's desk in slow motion. I stood there for a few seconds. Slowly, she raised her eyes.

"Your mother is a remarkable woman, Tom. I can't believe how she does it, ten children in the house now," she said.

"Yes, Ms. Lawrence, my older sister Maureen is in Kentucky studying to be a nun." Which I thought might give me some points.

"I don't know whether Maureen would put it exactly that way."

"You know, Tom, you really should have done better, grade-wise. I trust your mother gave you a long talk."

"We talked about my grades, and I said I'd try to do better, Ms. Lawrence."

"I think if I were your mother, we'd talk about it a whole lot more. There's no excuse for you not to get all *As* and *Bs* if you would just apply yourself, Tom. This is excluding handwriting and art, which you cannot help. Is there anything else you and your mother talked about, Tom?"

"Umm, I could be less of a slob at my desk, Ms. Lawrence."

"I didn't say that, Tom. More orderly is the term I used."

"Well, Ms. Lawrence, I think my mom looked at my desk and a slob might have been her interpretation."

"Did she say anything more, Tom, like how the paper route was going?"

"Uh, she said something about discussing the paper route, Ms. Lawrence."

A long pause followed. "I'm waiting, Tom." *What does she want me to say?* I thought. *She's got the goods on me? I know it, she knows it, and Mom knows it. I'm not going to incriminate myself any further.*

"I don't know what you mean, Ms. Lawrence."

"How's the paper route doing, Thomas?" she asked tersely. Ooh, that Thomas again. How in the heck am I supposed to know? I hope the arrears have been paid with some of the delinquent customers, but I suppose someone else is handling the route. "I suppose it's still doing okay, Ms. Lawrence."

"How do you know, Thomas, you haven't delivered one paper in six weeks!" she said.

I looked into her accusing eyes, and there was that fiery stare again, not as mean as when she stuck her finger in my

59

belly, but she was ramping up. Was that last comment a question? What answer does she want? She certainly wants a good one; she addressed me as Thomas again. I have to think of an answer, and quick too. She's staring. Options: "I am sorry, I will never do it again"—no, inappropriate. No, please not the woodshed; "I will be good, Mom," or "Yes, Dad, bunk fatigue and I'll think about what I did." I know this never works with my parents and probably won't work with Ms. Lawrence either, but in answer to her question, "How do you know, Thomas? You haven't delivered one paper in six weeks!" my response was "I dunno."

"You don't know...spectacular answer, Thomas! In all my years, I don't think I've heard a better explanation for a student's actions! Maybe I did not make the question clear. Is that the problem, Thomas? You are a bright boy, aren't you, Thomas? One would not know it from your last report card, but you have ample brains inside that head of yours. Let's see, now, why did you lie to me regarding the paper route, knowing that you retired from the business six weeks ago, Thomas?"

Now she had fully formatted the question. Now I could think about it and, upon due reflection, produce a solution that would get her to stop calling me Thomas.

Consider the question: Why did you lie to me regarding the paper route deal? Whoa, whoa, whoa—lie? Lie to Ms. Lawrence? No, no, no, that was incongruent. If she had rephrased the sentence to say, "Tom, why didn't you tell me you quit the paper route?" well, I would have to think fast. As soon as we get "lie" thrown out of court because of lack of substance or some other fancy excuse used by lawyers on

TV, the pertinent question would be why didn't you tell me you quit the paper route six weeks ago?

I could explain it mathematically like if A=B and B=C then A=C. If a cat is a mammal, and a mammal is an animal, then a cat is an animal. No, that might warrant a serious whopping.

"I'm waiting, Thomas," I heard her say.

I hate to do this to you Ms. Lawrence, but I need some more time to think. So my answer was "I dunno" again.

"Thomas, if I hear another one of those 'I dunnos,' I'm going to scream! Certainly, you know why you lied to me, and I want you to fess up!"

"I did not lie to you, Ms. Lawrence. When I talked to you earlier in the term, I did have a paper route, and I was contributing most of the money to my family. The fact that we dropped the route six weeks ago is true also and the fact that I did not tell you also is true. I have no excuse for not keeping you apprised of the situation, except I knew that when we dropped the route, I would be sitting here after school every night."

"Would it have been better if I'd said I had no excuse for being detained after school from here on out? But knowing the situation with homework and me, it didn't seem like a clever idea from my side of the fence."

"Ms. Lawrence, you can knock me around, I probably deserve it, but that's the truth."

"I would never touch any of my students, Tom! I have no idea what made you think I would hit you, but let me assure you that you are wrong. I am just disappointed in you, Tom. I gave you a break in the first place, you know. I could have just said too bad about the paper route."

"I know, Ms. Lawrence, and I want to thank you for showing kindness toward my family. When I came up and talked to you about the paper route problem, I had no idea that my parents were thinking of dropping it. I'm sorry if I hurt you, Ms. Lawrence. I don't know if most girls would have told you when they quit the job, but I am a boy and I'm going to go out on a limb and say most boys would have acted the same way as I did, Ms. Lawrence."

"It's still wrong, Tom, regardless of who is sneaky or does the right thing. How are we going to correct this problem?"

Can't she just think of a way to punish me? I find it highly distasteful to have to figure out how to square things between us.

"I guess I'll have to stay after school for the six weeks I missed, Ms. Lawrence," I said.

"Do you think that's an appropriate punishment?" she asked. "You were very sneaky, Tom."

"I dunno," I said.

"Thomas, what did I say about the I dunnos? I'll tell you what. You stay after school each day until I tell you the punishment is over, does that sound like an equitable arrangement?"

"Okay, Ms. Lawrence." Good or bad, at least the matter was settled. And so, at the beginning of November 1964, I sat with Ms. Lawrence after school every day.

I'll never know whether I fulfilled the deal that year because I was still sitting with her until four o'clock or four fifteen each day when June of 1965 rolled around, and we were dismissed for the summer. I'll say yes, the contract was fulfilled, but unfortunately was extended due to lack of written homework during November through May. I know most people would be distressed about spending an extra hour at school with their teacher, although it was of their own doing. Really, it was not too bad for me once I got accustomed to school starting at eight forty-five and ending at four fifteen. After all, due to my craftiness, the punishment started in November rather than the middle of September, didn't it?

Ms. Lawrence was my favorite grade-school teacher. She was a pretty young woman, and although I was being punished, she talked to me in a kindly fashion about the benefits of striving to do your best at learning. I often cleaned the chalkboards, whether to be helpful or just to break the boredom of sitting there pretending to do the prior day's homework, I don't remember.

On the last day of school, when Ms. Lawrence handed out the report cards, I turned mine over to read the most important thing: "Promoted from grade six to grade seven." Yet there were no words in the "promoted" section. It was blank. If she wanted to retain me, why hadn't she scratched out "promoted" and entered "retained in grade six" in its place?

As I considered this conundrum, Ms. Lawrence mentioned a few names of those—mine included—who she wanted to see after dismissal. What really concerned me was that the names were not from the top academic tier. You know what I mean, not among the ones who raised their hands as high as possible, sometimes standing and calling "Sissstter," or in this case "Ms. Laaaaaaawrence," when she posed a question. Did I flunk? Will I be demoted to my younger brother Larry's room? I'd run away from home rather than face my parents if this were true. I was the last one on Ms. Lawrence's list that day. Walking to her desk, I was a man walking the gauntlet.

"Hand me your report card, Thomas."

Ooh, Thomas, again, as I handed her the card. Should I cry and beg her not to keep me in the sixth grade? As she gave me the completed report card, she gazed up at me with twinkly eyes and a big grin. She had written those longed-for words on the card, "Promoted from grade six to grade seven."

"Gotcha, Tom!" She must have thought. She must have seen my look of anguish disappear, replaced by a joy only matched by waking up on Christmas or a birthday. Yep, she got me good this time, at least as good as the anger she must have felt at being snookered when she heard from my mom about the paper route deal. As she handed me my final report, I thought I heard a chuckle from her direction. She might have said, "Have a nice summer, Tom"—not Thomas—although I can't remember for sure. I left the room, and I'll bet I was halfway down the stairs before she finished her goodbye. She was not going to change that seven to a six!

6

Burnt Bacon

Mom and dad wondered for a time what I was going to do with my life. I certainly could not choose a career that required two hands. While my study habits improved as I continued through school, there was no excuse for my bad habits. I am not proud of my laziness. I did manage to earn a master's degree and worked in the accounting profession until I was fifty-nine. I want to thank all my teachers along the way; I appreciate their efforts. It might not have appeared that anything was getting through my head, but enough soaked in so that I could work and provide for my family most of my life.

My older brothers, Bill and Dan, started out with the paper route around 1960 or 1961. On Saturday evenings, Dad drove them around on their route because the paper was much larger than on Mondays through Fridays. I don't recall whether the papers were delivered to our house on

Saturday or whether my father had to fetch them at Thirty-Ninth and State streets and bring them home for assembly. I can remember watching the Jackie Gleason show while my older brothers wrapped rubber bands around 150 papers.

When they were finished, Dad helped them load the papers into our beat-up old car, which always seemed to be on its last leg, and then to Thirty-Ninth Street to start their route. I always went with him on these trips, just to hang out with him, even if almost nothing was said. He was my friend and my dad. I clearly remember the aroma of his Lucky Strike cigarettes, which to me was pleasant. I never took up the nasty habit, partially because it seemed like a waste of money, but mostly because of what I saw it do to my father. Smoking made him an old man before he was fifty.

After Bill and Dan finished delivering the papers, occasionally Dad took us for rides. Sometimes the rides would be short, up St. Clair Avenue to about Fiftieth Street, where he would turn right, do some squiggly turns, and finish on State St., passing East Side high school near Henry's Hamburgers. Then we would go home via State St. to Alhambra Court. I always wished we had stopped at Henry's for a snack, but I was too afraid to ask. He had taken time out to give me a ride. I didn't push it, as had I started begging, next Saturday I might have been stuck at home with Larry and John.

Sometimes he'd take us to Circle Drive on the bluffs where we'd stop for a minute or two and look out over the Saint Louis skyline. You could see how the Gateway Arch was being constructed; I always wondered whether those two sides would meet someday. Inevitably, sports talk would start—football or boxing or who would win the American League Championship in baseball. (Dad was a rabid St. Louis Browns fan.)

"Do you think Arnold Palmer is the best golfer in the world, Dad?" Bill asked him.

"Well, I guess he is now Bill, but there've been a lot of good golfers through the years, son." *Palmer*. Where had I heard that name?

I would not ask Bill or Dan; one little fumble of a word to any of my siblings would be remembered by them for future harassment of me for three or four days. I don't blame 'em; I'd do the same, except I would string it out for a week.

I thought about it. *Palmer, Palmer*, where had I heard that name? Wasn't Mom's family name *Palmer*? Didn't Grandma address her husband most of the time as AC? His first name could not be *Arnold*, could it? I carefully approached mom and inquired in the sweetest voice I could muster, "Mom, wasn't your last name *Palmer*?"

"Yes, Tom, my maiden name was Palmer, but now it's O'Connell," she answered.

"I heard Grandma call Grandpa AC, Mom. What does the AC mean?"

"He's Grandpa to you, Tom, and if I ever hear you calling him by his first name, it's off to the woodshed for you, Buddy."

"I know, I know, Mom, I wouldn't ever call him by his first name. I was curious if he had a real name or if it was just AC."

"Well, his name is Arnel Carr, if you need to know, Tom."

His first name is Arnold! I thought. "Thanks, Mom, I just wanted to know. But I'm always going to call him Grandpa, Mom. He's a nice man. I like seeing him when he comes here from Texas."

From my seven- or eight-year-old perspective, Grandpa was Arnold Palmer. But surely, he could not be *the* Arnold Palmer. I had heard you can play golf when you're an old man, but my grandpa must be more than seventy-five years old. The poor old guy needs to use a magnifying glass to read regular sized words! Still. Arnold Palmer? A famous grandfather?

My mom was born in Pollock, Louisiana, and moved to Waco, Texas, when she was three. My grandparents lived in Waco the remainder of their lives, from which they traveled to visit us about once a year. It was June when I next laid eyes on my famous grandpa. I was puzzled because there was a fancy golf tournament happening about that time of the year. Grandpa was skipping it this year, I thought. He only has one daughter, and she must be important enough to him to forego the tournament.

That year, he fixed our back porch. At one point, he had torn away the entire steps so that you were forced to jump about three and a half feet straight down from the porch to the yard if you wanted to play a little horses or practice your dribbling on our basketball court that Dad set up for my older brothers. I wondered about how Mom would get to the backyard to burn the trash. Would she go for it and attempt a successful jump? I would have given a month of my allowance of six cents a week to be in the audience for that event. It'd be worth the nightly trip to the woodshed for a week to see Mom fail the attempt.

After ripping my pants in three or four places for the sheer joy of mounting our back porch without the steps and leaping off, only momentarily believing that I could fly, I noticed my grandpa was preparing to finish fixing our porch.

I thought about telling Grandpa that it was hot today and that tomorrow might be a better day to complete the project. I wanted to do more jumping and climbing, and see Mom try her jump on the way to taking the rubbish to the barrel.

At seven or eight years old, I was fearless. If there were a couple of ripped-up old mattresses, I might entertain the thought of somersaulting off the old porch and landing on top of them. I cannot imagine ever being that stupid now, but I am more than sixty-nine years old now, not seven.

After eight or nine jumps off the porch, I approached Grandpa cautiously. "Grandpa, why does Grandmother always call you AC?" knowing full well the answer to the question. My grandpa had this way of starting a comment, a long, drawn-out Texas drawl, although he had spent most of his growing-up days in Louisiana.

"Tommm, that's my name—or my initials anyway. Grandma's called me by those initials for a quite a spell now."

"What do those initials mean, Grandpa?" I asked to confirm that his first name was Arnold, and that Mom was not trying to trick me.

"Arnel Carr Palmer, Tommm, that's my given name."

"Car," I asked, "spelled like the new Green 1949 Pontiac that you gave my parents?" (An eleven- or twelve-year-old car was right off the assembly line for my family.)

"No, Tommm, it's a family name spelled C-a-r-r. I wanted your mama to give one of her sons Carr for a middle name, but she wouldn't budge an inch, so I reckon Carr will die with me."

"Grandpa, are you the Arnold Palmer, the famous one?" I asked.

"I don't know what you mean, Tommm. I'm Arnel Palmer from Waco, Texas, and I taught chemistry at Waco High. You must have me confused with some other Arnel Palmer, son."

A plain old Chemistry teacher. Drat.

In a last-chance shot from far beyond half court, I chucked my best and asked Grandpa if he'd miss an important golf tournament if he didn't pick up his clubs and haul them to the competition.

Grandpa's chuckle turned into a hardy laugh. "Tommm, I hate to burst your bubble, but I have never even hit a golf ball. Did a lot of fishing in my day, but never any golf. My name is even different, Arnel instead of the famous golfer Arnold," he said. "I reckon, that if I was related to him, I might be his granddaddy since I was born in 1885, Tommm."

"That's okay, Grandpa," I said. "I know you could have done anything you really wanted. I love you, Grandpa, even though you were just a Chemistry teacher." I don't know how long it took Grandpa to finish his education, but he eventually earned a master's degree in chemistry.

I didn't particularly care for high school chemistry, maybe because I did not understand it, or perhaps because it took too much effort to understand. This gave me a respect for Grandpa's intelligence and explained why my mom was brilliant. "The apple doesn't fall far from the tree," as the saying goes.

Often when my grandparents made their annual visit, three or four bushels of apples and peaches came along for the ride from Waco. Fruit was a rare commodity for us, and I loved to watch Mom peel, slice, sprinkle sugar on the peaches and let them sit for a while in the refrigerator until the heavenly juices smothered the fruit. Mom also made chunky applesauce, which I imagine was more labor-intensive than the peaches. Either way, the peaches or the applesauce, let me tell ya, Buddy, that was high living.

Grandma and my mom never saw eye to eye, and Mom gave no quarter to her mother. I tried to avoid Grandma; she scared me if you want the truth. First thing every morning she heated water, cracked open some eggs, and submerged them in the hot water surrounded by this horrifying contraption. Then she would burn some bacon for Grandpa. Whether she was talking with Mom and not paying attention to the bacon, or Grandpa liked it burned, this happened every morning. I've come to believe Grandma burned her husband's bacon on purpose which is repugnant to me. If she and Grandpa had had a tiff, I could understand her thinking, "Okay, AC, you're getting some burned bacon today, Buddy." Maybe she was tired of fixing his breakfast every time they came to East St. Louis to visit their daughter, and she was trying to give him the subtle hint that tomorrow he might consider cereal.

Last but surely not least was the toast. Grandma took three pieces of bread, two for him and one for her, dropped them into the toaster, and pushed the lever down, set to toast the bread to a nice golden brown. When it popped up, she pushed the lever again, and again, and again, and again. Smoke rose from our toaster, and I'd run in horror to fetch the bucket in case of fire. When the toast was completely black, she sometimes pushed the lever one last time to make sure it was done to her liking. She would remove what I assume once was bread, and promptly go to work on the poor fellow with a butter knife.

Tiny flecks of black ash flew all over the counter, which further confirmed I better not make Grandma angry, or she might commence to work on me like the poor old burnt toast. Sometimes you could see remnants of toast when she was finished working on it, but usually, it would take a good deal of imagination, or more scraping with the butter knife, if you wanted to see what this food was supposed to be before being burned at the stake.

Then Grandma presented her poor old husband AC Palmer (no relation to the famous golfer) his breakfast. One poached egg (brilliant description, except I never am going to be the poacher) two pieces of burnt bacon and two pieces of toast blackened to a crisp. Funny, there was never any perceptible change on Grandpa's face when he sat down to his breakfast. Instead, always a "Thank you, Annie, sure looks good." Sometimes from a safe distance, I'd watch Grandpa eat, to see whether he'd chuck a piece of that burnt bacon on the floor when Grandma wasn't looking. Nope. He would eat every bite of that breakfast and seem to enjoy it. Poor Grandpa, either his taste buds were shot from seventy-five years of living, or his wife had put the fear of God in him because she had plenty of butter knives available for grumpy old men.

After Mom suffered numerous disagreements with her mother each day, Grandpa would finally chime in, "Annie, it looks like we've worn out our welcome. I reckon we'd better go back to Waco." I guess Grandma had become a goat in my mom's eyes a long time ago…or there was only one true boss at our house.

7

The Shoes

My family moved from Thirty-First Street to 783 Alhambra Court in 1958. It was not long before Mom landed a job substitute teaching at Clark Junior High.

Mom was a wizard, a magician when it came to the finer things in life. I am not talking about trips to the woodshed—sometimes multiple trips if my younger brothers and I were not careful. I am talking about a clean slate for the day and "Top of the morning to you, ma'am," with Mom fixing us toasted apple butter sandwiches cut on the diagonal! Let me tell you, I was a king on those days, at least until I commenced to torment my younger brothers, which did not last much past breakfast.

I don't know how she did it. When I want a slice of toast, I am capable of dropping the bread into the toaster and pushing the little thingy down. When the toast pops up is when I'm stymied. I'm chasing the darn toast all over the counter while trying in vain to apply the margarine. Seems my right fist has no influence on the wily little rascal. The toast is stationary until I place my fist on the lower right quadrant of the toast and attempt to spread the margarine with my good hand. The chase is on from there, with my right fist (God bless its soul) having not the least idea of the meaning of stability.

Oh, I do the job eventually, but the toast is stone cold when completed, and I wonder whether I would rather have plain old bread and butter than stone cold toast. Mom, on the other hand, could negotiate four pieces of bread in the toaster at once. With three hungry boys to feed at least three sandwiches, on average, two slices of bread in the toaster would be unworthy of the task. When the toast popped up, she sprang into action with catlike speed.

Apparently, Mom inherited her mother's knifing skills that she used to remove the ash from the poor burnt toast she fixed her husband every morning. Either this was the reason for her rapid-fire buttering of the toast, or my mom was born with the skill, honed by thousands of repetitions. After buttering all four slices, she deftly applied store-bought apple butter, a tricky procedure at best for me. Apply too much apple butter and you ruin the sandwich, too little and you have two pieces of toast with nary a taste of the apple butter. Mom completed the process to perfection every time. She slapped the two pieces of toast together, cut them diagonally, and presented them to the next hungry boy waiting in queue.

When I took the first bite of the toasted apple butter sandwich, sliced into two in a manner reserved only for kings, the masterpiece was warm, with each component of the sandwich perfectly aligned with my taste buds. I remember those sandwiches quite fondly, although it is more than sixty years since my mom prepared them for my younger brothers and me.

That's one of the reasons our babysitter and I did not see eye to eye, from the first day she came to our house to watch us while my mom taught school. The babysitter had no toasted apple butter sandwich skills. Oh, she made the effort, I will give her that, but if I were grading her, she'd get a D on her report card. I should have been satisfied. It was food that she provided me, but when you're a king suddenly demoted to a snotty-nosed peasant boy where toasted apple butter sandwiches are concerned, it is a blow few people can bear.

I do not know what she was doing when the toast popped up. Snap to it, lady, time's a wasting, and the bread is quickly cooling. When she would finally decide to resume making the sandwiches, she moved in slow motion taking the bread from the toaster and then put way too much margarine on the toast. Not blessed with my mom's knifing skills, she would take one or two swipes at the margarine, followed by the application of far too much apple butter. As a final indignity, she cut the sandwich into two rectangles and slapped it down in front of me. I recall saying, "My mom always cuts them cornerwise," to which her reply was "I'm not your mom and eat that apple butter sandwich or you're not going to like what I do next, Tommy." What gives with this old lady?

She was at least as old as my mom—ancient. Didn't Mom have a talk with her about how obstinate I could be at times? Maybe the babysitter was trying to assert her dominance over this five- or six-year-old boy. All I know is that I did not like the lady from day one, or her apple butter sandwiches!

A couple of evenings after Mom started substitute teaching, I was watching a movie about some men who were chasing a guy who had double-crossed them. The bad guy, who was a bit of an antihero, continued to escape his comeuppance. I'm not sure if I fell asleep for a while, but the next thing I saw was another escape scene. The pursuers fired their guns indiscriminately at our clever antihero. It looked like he was a goner. Suddenly, he dove to the ground, skidded a few feet, and lay motionless, letting his pursuers think they had rubbed out their double-crosser. The gangsters kicked the motionless body a few times to be sure he was dead and, satisfied that the task was achieved, sped away in their 1920s souped-up car. A few seconds after they left, up popped the grinning double-crosser. Foiled again, you suckers! I took note. Forevermore, I would know how to hoodwink my adversaries in a pinch: play dead.

Cash was not readily available in the O'Connell household. Oftentimes, as soon as we outgrew, or in my case, destroyed, our clothing, we inherited our older brother's or sister's clothes, which at times were in about the same shape as the clothes we were wearing before the upgrade.

The only item of clothing that had my mom thwarted was shoes. There was nothing salvageable to be handed down to younger brothers. Tennis shoes were cheap—two pairs for $5 at Hill Brother's. To a certain extent, you get what you pay for, as they say. I blew out the entire right tire on one pair of shoes, after only a couple of day's use. Mom was not pleased when I showed her the sole hanging by two or three inches from the upper shoe.

We tried to keep our shoes in good repair for the longest time possible. But first, the sole would be eaten away until you would need a high-powered microscope to see any semblance of tread. In a few more weeks, the sole would mysteriously disappear, then the foam rubber, or whatever lived between your foot and the ground, would begin to vanish. Then came the battle between your bare foot and the rocks that always worked their way into your shoes to make mincemeat out of your socks. Often, I wished I were a cat with those soft little pads on their paws, with nary a thought about crossing a rocky outcrop. I tried keeping my feet intact by placing cardboard inside the shoes, knowing this was at best only a temporary fix. Finally, I had to beg my mom for new tennis shoes, not because I really wanted them, but because I was weary of cutting up empty cereal boxes for the fix-up job. I'm sure Mom would've given in a long time before she did, had she a few dollars in her pocketbook. But she needed to weigh my new shoes against the luxury of eating.

I was fighting the same old battle with the shoes one day while Mom was out substitute teaching. I had already given my shoes the temporary fix five or six times, so I figured it was time to pester Mom about a new pair. What was I thinking when I asked the crabby old babysitter her opinion about my dilemma?

What did I expect her to say? "Sure, Tommy, just let me get my pocketbook and I'll run out and buy you a new pair of shoes." If I had thought about it first, I would have realized how foolish it was to get her involved in my problem. Mom made only twenty dollars a day, so I reasoned that the crabby old woman got five dollars per day to watch us. Was she going to take her five dollars to Hill Brothers and buy one of my brothers and I a new pair of shoes—you had to buy two pairs to get the deal?

Plus as far as I knew, she did not have a car. Was she going to walk two long blocks to State Street carrying my baby sister Eileen with three wild boys in tow—boys who'd be running amok on the streets, dodging cars and almost giving her a heart attack? Would she walk all the way to Fifty-Ninth Street? (Alhambra Court was really Thirty-Fifth Street.)

"That is really a sad pair of shoes, Tommy," the babysitter said. "Don't you have another pair to wear?" I tried to imagine myself having two pairs of shoes at a time. *Wasteful*, I thought, but a second pair sure would come in handy now.

"I don't have a second pair of shoes that fit," I said.

"Tommy, certainly in a house full of children you can find a pair you can wear until your mom can take you to buy new ones."

"My feet are too big to fit in Larry's or John's, and besides, then *they* wouldn't have any shoes," I said.

"Well, what do you want me to do about it, Tommy?" she asked. I suddenly realized to whom I was talking at that moment and realized that of course she is not going to help me. If she had brought a bag with ten pairs of new tennis shoes exactly my size, she would not have given me a single pair, the grouchy old woman. She was persistent; I'll hand her that.

Our house was not too orderly, so she had to pick up many piles of clothes tossed in corners in her quest for shoes my size. A pig would be embarrassed to call the back of the basement his residence! It was Larry's, John's, and my room, as well as the final resting place for junk of all types. Finally, after a bit of hunting, she picked up some clothes in the back of our basement and unearthed a pair of black-and-white hard shoes waiting to be worn.

"How about these, Tommy?" The hunt was over, at least from her perspective. The shoes were my size. She seemed proud of herself for finding them.

I knew exactly where those black-and-white shoes were. I had stepped on them about two months prior, underneath the same pile of clothes where the babysitter found them. Although those shoes might have been a viable option in a utopian world, I had disregarded them as a solution to my problem. I was aware that they had some good wear in them, from my examination from afar, but they were girls' shoes, which removed them from the mix altogether. I remembered seeing the same shoes on my sister Anne's feet; ergo, it was completely preposterous to propose that my feet would touch a shoe worn by a girl! Moreover, if my older brother Dan had been the original owner of the shoes, the moment Anne's feet went into them, they'd be deemed girls' shoes and thrown in the null set, never to be worn by any self-respecting boy.

"What about these, Tommy?" the babysitter inquired for the second time. "They look about your size. Let's try 'em on!" I looked at her for a few seconds, giving her ample time to think about the ridiculous question she had just asked. "Well, how about it, Tommy?"

"No! Those're girls' shoes!" I exclaimed.

"They're not just girls' shoes, Tommy. Both girls and boys wear saddle shoes, and they're real nice. Let's try 'em!"

Was she nuts? The heels were a good inch to an inch and a half high, and everyone knew the colors black and white were for sissies!

"Nope. I saw Anne wearing 'em last year, so those are girls' shoes."

My six-year-old belligerence—a six-year-old boy telling her what he was or was not going to do made the babysitter hot under the collar. I wasn't trying to make her mad; I simply was not going to wear girls' shoes.

"I don't care if they're boys or girls' shoes, you're going to wear 'em, Tommy!"

"No, I'm not!" I shouted. She made a couple of quick steps toward me, and the chase was on, around and around the basement.

Our big beast of an oil furnace in the middle of the basement was fed by a pipe from the oil tank. It measured about four feet square and rose to the basement ceiling, with ductwork spreading to all areas of the house. Occupying another two or three feet toward my older brothers' room was the water heater, with a chimney to remove the oil fumes. The whole setup, as I remember it, was about ten feet long and four feet wide. Next to the chimney was my mom's washer and dryer. There was only about a foot and a half clearance between the washer and dryer and the chimney. As you made the swing around the chimney, you'd have to jam on the brakes when approaching the curve to avoid crashing through the plasterboard wall of the aqua stinky room.

The aqua stinky room was the prior sleeping quarters for my younger brothers Larry, John, and me. Due to some disagreements between my younger brother Larry and me, my father needed to replace, on more than one occasion, various sections of the plasterboard wall. After three or four instances of repair work foisted upon my father, we were banished to the back of the basement. I recall a secret passage to the stinky room, the last section of repair work that Dad left open for future disagreements between his boys.

If you timed a zig off your left foot before you crashed into the washer and continued at a precise forty-five-degree angle, you'd have a good chance of making it into the stinky room without losing much speed. Once you made it there, you'd be in a peck of trouble! Even if you executed a complete roll off the stinky room wall that you were approaching in four or five feet, you would crash into a double-sided wall, which would hurt for sure. If I were stupid enough to attempt the "zig" a few times, I think I would have had a better-than-average shot at having my stroke at age seven instead of nine.

When an older brother was trying to impress upon me, corporally, mind you, that he was lord of the manor, and I was no more than a serf and should be satisfied to live in his kingdom, I felt my best option would be to head for "the circuit" at the back of the basement. I realized it would end badly for me, but if I could get to the circuit, I might prolong the inevitable. If I had a good lead on him, the chase would begin. I would gallop at full speed for about eight feet, hit the brakes, and cut hard right for four feet, igniting the thrusters for another eight feet, followed by braking, pressing hard to the right again for four feet and igniting the thrusters once more.

I had no illusions of running faster than Bill or Dan. If we were outside in a dead outrun, there would not be any contest. They were five and six years older than me, and exceptionally fast for kids their age. Inevitably, they would catch me during the chase around the chimney. Sometimes it would take some doubling back on the road I covered, and I'd run straight into their clutches. I was lucky, though, as there was so much age discrepancy, they never hit me. They'd tickle me for about five minutes straight until I couldn't breathe. Never anything worse than that.

When I reached the circuit, I had a short lead on the babysitter. Will she really engage in a race-around-the-chimney game with me? She had to be over forty years old, and it looked to me that she had not run in twenty years. Would she try to catch me? Good luck, lady. I ran forward toward the washer, and when I turned the corner at the chimney, I knew it had to take the wind from her sails. I waited to see if she were chasing me. When she rounded the chimney, she was madder than an old wet hen.

She shouted, "You get over here right this instant, Tommy!"

Yeah, so you can put those girls' shoes on me. No way, lady! She quickened her steps again, so I ran to the chimney and looked back to see if she was continuing the chase.

She rounded the furnace looking winded but continued the chase. I had to admire the old lady for her tenacity. When she passed the halfway point, I rounded the chimney again and ran to the furnace to see if she was still in pursuit. One or two seconds passed: no lady. *Oh, the old double-cross*, I thought, as if I'm going to run smack into her hands. I peered around the furnace. There she was, blocking the path between the washer and the chimney. I was tempted to put my hands to my ears and wiggle my fingers while saying "Nyeah-nyeah," but luckily, I felt sorry for her. She was already mad enough without the taunt. Again, she demanded that I come to her this instant.

"I'm not wearing those girls' shoes!" I shouted. She charged toward me again. I cannot really say she was running; it was more like a quick shuffle. Looking back at age sixty-nine, the spirit was willing, but her body said, "No way!" I darted through the back of the basement and through the red room and stood near the steps, watching her chug to the chimney. I had two options: run up the stairs or continue the chase through the aqua stinky room.

I do not know why I elected to continue the chase; did I want to break her spirit, or was it just for the exhilaration of the chase? I ran into the stinky room and quickly exited by the secret passage created either by brother Larry or me throwing the other one through the plasterboard wall. I often wished that I could see the look on the babysitter's face as she turned into the stinky room and saw the hole in the wall into which I'd escaped. I knew she thought she had me now, the little stinker, until she spied the secret passage into the back of the basement. I waited at the furnace as I heard her stumble through the secret passage, her body glancing slightly off the chimney. She was tired now; I heard her breathing heavily as she leaned on the washer to balance herself. She gave out a meek, "Come here this instant, Tommy" as she gathered herself near the washer to continue the chase.

For the first time since my mom started substitute teaching on a consistent basis, I admired this woman. She must have known by now it would be a frigid day in July before she caught me, and that I could play chase-around-the-chimney for hours, yet she made a valiant effort to catch me. As I trotted toward my older brothers' bedroom, I thought of a way to end the game. She was old; I did not want her to wrench her back or injure a leg. Suddenly I remembered the gangster movie and how the antihero hoodwinked the gangsters.

Quickly, I decided to reduce my trot to a quick walk so the poor woman could catch up to me. When she lessened the distance between us, I planned to start running again, through the red room, make the left turn into the stinky room, and then do a belly flop on the floor and remain motionless. She might kick me a couple times, but seeing no movement, she would assume I was dead and go upstairs to resume her babysitting duties with my live brothers and sisters. A great plan, I might say, although it was not original.

I put my main plan into action, let her almost catch me, ran again through the red room, took the hard left, and dove to the stinky room floor, skidding an impressive two or three feet after hitting the tile. I wished at that moment that my dad had put more cushioning than a one-eighth-inch tile over the concrete floor. My body lay motionless while I waited for the kicks from the sitter. Several seconds passed before she hoisted me to a standing position. As she swatted me several times, I realized, this was not exactly how it happened in the movie. After the spanking, I heard, "Now. Put on these shoes, Tommy, and I mean now!"

I broke away from her, and as I exited the secret passageway through the stinky room I shouted, "No way, ma'am!"

Why did we call the aqua room the stinky room? It might be that sometimes the room smelled like rotten eggs or sulfuric acid. There was a little sink that might have been the perpetrator, which likely was connected to the drainage system.

I ran to the back of the basement behind a makeshift table that my dad devised as an additional storage space for sundries. As she slowly reached the opposite side of the table, she pleaded, "What difference does it make whether they're girls' shoes or boys' shoes, Tommy?"

"If you don't know, ma'am, I know you were once a girl, without even seeing you or knowing your name."

"Fine, Tommy, I'm through with you and the shoes, but don't think I'm not going to tell your mother about this."

I don't recall getting into too much trouble with Mom regarding this episode. She well understood the repercussions of my wearing girls' shoes; she was never as mean to me as the sitter. This further confirmed my opinion that they were girls' shoes. My mom knew it and the babysitter should have known it. Ms. Ko—oh, I almost blew it and told you her name. She has passed by now, God bless her soul, but one of her daughters might try to squeeze my feet into a pair of those black-and-white oxfords to make things square with their mother and me. The only problem would be those shoes would have to be women's size 16 to fit my feet nowadays.

8

The Caddie

My mom assumed I'd be involved in every altercation that occurred in her house, and it annoyed me when she would shout my name when I was innocently eating a bowl of cereal in the same room where she was boiling potatoes or cleaning the counter. To be honest, though, if she had blurted out, "Tom, stop it!" during any altercation that occurred, 90 percent of the time she would have been right, to merit a solid B-plus average on her report card.

I was thirteen or fourteen when Uncle Laur gave me his starter set of golf clubs. My father's younger brother by sixteen months, Uncle Laur was a busy man who no longer had time for golf or any other leisure activity. The starter set included four irons, a three, five, seven, and nine, a putter, a driver, and a spoon (three-wood). Since I was right-handed before the stroke, you could say I was left-handed after the conversion, or more appropriately, I use my left side for everything I do. My uncle Laur was left-handed from birth, which made the gift of the clubs perfect for my use.

Dad and Uncle Laur did not reason it might be a good idea to introduce me to golf because either of them had a vast knowledge of the sport. Dad might have hit a couple buckets of balls at a driving range at some point. My uncle had more experience in smacking the little ball around the green. Their rationale was that I would not have to spot most people so much on this sport, seeing that I could use chiefly only one arm and one leg. It did not matter to me how good I was at an activity. The only thing I demanded of myself was the absolute best I could do under the circumstances. If the mark came up a little shy of the optimum efficiency set by an objective person (me), I was not a happy camper. This was a frequent happening. Or let's put it this way: I was not going to be the next Arnold Palmer.

The human body is a fascinating piece of machinery, coming equipped as it does with two hands, two arms, two feet, and two legs. The arms, hands, legs, and feet (let us call these the extremities) are simply cogs of the machine that take orders from the central processing unit. The extremities do their best not to deviate from anything the CPU tells them, nor do they have a mind of their own. If the CPU's container is compromised (perhaps recklessly) and can only direct one half of the extremities to do their jobs, the other half sits idle, ready to act on the orders of the CPU and wondering what in the heck happened to the instructions it had previously received numerous times a day. After months and years of inactivity, the idle extremities conclude it is time for bed and atrophies over time.

Since the clubs were left-handed, it should not have mattered that my right extremities had gone to sleep some time before this, and being stubborn like the rest of my self, refused to wake up. Unfortunately for left-handers, the right side is where the power is generated and the transfer of weight from left to right ain't gonna happen with *my* right leg. I could modify the swing pattern by converting to right-handed. This would give me beaucoup power from my left arm, but it would rip to shreds the inactive muscles of my right arm, wrist and hand and might tear off the hand and send it flying down the fairway, hopefully straight. Even though it has not helped me much these last sixty years, I'm fond of my right hand. Its lack of performance is not its fault. The fault lies totally with the CPU. Hmmm, on second thought, I think I'll become a mediocre left-handed golfer, as I preferred that to searching for my right hand somewhere down the fairway.

My uncle Laur took me to the driving range a few times, so generally, I did not whiff anymore. Funds were low, so my uncle bought a few whiffle balls the approximate size of golf balls. I made holes around the outside of our house. It was exciting when the ball flew over our fence and into the backyard (another successful fairway hit) or over a bush in the backyard, to land just short of the garage (the green).

Something was missing, I thought. A caddie! I needed a caddie. One who would carry my clubs and hand me the proper club for the shot. One who would work cheap, i.e., free, just to hang out with his older brother—my little brother, Mike, eleven years younger! Yes, he would do it;

well, at least until he found out that carrying clubs for the sheer fun of it was for the birds. We walked to the left side of our house, I shoved a tee in the ground and placed a plastic whiffle ball on top.

"Give me a driver, my young man."

Mike, with a smile on his face, said, "Tom, I'm not a young man, I'm only four. What's a driver?"

"It's the longest stick in the bag with a chunk of wood on one of the ends."

Mike looked into the bag and whipped out a driver on first try. From there, things get a little hazy regarding the first—and only—day with Mike as my caddy. I'm sure I told him to stand back at least five feet to save his poor head when I swung the club. I took the driver, pried open my right hand as best I could, and then worked the club and the right hand for a good ten or fifteen seconds until they became one, or as best I could do within the time constraints so as not to get penalized a stroke for slow play.

I am a tall fellow, with the arm length to make a gorilla accidentally break one of the commandments: "Thou shalt not covet thy neighbors' goods." Furthermore, I could not follow through from my left side to my right. One of my axioms after nine years and two months of life: you do not hop around on your right leg unless you're willing to suffer the consequences of falling or wrenching your knee any time you try such foolishness. Also, there is a direct correlation between age and getting seriously maimed when I play the fool by trying to perform tricks solely with my right leg. Maybe if I had actually told Mike to step back a bit, I should have said seven feet instead of five. If I pondered it more, I'd have realized that a four-year-old has no concept of distance. I should have watched the little guy a tad more closely.

As I took my backswing, I heard a resounding clunk, which I was sure could be heard a block away in every direction, followed by my little brother's high wail as he ran to our mom to relieve his pain. As I entered the house, Mom already had a washcloth wrapped around a few chunks of ice on Mike's head. Obviously, she thought I'd deliberately socked my youngest brother in the head with one of my clubs. There was no sense denying it; I'd been found guilty in absentia in Mom's court long before I entered the house to check on Mike. Hopefully, he knew it was purely accidental.

Regardless of the situation, Mom always gave me the benefit of the doubt. She never gave up and she always supported me. She loved me in a way that only a mother could. I was never a goat to her—always a lamb in her eyes, and she was proud to call me her son.

Mom was born on August 31, 1921, in Pollock, Louisiana. The family moved to Waco, Texas, when she was three years old. Her father always said an ideal family would be one where each brother and each sister would have at least one brother and one sister, a minimum family size of four siblings. It did not work out that way for my mom. She was an only child and, hence, grew up extremely lonely. Her dream was to bear at least one son so that she could watch him play football. For Mom, Texas and football were always in the same sentence. With six sons, she ended up with five potential football players. Football was out of the picture for me after the stroke.

My father was a big sports proponent. But he did not allow his sons to engage in boxing or tackle football. He liked *watching* both sports as long as his sons were not on the team. Dad was a worrier; he did not want to see his boys hurt.

Both with college degrees, my grandparents emphasized education. Mom graduated from Baylor University at age nineteen with a degree in biology and one course short of a double major in mathematics.

Her interest in biology might have been the reason she had a pet alligator roaming around her room at home. She was horrified when she came home from Baylor and found him frozen on the back porch. Did the alligator meander onto the back porch on a cold Texas day? Or was he helped out the door? Trust me, if I had a three-foot long alligator snap at me while I was cleaning my daughter's room, either the alligator or Annie Palmer would have to go. Call me self-centered, but I am partial to my arms and hands, including the poor, old right ones.

Mom was offered free additional schooling at Arizona State and Colorado for postgraduate work, but she was young and anxious to get out into the world, so she accepted a teaching job in Jasper, Texas, where she met my father in 1941. I do not think they planned on eleven children, twelve counting the miscarriage, but each of their children were thoroughly welcomed as soon as Mom and Dad knew that she was pregnant. As he held his dead baby and wept, my father named the potential baby Jerry or Jeri, the sibling I never knew. My parents always struggled to make ends meet but always demonstrated plenty of love and affection for each of their sons and daughters.

Mom was great at stretching a dollar until it cried uncle. I can't imagine how she did it, even with financial help from my brothers and sisters. One Christmas, she won a toy tank, "Tiger Joe" from the IGA food store, which she gave to Larry, John, and me. She was proud that she could give us something that she never could afford. I won't forget the look in her eyes when she presented us her gift—the best look ever of any child opening presents on Christmas morning. Never did I see or know of my mother buying or wanting a new dress or even some halfway decent jewelry. Anything of a material nature was always for her children or husband.

My dad had to collect from his clients the monthly or weekly amounts due on their life insurance. Mom helped Dad reconcile his insurance accounts weekly, which sometimes took hours if you were lucky, and they balanced the first time. Dad was grumpy when the reconciliation was off and sometimes directed that grumpiness toward Mom. Never did she utter what most people would say when unkindness was thrown their way, something like "You can darn well do this yourself, Buddy. Here I am among the hundreds of other things on my plate, trying to help you." Instead she sucked it up, took the high road, and encouraged him: "Don't worry, Bill, we'll get this reconciliation figured, honey."

Evelyn Palmer could have done anything she wanted to do. She was a genius. Instead, she was pregnant more than one hundred months of her life, and having to put up with me, which was no bargain with ten additional sons and daughters, always wondering where the next dollar would come from. But it was she, not Dad, who shaved every nickel and dime to its utmost potential.

I always felt her tremendous capacity for love. Never did I feel cheated because I did not have all the niceties like other folks. I always felt safe knowing that I had the greatest gift of all—twelve people I could count on to be in my corner, especially Mom and Dad. Yes, sometimes I thought Mom was hard on me, but I know I'm a better person for her love and attention.

When most of her children were grown and either married or ventured out on their own, Mom started secretarial work for the Religious Education Department of the Belleville Diocese. Ironically, she hated teaching and always claimed her parents forced her into it. She worked for the diocese until she was just past seventy-five, nurturing many friendships and always talking about her children and sharing how proud she was of all of us.

As time passed, I finally began to put more effort into my studies, so that I did manage to graduate with a degree in accounting. With this degree, I made my contribution to society for thirty-seven years. In the light of my own marriage and two children, I realize how lucky I am to have been raised by Evelyn Palmer, surely the most precious gem of all.

When the St. Louis Cardinals left for Phoenix, I tried to compensate her for all the trouble I caused as a kid by taking her on a number of outings to the Kansas City Chiefs and later to the Indianapolis Colts. My wife Mary and I took our mothers out to New England for a couple of weeks soon after we were married, which was important, as Mary's mother died shortly thereafter. We took her and our children on several three or four-day excursions in the Midwest. The best part of those trips for Mom was treasured time with her grandchildren. She had so much room in her heart for Lisa and Tommy.

When Jackie Smith and Dan Dierdorf were inducted into the Pro Football Hall of Fame as St. Louis Cardinals in 1994 and 1996 respectively, my brother, Mike, and I took her to Canton, Ohio, for the ceremonies. She was in a high state of excitement all through the trip. Had I detested football, which I certainly do not, it would have been worth the trip anyway, just to see Mom's eyes in Canton. This may sound ridiculous now, with all the facets of football reported on cable, but she adored the twenty-odd minute reels of various teams. Her favorite reel was the Cardiac Cardinals in the 1970s, which she watched four or five times. The elder projectionist said to me, "Your mom sure does like football, doesn't she, son?"

I nodded with a big grin and said, "Mister, she sure does!"

The induction ceremonies were awesome. We would arrive at the Hall three or four hours early, park our car, and walk the five or six blocks, folding chairs in hand while I was obliged to quicken the pace to catch up to Mom! We placed our lawn chairs as close as we could to the stage and waited in the late summer heat, eagerly anticipating the event. The behemoth men, many brought to tears, explained what an honor it was to be recognized in this way and they openly shared their struggles. Each new inductee had something special to say about his mother, of how important she was to his success.

I hope I gave back to my mom a little bit of what she gave to me. Her love can never be fully repaid; how could it when she gave me life and she attended to my every need from birth onto adulthood? How could the debt be settled when she made me feel safe and warm as only a mother could? When I ran to her for comfort, she was always there. She taught me right from wrong so that those parts of me that are honest and honorable are in large part a reflection of her. I love you, Mom.

9

The Bonfire

I was born on January 10, 1953, exactly thirty-nine years after my father, who always told me I was the best birthday present he ever received. We were always close; I respected and admired my father as a father. He was a deep friend to me, a man who would stand with me, always be with me when times were rough, and who genuinely liked hanging out with me. Any person who was raised by my mother and father and knew how much they sacrificed for their children would respect them as parents, but I also had one of my best friends in my dad. There were a few tussles along the way, with words only. But words can cut, wound, and ruin a friendship. When all the words were bantered about, a cut here an insult there, enough to make me steamed, I remembered who I was hurting with my words: a man who would die for me or any one of his children, a faithful friend. I knew the hatchet must always be buried; our friendship always preserved.

Sometimes, the fire must smolder for a few days, lest you stomp on red-hot coals absentmindedly while forgetting to put on your shoes. When it was safe to approach, I talked with the man—my father, my friend—and apologized for any mean comments. Sometimes saying I'm sorry is the hardest thing to do. You and I believe we are right all the time, don't we? Yet sometimes the greater person is the one who forgives and forgets, as my father always did with me.

My dad always owned junky cars. These cars were ready to take their last breath when Mr. O'Connell acquired them. In the early 1970s, he acquired a cool-looking fire-engine red 1957 Chevy with those big fins on the rear. It cost $85 tax included. Now in 1973, $85 was certainly worth more than $85 today, but had I been the seller of the Chevy, I would have suffered several sleepless nights of shame for selling it even for that amount to Bill O'Connell.

My dad was not a tidy man, at least regarding his car. He carried around that huge insurance book for his clients, which weighed at least twenty pounds. For some reason, he removed pages from the big book and threw them in the back seat of his car. I imagine these excess pages were not needed; my mom and dad would never have been able to reconcile the weekly accounts if this were true. Instead of occasionally cleaning out the back seat, he would continue to chuck the used insurance sheets into the back. I do not know the average number of sheets he threw in the back seat per day, but there probably were thousands of them when the car bit the dust and Dad needed another car, which usually was biannually. He was a little more than six feet tall and did not weigh more than 150 pounds most of his life. I imagine if the car could have talked, it would have said, "Hey, Pops, how about ditching some of these old insurance sheets? They're killing my rear end! At age fifteen, I do my best to keep up my end of the bargain. So get these fifty-pound bags of cement off my back, or I'm going on strike."

Eventually, the bright red '57 Chevy with the big rear fins petered out and went to the place where good cars go—those that gave their all for my dad. It was not that my dad was mean to them, mind you; he always gave them ethyl for sustenance and filled them with brand-new oil when it was time for the oil change. But each of Dad's old cars had already worked twelve to fifteen years before he acquired them, and he put only tough city miles on the poor things every time he drove them. And there were those unneeded bags of cement, which in my mind, finally finished every car.

It was one of those miserably sweltering summer evenings shortly after we moved from the house on Thirty-First Street to 783 Alhambra Court. The new house, at least for the O'Connell's, offered two bedrooms, a halfway decent-sized living room, a humongous dining room, a not-too-big kitchen and one bathroom. My parents took one bedroom, and my sisters took the other. My brothers' and my accommodations were in the basement, which was a little cooler than the rest of the house, but not by much. We did not have air-conditioning through most of my childhood, not even a window unit. On one of those days in East St. Louis when the temperature never fell below eighty at night, it was brutal in the house. I recall my little brothers lying as close as possible behind a huge fan, trying to absorb all the moving air. We did have window fans, which were supposed to circulate the air, but they didn't cool it, so they were not much relief from the heat.

At times, my parents took us for extended rides in the car for relief. Ethyl gas, the good kind, was inexpensive when I was a boy—fifteen or twenty cents a gallon—so the rides were a cheap way to cool off. All my siblings, including me, would pile in stacked two or three deep in the back seat. I would always get stuck on one of my older sister's laps, probably because of the altercations that were sure to ensue if I were placed elsewhere. Seat belts were not invented yet, so Kathie or Maureen had their girls' arms around me. I understood I had to compromise to be included in the mix for the ride. Mom and dad would take the front seat with one or two of their younger children between them, Dad securely holding the youngest child on his lap with one arm, and another between him and my mom. Mom was prone to car sickness if she did not drive. We all rolled down our windows as far as we could for maximum coolness. That was our air-conditioning. Mom backed slowly from our driveway or away from the curb. We usually made our way to St. Clair Avenue and over a viaduct, to leave East St. Louis proper.

We would pass the Stoplight Restaurant, which had good chicken, we heard, and the minimum-security prison of Assumption High School on the other side of the street. I might have said it felt like a minimum-security prison when I was there, but it was not that bad with the Brothers of Mary doing most of the teaching. I would have liked it a little better if there had been about 50 percent women in my high school instead of none. Oh, I'd be afraid of 'em at first, but hopefully, after about two years I would have been comfortable enough to engage in short conversations, maybe even making good friends with some of them. I have a right to dream, don't I? In any event, girls would have vastly improved the scenery, although it might have decreased Assumption's academic standing, at least among the guys.

As we passed the stoplight, St. Clair Avenue became US Route 50, and the speed limit went up to fifty-five or sixty. We were technically in northeastern East St. Louis, where there appeared many farms on the left side of the road. Mom would increase her speed to the appropriate level, and it felt wonderful to have the air blowing about me, albeit in eighty-plus-degree heat. Often, my dad called Mom a jockey and asked her to slow down as he stomped hard on his imaginary brake on the passenger side. Now I had ridden in a car with both parents driving, and if a jockey were defined as a person who scared your pants off while at the wheel, my dad would undoubtedly win easily. His feeling of helplessness as a passenger might have spurred the term "jockey." Though she never said a word, I don't think Mom much liked the term as applied to her.

Usually we would pass the French Village Drive-In and start to climb the mountains, or what I called mountains as a young boy. They were only bluffs, a hundred feet high, but one might excuse a city boy for the error when an elevation rise of three or four feet at the property owned by the Boyers was a big deal around our neighborhood. Sometimes our route would pass the giant Collinsville Ketchup bottle, also at least a hundred feet high. I wished we could have stopped there so I could have climbed that ketchup tower to the top. I knew I could do it if my dad gave me a chance, climbing cautiously up those girders, of course. Sometimes we'd head south on the same road to Belleville and eventually see the square, which was a round-about with a fountain in the middle where the water magically changed colors as it danced up and down.

Occasionally, we would take an alternate route from the bluffs, and then up we would climb, turning right about halfway up, and onto a narrow road. Around and around we would go, always up, up, to turn onto Circle Drive and stop at a clearing to overlook East St. Louis and the St. Louis skyline. The buildings were not as tall then, and there was no giant arch by the Mississippi River, but the scene was impressive to me as a boy.

On a couple of occasions, we stopped at an A&W Root Beer drive-in at Eighty-Ninth and State, where my parents would buy each of us a tiny glass of the famous root beer, so cold that there was frost all over the glass—high living for this American boy. Often, we would wind home through East St. Louis. Past Robert Hall, the National Bottling Company, where my uncle would buy all the sodas for the Altar Boys Summer Picnic and Hill Brothers Shoe Store where you could get two pairs for five dollars. Mom would take us around a bend on State Street past Custard's Last Stand, past East Side Senior High School and Henry's Hamburgers. If we were lucky, there was a train crossing around Forty-Second Street, and I would get to count the passing cars—that is, if the gates were down and you could see the locomotives pulling the cars. We'd pass American Lumber Company and Dairy Queen on Fortieth Street, past Tri-City Grocery store and finally hang a right on Alhambra Court where the pillars stood, or at least a sculpture that I defined as pillars. I always had a sense of adventure on those cooling rides. I liked them mostly because they were a family event, as I genuinely liked my siblings most of the time, and appreciated the time and effort of my parents, who sacrificed much for their children. They always took time out to do something enjoyable for us.

The house at 783 Alhambra Court was equipped with a big front porch, completely screened when my parents acquired it. I do not know how long it remained screened; time passes slowly for a child. A young couple with one or two kids could have kept the screens intact for many a year, but a mom with nine children had little chance. I imagine she warned us about the screens. It is not as if one day my brothers and I decided the screens had to go and summarily ripped them off.

It was a mix of little incidents. For example, a lad attempting to circle the porch from outside the screens, only to have one or two of his brothers hit the inside of the screen with enough force to knock him down from the three- or four-foot-high porch. A dispute over the above action might have led to some abuse to the screen, solely due to it blocking the porch proper and our front yard. Mind you, this did not happen every day, so no one could be clearly targeted as the perpetrator, i.e., "Tom tore off all of our front porch screens, Mom," but I will tell you in three, four years max, our front porch was void of all screens.

The screens and the wooden frames to which they once were attached were relegated to our garage, where they were waiting to be repaired once my parents had enough money to buy the parts. I revisited our house at 783 Alhambra Court a couple of years ago, and whoever lives there now has a fine-looking front porch, but unfortunately, not a screen is to be seen to seal out the summer bugs. On the bonus side, I found a way to occupy my summer hours by using the screens to filter the cinders in the garage, so that only fine cinder dust remained. It was cool to feel the smoothness of the cinder dust minus the rocks. I guess I *am* a relative of Romulus or Remus, and I do long for a dusty cave where a docile she-wolf and I could become friends.

Shortly after we moved to the house, when the porch was still screened, my family sat out there on many a scorching summer day. At first, I wouldn't be caught dead lazing there like an old person. Instead, I'd be out in the front yard playing freeze tag; red light, green light; or "Mother May I?" (Shhh, that last one's a girl's game or at least one for sissy boys.) "Chase" around our house or even engaging in a mellow game of hide-and-seek. As the evening waned, Mom usually corralled us younger kids onto the porch. We were hyper, racing from side to side on the porch, poking at the poor old screens on either side. Mom would threaten to haul us to the woodshed if we didn't settle down. Slowly but surely, most of my siblings shuffled into the house.

I sat on one of the coveted lawn chairs, nearest to Dad, with him rocking and me, as close as possible, watching lightening bugs or listening to the locust chirp from the giant trees across Alhambra Court. No talk was necessary. I sat next to my dad, my friend, a man I always could count on. Yes. He was a man I could ask anything and know his answer would be the truth as he saw it—no phoniness, no shallowness, the most honest person I've ever known, bar none.

One evening, a new car turned down Alhambra Court and slowly drove past our house. "Dad," I said, "look at that car! Just think," I said, "in twelve or thirteen years, we'll own a car just like that one!" Dad heartily chuckled; he must have repeated my line to various folks eight or ten times. "Yes indeed, Tom, in twelve or thirteen years, a similar car will be ours."

Dad didn't care how worn and ratty his cars were. Cars were only a means of getting there; if twelve- or fifteen-year-old wheels would do the job, that was all he could ask. He never owned a suit. All he owned for dress-up was a loud sports jacket that Mom should have accompanied him to buy. He didn't have the cash to buy a thing as fancy as a suit. Whatever he could wear to his prospective clients was fine with him.

In the fall, Dad often built evening bonfires in the backyard. We had a gigantic tree, maple, I think, but do not quote me on it. The prevailing thought was the tree had as its origin four trees, which grew together, so that the base was six or seven feet in diameter, with four trees diverging from the trunk at about seven feet high. At the point where the trees showed their separate identities, there was a natural shelf where two or three people could rest and share their opinions of current events. There was a sitting side where one could rest between two of the divergent trees. Of course, there was always a fuss about who called dibs on the sitting side, but possession was always nine-tenths of the law when it came to such matters.

Storms in preceding seasons knocked down branches of various lengths and thicknesses, which served as good kindling for the fire. Dad gathered scraps of wood from the garage, leftovers from various projects. Sometimes he would bring some scraps home from work, enough for the fire to roar for several hours.

Our house was built about 1920 and originally heated with coal. The coal bin was about eight feet wide and twenty-five feet long. When most of it was filled with coal, stoking the furnace must have been a pain. Luckily, our house was blessed with oil heat. The oil tank was huge and must have held several hundred gallons.

Dad would go to the basement to fetch oil to kindle the fire. A bright idea for starting a bonfire? I don't know, but Dad was careful, and his eyebrows were intact after each ignition.

When he threw the match on the kindling, it would slowly ignite with the fuel mixture. The fire leaped and danced and grew with the oil. Dad added progressively bigger chunks of wood once the kindling was started, and before you knew it, we had an impressive roaring fire which seemed to burn by itself with little help from outside sources. Periodically, Dad helped the fire along by taking partially burned wood chunks and throwing them into the center of the fire, always mindful to handle the cool end of the wood.

At the house on Thirty-First Street, we burned our trash. Once a month for fifty cents, Mr. Crawford stopped at all the neighbors to pick up the ashes and dump them into his old truck. Ash collecting looked like a good deal for Mr. Crawford—fifty cents for every barrel he dumped, and for me, this was an opportunity to get filthy. It was hard work, and he had a hired hand to help. I can't imagine that he fared very well after paying the guys who owned the ash dump. Anyway, one day I noticed a two-foot-long rounded, ribbed scrap of metal sticking out of our barrel. *Hmmm*, I thought, *I didn't yet know what I could do with this item, but surely there was something I could poke, if only one of my younger brothers.* I pulled it out to further examine my find. I don't remember my exact reaction time, given the event was a complete shock. I do recall that my hand sent a message to my brain, saying, "I think we should have waited longer before picking up this iron!" My hand quickly released the white-hot bar, but the damage was done. For a long time, the palm and fingers of my right hand looked like the padding on the underside of our cat's paws.

When the evening bonfire died down to glowing embers, Dad sat in his lawn chair watching the fire, chatting with Mom and my older siblings. At times Mom emerged from the house with marshmallows, or on rare occasions, hotdogs to roast. With good reason, she allowed us younger boys only the joy of burning the marshmallows. As the hours passed, most of the crew headed indoors with Mom until Dad and I and a couple of stragglers were the only ones left around the fire. There were bits of conversation but mostly there was silence, sitting, thinking, me and my friend, looking into the glowing embers and listening to them pop. Here was contentment and true peace within myself, me in my hand-me-down clothes and raggedy Hill Brothers shoes, sitting with the man who would always be there for me, who would shoulder my burdens anytime, anyplace, who would shield me from any harm or worries—true peace, true peace.

At around noon on another sparkling day in the midst of summer, the sun was blistering hot. I do not know what spurred such a thought on that bright day. Maybe it was fond memories of true peace, but with an enlisted younger brother, I decided to start my own bonfire. In the backyard, we gathered all the sticks we could find. I'm not sure who had the bright idea of attempting this feat inside the garage. It was probably me since I was the brains of the outfit. We had the kindling in our arms: why waste the effort to scrounge larger chunks of wood and haul them to the backyard, when we had all the makings of a good fire here in our arms? As we stacked the kindling into a neat little pile, a problem struck me. We did not have oil.

God only knows what a mess a moron could make if he didn't have the good sense God gave him not to attempt a bonfire indoors. Thankfully, we didn't go into the basement for oil. Instead, we chose an alternate helper, and began to stuff newspaper into the kindling. We carefully stacked the larger pieces of wood around the kindling. In case the fire needed extra help to ignite, we threw in what paper remained of the Sunday edition.

Since we had no oil (thank goodness) would the fire fizzle after the paper was consumed by flame? But no worries; because of my dad's chain smoking, we had an abundance of matches. When I struck a match and applied it to the makings of our bonfire, to my amazement, it took hold in a flash, perhaps because paper is a good fire starter, especially when applied to dry wood and kindling.

Within a minute or two, we had a roaring indoor fire, and I wondered whether we should have taken the time and effort to set our bonfire in the yard. Furthermore, the fire was not set in the middle of the garage but in the right corner near our junky cars. I think we might have applied a little too much fuel: flames licked the eight-foot ceiling. Any solution? Any way to tame this bonfire? Well, we could tear apart the boards of our fire and stomp on them until they went out. This method I immediately rejected, as I did not want my hands to look like the underside padding of a cat's paw again. Applying water to the fire might work, but let's save that for a last resort. What now, Tom? Think, Buddy, think!

When it is someone's birthday and they finish singing the birthday song, sometimes you can blow out the birthday candles if you inhale a huge amount of air. If we had enough wind, my brother and I could blow out the fire. Quickly, I spied two old, worn bath towels, gave one to my brother, and shouted, "Wave it at the fire just as hard and fast as you can! We're going to blow out the fire!" Let me tell you, I do not know the mechanics of fanning—that is, the point at which the wind blows the fire out versus the point at which it infuriates the blaze, making it grow by some geometric rate. All I know is our efforts went for naught, and the flames were now leaping off the fire and onto the walls of our garage.

Well, this is it, I thought. I am washing my hands of this fire. The fire that I started with my comrade is burning down our garage, and I am relegated to a mere reporter of the incident to my older sister Maureen.

"I don't know how it started, Maureen, but someone better get to it fast, or there won't be any garage a little while from now."

I hate to say it, but I was a big liar in those days, especially when it came to matters of setting fire to one's garage. Actually, I did confess many times to Maureen. I don't remember getting into much trouble with Mom that day, so my older siblings must have stopped it with enough dispatch that it did minor damage. I have often wondered on that beautiful summer day whether there was anyone home in my noggin.

10

Perceptions

My father was one of the most articulate people I've ever known, and I loved to listen to stories of his life. The man had a phenomenal memory, colored with intricate details. He did well in grade school and finished in seven and a half years before entering Cathedral High School in Belleville, Illinois. Dad was not interested in furthering his education. While his mother had to force him into high school, he did everything he could think of to get booted from the secondary system. This included cutting classes and hanging around the backyard of the bishop's rectory to debate with him the importance of education.

Dad begged his mom on numerous occasions to let him quit school so he could make his way in the world. At age thirteen, he already had eight years of schooling under his belt, versus Pop's three years. He argued that "Pop did all right, didn't he, Mom?"

"You've always done well in school, Bill, and you'd better bet you *will* graduate from high school, even if it takes twenty-five years!" replied his mother. "You know your younger brother Laur won't make it," she explained. On the contrary, three years later, Dad's younger brother Laurence joined the priesthood after graduating as class valedictorian from Central Catholic in East St. Louis.

Dad was an athlete. As soon as he started throwing a baseball, Dad developed a tremendous right arm for pitching and throwing for long distances. He had to develop this skill. No one reaches their ultimate potential without hours and hours of practice, but he had the knack.

In 1927, you did not need to have much schooling—only the desire to achieve a good life. It was Dad's desire to pitch in the Major League and strike out the best players in the league. If baseball did not work out, Dad thought, he could always fall back on a job at the railroad like his older brother, Tom. There was plenty of time to pursue his dream.

In Dad's junior year in high school baseball, he threw three no hitters. In one game, he managed twenty-three strikeouts in seven innings; two runners reached base because the catcher let the ball get past him. Rising fastball, curveball, sinker ("drop ball" is what they called it then) and screwball were all in his repertoire. I don't know how far the man could throw, only that he won a five-dollar bet with his older brother, Tom, when he threw a baseball from home plate to the top of the right field pavilion in Old Sportsman's Park, where the Browns and the Cardinals played ball. The base of the pavilion was 310 feet from home plate. Suffice it to say when my father played right field, it took either an aggressive or a foolish player to attempt to make it from first to third when a solid single was hit to right field.

One day during his senior year, Dad was watching Cathedral play a home football game. He had never played football, but it didn't take much convincing to get him into a sandlot game. Dad liked to compete in anything resembling athletics and, regardless of any knowledge or lack thereof, would play full bore. While attempting a tackle, he rolled onto his right shoulder; two or three guys piled on, at which point there was a sick, crunching sound that came from his shoulder. *That did not sound good*, he thought. He never revealed whether or not he exited the game promptly. But he did tell me that event ended his pitching career.

After eight or ten fastballs, his right arm ached enough to convince him not to throw for a while. There were no surgeries in 1930, at least to return a golden arm to its original pristine condition. "You threw out your arm" was what they said, although Dad knew well what had caused it. He continued to throw incredible distances. Still he had his curveball, a drop and a screwball, but no fastball, which was what the Detroit Tigers wanted to see from him. After throwing a couple of fastballs to a big-league batter, Dad began throwing his junk. After being warned a couple times that they only wanted to see his heat, the Tigers wished him adieu, which was a pleasant way of saying, "Scram, kid!" They didn't care if he were the next Walter Johnson. If he couldn't follow orders, he was out. I know it must have bothered him for a long time. His dream had been to strike out Babe Ruth. He never lamented about it, though. It was just a piece of his life, and he'd often smile when he told his athletic tales—God's wonderful gift of the golden arm and those rewarding times.

Shortly after we moved to Alhambra Court, Dad decided to erect a basketball goal in our yard, surrounded by a sizable area made of medium-sized rocks. In his formative years, he'd played primarily soccer and baseball. In his junior year, Cathedral started a basketball team. Since it did not conflict with baseball, he joined. At six-one, tall for a man in 1930, he was quick and coordinated. After some practice, he mastered dribbling. When he had the ball and had spotted a lane to the basket, he turned on his speed and often attempted a layup. When he put up the shot, depending on how fast he was running, the ball would crash against the backboard and fly six or eight feet from the basket. He felt like a clown at those times, and he wondered, "This sport can't be that hard, can it?" He had the tools, didn't he? Well, Dad, you had ample tools, but you did not have the foggiest notion of how to shoot the ball instead of throwing it.

I don't know how long he worked at perfecting the art of shooting a basketball, but that first experience must have had something to do with his erection of our basketball court and the demise of the grass on two-thirds of our backyard. He liked watching basketball and knew the rules of the sport, so he made the dimensions accurate. I was not part of the crew that constructed the rim and backboard. Since I was only five or six, I watched the construction from afar. When it was finished, the rim was sturdy and level, standing ten feet high with its two posts secured in cement. If you wound up and threw a basketball as hard as you could against the backboard, the posts would sway a bit, but for a guy who sold life insurance for a living, Dad did an excellent job.

After the goal was up, he ordered at least two loads of good-sized throwing rocks, which were great also if you had a hankering to zip your little brother in the hindquarters. Chat is what my dad called the mixture. He spread it from our small back porch to the large thornbush and entrance to the garage along the drive. A light shined off the garage into our backyard at a perfect angle to illumine the back-board, so I was able to take thousands of shots after sunset.

The chat needed to be pounded flat by constantly dribbling the basketball all over the court, which my father left to the ones he lovingly built the court for, his sons. It was tricky at first for me, attempting to dribble with enough force to help level the court. Scores of times I made the attempt, only to have the ball bounce away as it hit an errant angle of the chat that had been shoveled there by Dad and my brothers. I don't recall how long it took for the court to become smooth. Long before that, I honed my dribbling based on the angle of the rock and knowing the direction of the next bounce.

I don't recall how long it took for me to try dribbling with my left hand. I am right-handed, and I make no boasts about being ambidextrous. The court was well flattened by the time I first tried dribbling with my left hand. The first few times, I looked like a clown on the makeshift court. It took plenty of time before I got comfortable dribbling with either hand. I enjoyed the challenge.

I started practice throws toward the rim shortly after Dad completed the court. Tall for a boy my age, I could hit the rim, provided I was not too far away. I took hundreds and hundreds of shots to the corner of the rim. I learned through repetition where to bank the ball into the basket. When I was more to the center of the court, I aimed over the front of the rim. Soon after I moved to the center of the court, I imparted a clockwise spin off my fingertips using my wrist when I attempted a shot. I loved the sound of the basketball singing as it ripped through the net. In truth, there were many more dinks off the rim and bangs off the backboard than singing balls, but that sound, that sound, made it worthwhile to put up countless errant shots.

I realized I had found the key to shooting a ball and not throwing it to the basket and hoping that it would go through the basket.

It was after this revelation—spinning the ball with my wrist before releasing it—that I began using this technique for all my shots. Some of the shots were short, barely hitting the front of the rim, but the spin took most of the velocity off the ball as it danced around, touching all parts of the rim and falling into the basket. Likewise, if the ball was misaimed and hit the left or right side of the rim, sometimes the dancing happened again, and after its circular path, the ball fell gently through the basket. It did not happen every time, mind you, but it was fascinating when it happened. For a brief time, I thought that I alone held the secret art of shooting a basketball.

Often in scrimmages with my older brothers and neighbor boys, a kid would dribble toward the basket for a layup. So I practiced that skill, dribbling to the right side of the basket and laying the ball with my right hand off the backboard in hopes of making the basket. I'd dribble to the left side of the basket and lay up the ball with my left hand off the backboard. This, too, I practiced hundreds of times until I became skilled from either side.

At the St. Patrick School gym, I got to practice with my father and older brothers. While my brothers scrimmaged on half the court with my cousin and some kids they knew, Dad and I manned the other half. I must say it was mostly I who used our half of the gym, if you exclude the bounce passes, I took from my father while running to the hoop…and the balls he fetched while I took foul shots.

By the age of nine, I had the fundamentals squared away. I could dribble with either hand and switch hands off the dribble at will. I could shoot layups with either hand and make the basket at least 90 percent of the time, plus make three out of four foul shots. It was the early sixties, and I showed good potential. With hundreds of hours of practice on our makeshift court at home, I had a jump on most nine-year-olds. I thoroughly enjoyed basketball, whether perfecting my skills alone or with others. It would not have mattered to me whether I showed promise in the sport, or if I stumbled all over the place when dribbling. I have a true love of the sport, and I hope my dad knew how much pleasure I derived from that little kindness he did for his boys.

When I had my stroke two months after my ninth birthday, Dad grew closer to me. He drew me in, wanting to let me know he would always be there for me. I had lost the good side of my body, and he could not imagine how depressing it would have been if it happened to him. For me, the day after I lost the use of my right side was just another day.

When I became cognizant again, I never thought about what happened to me, good or bad. I lost my right side and so I converted to my left hand as best I could. To me it was no big deal. It was a challenge, mind you, learning how to walk and run again and converting my clumsy left hand and arm to throw, shoot baskets and write again. When I met those challenges, the euphoria I felt when I heard the basketball sing again as it fell through the net was awesome! The ecstasy I felt when the wind blew through my hair as I learned how to run again was a gift from God, and I am grateful to Him each time I think of it.

My father must have had a vastly different idea of what was happening in my mind. He saw his vulnerable son picking up the pieces of his shattered life and having enough guts, enough spirit, to continue and reconcile the struggle, to make true peace within himself. Dad said I became a man that day. I did not cry or mope or ask God why me; I accepted the loss of a side and went on with life. On all the occasions he said I'd grown to a man that day, I thanked him, but I also said there was no reason to cry or mope or plead with God.

"Dad, I don't care that I've lost a side. It doesn't matter to me. I can do everything other people do." I'm not sure he believed me.

A couple of years after the stroke, I got into a verbal fight with a classmate on the playground. I don't recall what the tiff was about, but we eventually degraded to name-calling. After a few choice names, he called me a crippled bum. Man, I never thought of that one. I'll have to remember to call one of my brothers a crippled bum before the shoving and punches ensue. He wouldn't stop repeating "crippled bum." I got angrier and angrier. The fight finally got down to a "No, I'm not," "Yes, you are," "No, I'm not" scenario. That name *crippled bum* really got my goat! It should not have riled me, as to me, it had no bearing in fact. When I called my brother a big pig, I knew he was not a pig; it was only an epithet. But that kid wouldn't stop calling me a crippled bum, so I socked him in the right eye. He ran away bawling, with a healthy shiner that lasted about a week. I should have remembered the old saying, "Sticks and stones will break your bones, but names can never hurt you."

Dad didn't get home until eight or nine that night. I let him rest a bit and then approached him in his rocking chair. Dad was never a bully, but he stressed to all his children always to stand up for ourselves and never to let anyone use us for a personal punching bag. It is important always to try to have a good relationship with one another, he said, but when someone's bullying you every day and you do nothing, life can be miserable for you, both physically and the way you perceive yourself.

Maybe this was the reason I told him about the incident. I should have known better since it was I who threw the first punch. I told him about the argument and the end result of the poke in the eye and then waited for his response. I don't know what I expected him to say, maybe

"Way to go, Tommy, bet that boy will run from you next time he sees you!"

"You hit him first, Tommy?" he said. "He didn't push you or come at you in such a manner that you knew he was going to hit you, son?"

"Well, Dad, we were having this huge argument and then it got down to name-calling, and he kept on calling me this same name over and over again and…and…" Oh, help me, mind, give me a solution that doesn't make me guilty!

"So you clocked him right in the eye for a stupid name, Tom? What have I always said about bullying, Tom?"

I was on the defensive now and my opponent was Dad. I knew who would win. I tried to produce a good response to that last question.

"Haven't you realized by now the adage 'Sticks and stones will break your bones, but names can never hurt you' bears much weight? What name could cause you to lose your temper to the point of punching a guy in the face, Tom?"

He looked at me eye to eye, expecting an answer. This was not what I thought would happen when I began this conversation. He had asked me a simple question, so this superseded all other questions, at least for now. He took me off the hook—just a simple two-word answer. Yet I knew there would be more chewing out after I answered his question. I looked at him and he looked straight at me; I gulped and said, "He called me a crippled bum, Dad. I know this isn't any reason for popping a guy, regardless of how many times he said it."

Instead of chewing me out for hitting the kid, my dad winced, lowered his eyes, and instead of using five or six syllable words, the only word that he could muster was "Oh." I waited for more feedback, for him to raise his eyes and continue with the scolding that I knew I deserved. It seemed like minutes passed as I watched his downcast eyes and the hurt expression on his face.

"Are you okay, Dad?" I asked with "What the heck happened here" thoughts racing through my mind. Still there was not an answer from Dad—only silence and the downcast eyes.

Crippled bum? Was that the problem? It was a decent pick for name-calling, but it was just a name. I wondered if the word *crippled* bore more weight in my father's mind.

"Dad, am I crippled?"

"Well, Tom, you do walk with a pronounced limp, and you can't do much with your right hand. This was brought on by your stroke. It doesn't look like you're going to get much more use of your right side. So…" As he raised his eyes to meet mine once again, he said, "I guess you are crippled, Tom."

I tried to understand. I got from his eyes that he was waiting for my reaction. Me, crippled? How could that be?

"No, Dad, I am not crippled! I know I have hardly any use of my right arm and even less in my right hand, and I do walk with a limp, so most of my walk comes from the left side. But I can run, Dad! I can feel the wind through my hair, and I can shoot baskets with my left hand and hear the sound as the basketball rips through the net. I can't tell you how wonderful this makes me feel, Dad! I know I can't be as good as I was before the stroke, but that's okay with me.

"A crippled person is someone you pity, Dad, and I don't want anyone ever to feel sorry for me. There's no reason. I'm okay, having a stroke is part of life and you have to accept all that life gives you. I'm just a regular guy, Dad."

Eyes twinkling like a true Irishman, my father reached out, and while pulling me in for a long hug said, "How foolish of me, Tom. Surely, you're not crippled, son!" After the hug, he held me at arm's length as if seeing me anew. Again he said, "Don't pop a guy because he called you a name, son." But my dad's lecture had lost a lot of steam. I was grateful the kid called me a crippled bum instead of a big pig.

Life leads us to our ultimate destiny in fascinating ways. Few people start with a specific goal that smoothly unrolls for them. Most of us weave our way through life to a hopefully successful end. Our fruitful and meritorious goals can make the world a better place in some small way. Certain successes at life's end are meaningless to many, but golden treasures to others—goals that far outshine fame or gold. Those touched by such lives see them as true beacons of shimmering light, love, and meaning, never to be forgotten.

My dad never had a thousand dollars in the bank, yet his gold was wrapped in his eleven children, twelve, he always said, if you included Jerry or Jeri, who never saw the light of day or breathed one single breath. Dad was not an ace insurance agent, but he was always honest with his clients, sometimes talking down the amount of insurance they wanted because he could see they would struggle to make the premium payments in ten or fifteen years with two or three extra mouths to feed.

Dad was my faithful friend; one I could always count on to be there. He had tremendous faith that he and his family somehow, some way, would make it through our persistent financial problems. Love: did my dad love me? You bet! In the thirty-five years that I knew him, I never saw him cry. When he returned from Waco, Texas, with my mom and heard that I was in the hospital seriously ill, he fell apart, weeping to the point that my two older brothers had to help him to his room. He pleaded with God to give *him* all that happened to me on that Saturday night—to please let his son live. I'm certain if God had spoken to my father, he would have said, "He will live, Bill. Thank you for the offer, but your son, Tom, will be able to handle this." When my father was holding another child having a seizure and praying to his Maker to let it pass to him, did he love the child who, after the seizure was over, said "I okay now, Daddy!" Did he love the stillborn child, his twelfth child that he baptized while he wept? Did my parents' lives have meaning? Did they matter much? You bet they did their gold lives and grows each day.

11

Pop

My dad graduated from Cathedral High in Belleville in June of 1931, which I'm sure pleased his mother. In 1931, one out of three people were jobless. It was frustrating when my dad got a lead on a factory job, only to get there and find hundreds of people waiting in line for two or three positions. Most of the time, the employees responsible for hiring walked down the line and saw people they knew or relatives of employees they had already hired: they were the ones who got picked for the new positions. My grandfather was confused. He had worked seven days a week as a street-car conductor for many a year. How, then, was there not any job for his son, Bill?

Pop, my dad's father, was born in 1880 in a small town called Cahersiveen, Ireland, situated off the Atlantic Ocean in the far western county of Kerry. Pop had three years of formal education and, at age nine, traveled every day four or five miles out into the Atlantic Ocean to fish with his older brothers. Pop came from a large family, seventeen or eighteen children my father told me. Life was hard in Ireland; several of Pop's brothers and sisters did not make it past three or four years old. Tom Connell, Pop's dad, farmed a plot of ground and grew cabbage and potatoes to supplement the salt mackerel or whatever fish they caught for the table. Tom Connell was an honest man, fair and learned. There were many times when what Tom had to say, in squabbles over land or other property, was deemed fair for all involved. If Tom Connell said it was fair, it was fair.

Pop immigrated to the United States in 1900. He always remembered how hard his life was during the first twenty years. This was one of the reasons for Pop's work ethic. If you worked hard in this new country, you could make a good life for yourself. What Pop did not realize was how fortunate he was to have had a full-time job during the Great Depression. Anyone without a skill found it difficult to get started, regardless of how hard they worked. During my dad's jobless period, Pop constantly brought up matters of employment.

"I'm going out looking each day, Pop. No luck today, but I'll be going out tomorrow." It must have been extremely frustrating for my father that his own father assumed he did not have the desire to find gainful employment.

I graduated in 1975 with a bachelor of science degree in accounting from Southern Illinois University in Edwardsville. I did well in all my courses in accounting: nine *A*s and one *B*, and just as well in all my other courses. There were plenty of jobs available, unlike the period when my dad sought work. I didn't think I'd have much of a problem landing a job during the first few months of 1975, while I was completing my degree. I interviewed with all the firms I could, both in public accounting and industry. But no one was interested in my credentials. I learned there's more to succeeding in business than how many As you accumulate on your report card. Grades are important, as you do not want someone in accounting who doesn't know rudimentary math. But one of the key components of business is communication, as in so many environments. One of the better ways to test this is how fast you can think under pressure in an interview.

Looking at myself objectively, I'd say I do not perform well in interviews, as my articulation was destroyed by the stroke. During the intervening years, I gradually regained the ability to talk. Although I talk reasonably well, the ability to articulate new concepts in an interview and answer them in a clear and concise manner is not there. I realize this is difficult to understand if you don't have a similar problem. I'm not complaining, mind you, but that's part of the reason for my unsuccessful interviews.

I did not snag a real accounting job for an entire year after graduation, although I did find part-time work at St. Louis University. My dad was always supportive, never questioned my desire, never put pressure on me, always let me stay under his roof. He never made me think I was lazy, and he wanted to be sure that I knew I could always count on him to be in my corner—the one who would always be there for me.

I don't know how many months my dad looked in vain for work back in the Great Depression. His older brother,

Tom, worked at a railroad yard in St. Louis starting as a messenger at fifteen. Uncle Tom did well at the railroad, progressing to various positions, each requiring more responsibility. Tom had connections, not only at the railroad yard, but at companies he dealt with in his railroad years.

Tom visited his family during a discussion about strategies to help his brother, my dad, get a job.

"Tom," Dad asked, "do you have any leads on jobs? It's so frustrating to get a so-called lead, only to arrive at the company and wait in line with hundreds of other people for two or three jobs."

"Well, Bill, I guess I could get you hired handling freight. It's hard work and doesn't pay much. Frankly, I didn't think you were looking for that type of work, though."

My dad, looking at Tom in amazement, said, "Tom, I'll do anything! I don't care how hard the work is or how low the pay, I just want to get my foot in the door. I appreciate all the help I can get!"

"Let me see what I can do," Tom replied.

My dad started work at Columbia Terminal for thirty-seven cents an hour. The job consisted of manually loading and unloading railcars of anything from crates of shoes to gigantic barrels of Staley Syrup at seven hundred pounds a barrel. At this point, there were no propane or electric forklifts at Columbia Terminal. So with the manual loading and unloading of rail cars, there was a knack to picking up heavy loads.

Ted Walsh, who was dating Dad's oldest sister, worked for a while at Columbia Terminal with my father. For the first few months of his employment, my dad thought that Ted Walsh was the strongest man in the world. While Dad struggled to lift heavy loads of freight, Ted spun around the same weight and picked it up with ease, hauling it to its appropriate place. After a few months, my dad learned the art of balance, so handling freight became easier. It was exhausting work; I'm sure my father slept like a baby when the day was over.

He did not want to make a career at Columbia Terminal straining his guts. He had ambitions to become a lawyer, and I'm sure if he had attained the dream, he would have been an excellent attorney, what with his great gift of oratory. In addition to working all the hours he could, he attended night school for two or three courses a semester at Washington University in St. Louis. After a few months at Columbia Terminal, my father was in extremely good shape, with a twenty-seven-inch waist, smaller than his older sister's, which I imagine did not please her. At a little over six feet tall, he weighed only 142 pounds.

Because he was a hard worker, Columbia Terminal gave him all the work he could handle, sometimes eighty to ninety hours a week. What with night school and all that backbreaking work, my father was exhausted all the time, which started to break down his health. One day, they had a railcar of shoes to be unloaded. Dad and all the other freight workers relished this work. The crates of shoes were bulky, but they weighed only forty or fifty pounds, a light load. As he started to unload, my father staggered under the weight. He knew immediately that something was wrong.

After almost falling with a couple more crates, he went to the foreman: "There's something wrong with me, boss. I can't take the weight of these shoes. I don't know what the problem is, but I'm clocking out and going to see the doctor."

"You can't do that, Bill. You're leaving me hanging."

"I'm sorry, boss, but I'm no good to anybody in this condition. I feel like I'm ready to pass out. I'll be back after I see the doctor."

After a short examination and a few questions: "Are you short of breath, Bill? Do you have chest pains? What have you been doing? You're as thin as a beanpole and your heart's racing so fast I'm surprised you're not having a heart attack!"

"I'm working hard at Columbia Terminal for eighty to ninety hours a week and then I have night school at Washington University, Doc. I want to eventually become a lawyer. But it seems like I'm always exhausted. Today I was reeling under loads of only forty or fifty pounds. I almost passed out. I guess that's why I'm here. Something's dead wrong."

"Bill, I'm glad you came to see me today because you're only a shade away from a heart attack, and if you did pass out on the freight platform, you may never have woken up! Why in God's name are you working so hard for that many hours, and then putting night school on your plate?"

"Doc, it's the Depression. I was out of work for months and months! And who knows if this job will peter out? I'm low man on the totem pole. I have ambitions, Doc. I don't want to be handling freight all my life!"

"I understand ambitions, Bill, but right now, you're physically exhausted, and if you go back to Columbia Terminal or any job right now, you're risking your life."

"What do you want me to do, Doc? What are my options?"

"You're not going to like it, Bill, but if you want to be alive a month from now, you're going to have to quit working and drop your classes at Washington University. I'm going to give you some heart medicine, so maybe we can get control of that ticker of yours. That's what's worrying me now."

"You're not giving me any good options, Doc."

"Bill, take this as coming from a friend and somebody who knows a little bit more about medicine than you do. If you go back to work and ignore my advice, this might be the last day for you. Now you are a man, and you can do what you want, but I would hate to see the anguished look on your dad's face as he buried one of his sons. Your dad is a good man, Bill, my friend. Just remember, my eleven-year-old son can carry fifty pounds, the weight that made you stagger."

Dad took his advice, told Columbia Terminal he would not be returning for a long time, and headed to his parents' house at 625 North Thirty-Second Street in East St. Louis. He went to the kitchen where Pop was resting after his job as a streetcar conductor was finished for the day.

"You're home early, Bill," Pop said. "Didn't they have any freight for you to handle today?"

"They had plenty of work today, Pop," Dad said, and then he told him how he had almost passed out and how he could not handle the forty- or fifty-pound trips from the freight car. He told him about how he went to Pop's doctor and was told to quit work, drop the classes, and go home and rest until the doctor said it was okay for him to resume normal activities.

As his son told him the unwelcome news, Pop looked at his boy, a twenty-year-old in the best condition of his life, having been told to quit work and set his ambitions aside for an indeterminate time.

"It doesn't make any sense, Bill, you're in the best condition of your life and here my doctor says you have to quit work! You *are* skinny, Bill, and it might be better for your stamina if you picked up thirty pounds or so, but to quit? I don't know, Bill."

"Pop, it was really a blow to me. Your doctor threw a monkey wrench into my plans!" Dad left out the part about his being on the verge of a heart attack—that if he returned to work, it might be the last day on earth for William J., which had properly scared the young man.

"Maybe he meant to quit work for the rest of the day," Pop said.

"It didn't sound that way to me, Pop, I'm not mentally challenged. He was suggesting more of a permanent solution, or at least until he confirms that my body's healed."

"Let me go talk to him," Pop said. "He's my friend. Maybe you can rest for a week or so before you go back to work. This just doesn't make any sense to me, son."

"More power to you, Pop," Dad said. "If you can make that arrangement or find out that I totally misconstrued our discussion, that would be great!"

Pop went downtown to talk to his friend. It was late afternoon, and the doctor was about ready to leave for the day. "Hey, Doc, I want to talk to you for a few minutes about my son, Bill."

"I don't know whether it would be proper to talk to you about another patient, Dave, even if he is your son. Bill's a grown man, not your little boy anymore."

"I know it's none of my business, Doc, but it's just that he came home today with orders from you to quit work and school…and I just don't understand. He's in the prime of his life and jobs are hard to come by these days."

"What did Bill tell you about what happened today, Dave?"

"Well, he told me he was having some difficulty at work, and he came to see you. After examining him, Bill said you told him to quit work and to discontinue college for a while. I know he's been working long hours, and he might be burning the candle at both ends with the schooling and all, but to say he has to quit everything until you tell him it's okay to resume, it makes no sense! He's twenty years old, Doc, and in the best shape of his life! I just wanted an explanation, is all. Maybe my son could rest a week or so before resuming normal activities. I know he's skinny, but he's always been on the thin side."

Pop could see the aggravation starting to boil in his friend's eyes.

"Did he also tell you he was staggering under a forty- to fifty-pound load of shoes, Dave? Did he tell you that he almost passed out at work today? Have you looked at your son in the last couple of months? He's a beanpole, Dave, over six feet tall and he weighs only 142 pounds! Did he tell you that I was wondering whether I was ever going to get his pulse rate under two hundred beats a minute? Your son almost had a heart attack right here in my office, Dave, and yes, I told him to quit work and school until we can get things under control. The boy has had a total physical breakdown. Do you want him to die just to prove to you he's not lazy, Dave?"

"No," Pop said, "Doc, I didn't realize how urgent this is—and I certainly didn't know about his heart."

"I didn't think so, Dave. I wouldn't be your friend if you were that type of person. My advice to you is to stand with him and try to fatten your son up a bit. It was a bitter pill for *him* to swallow too, as I'm sure you can imagine. I had to put the fear of the Lord into him to understand the seriousness of his condition."

As Pop was returning home from the discussion with his friend about his third-born son, he remembered his constant badgering of Bill before he landed that job. Could it be that Bill was trying to prove to me that he is not lazy? When Pop entered the house and laid eyes on my dad, he fell apart. He put his arms around Dad and through his weeping he managed to say,

"Bill, I'm sorry, please forgive me. Here, through my lack of understanding, I badgered you day after day about finding work. After you found a job, you worked so hard you almost lost your life trying to prove to me you were a worthy son. Bill, I don't care if you never work again; there will always be a place in my house for you! I love you, Bill, and I'm so proud to call you, my son."

Dad did not know what to say. There was only one other time he saw his father cry and that was upon hearing his father had passed away in Ireland. Yes, he was glad to find a job. It relieved him of the nightly chats with Pop regarding gainful employment, but more importantly, it gave Dad some spending money and inspired him to go to college to become a lawyer. Pop never instructed his son to work eighty to ninety hours a week and add schooling to that.

"Pop, I love you too. It's not your fault. I took on the overtime and I went a little too far. I'll be okay, Pop. I just need some rest is all."

Pop worked as a streetcar conductor until he was sixty-five years old and forced to retire. He became a custodian for five more years at a senior high school until at seventy he was made to retire from his second job. Pop's work ethic was strong: he would have continued to work as long as he physically could. After he retired and started receiving pension checks from his prior employers, he told his wife, Annie, to return them to the company, as he felt he had not earned the money. She would routinely explain to him that the checks were for service he already had done for the company.

Pop had arteriosclerosis, the progression of which eventually robbed him of his mental acuity. He had good days when he could recognize his wife and all his children, but there were far more bad days when he did not recognize any of them.

Pop died when he was seventy-seven years old, which would have put my age at about four. I don't remember much about him. The few times I can remember him coming over to our house, I recall being puzzled. As soon as he would come into our living room and I was introduced to him, he'd say, "Well, Annie, I think it's about time we return to our house." He just arrived, I thought. Why does he want to leave? My parents could not explain; what *is* hardening of the arteries, and how did that influence his abrupt desire to go home just after he had arrived?

I know it must have been distressing to Dad and heartbreaking to the one who loved him most of all, Annie,

Pop's wife. Shortly before my pop was called to his maker, Dad stopped at the hospital to see how Pop was doing. His mother was there; it was one of Pop's good days.

"Hi, Bill, and how're you doin'?" Pop asked with an Irish brogue you could cut with a knife. Dad looked at Pop's sky-blue eyes that were twinkling as cognizant as they were when Dad was a boy.

"I'm doing fine," Dad said, "and it looks like *you're* feeling better too, Pop!" They talked a long while until it was time to leave the hospital for the night. Dad shook hands with his father and stepped back a couple of steps so Pop could say goodbye to Annie, who he recognized as his wife for those few hours. As she approached her husband, he gently took both of her hands, kissed them, and said "Annie, shor'n you're the best, Annie, shor'n you're the best." My dad's mom, tears running down her cheeks, said, "Dave, I love you too. You're the best person I've ever known."

My father sure was glad he stopped at the hospital that night. He must have told me that story four or five times. Each time he told it, I could tell it was deeply meaningful to him, although there was no crack in his voice as with many of his other stories.

Dad recovered from his physical breakdown, although I never asked him how long it took. I know he never spent another day working for Columbia Terminal or any other freight-handling company. He never took another college class nor became a lawyer. He took another path for thirty-eight years, minus four years and three months in the US Army for World War II. His career was more sedentary. I can only explain his life insurance work as a gigantic paper route where you sell an intangible and collect from your clients—where the buyer rarely sees the benefit, only another can reap the reward.

Life insurance must be one of the hardest things to sell. You cannot see or touch it, and when you die, the benefits go to another person. Still, it is an important financial asset for a family, particularly those living from paycheck to paycheck. Yet it takes some convincing to buy adequate protection for something you don't even want to think about, an uncompromising future that seems so distant, the client's death.

12

Patches

Sometimes, my dad and I talked for hours and hours on end, mostly Dad doing the talking and the storytelling, but that was okay with me. He liked to be heard. I felt fortunate that he spent the time with me. There are a lot of regrets in my life, lots of should-have-dones and could-have-dones. My father passed away more than thirty-four years ago, and I still relish and celebrate the memories of our times together. No regrets here, let me tell you.

My father had the Irish gift of gab. A considerable number of his tales were about the people he met along the way through the insurance business.

One client gave him a beagle pup named Patches. Since my father did not hunt, he gave it to us kids for a pet. Patches was a beautiful dog with reddish-brown splotches on a pure white coat. One would think that a dog loved by ten children and cared for by two genuine grown-ups would consider himself lucky and give out his fair share of love to the adoptive family. On the contrary, my dear friends, when he and my father arrived at 783 Alhambra Court, Patches appeared more than a little aloof, as if he were thinking "Is this it? Man, did I get screwed on *this* deal!" He didn't like the urban jungle, quite different from his prior abode. Gone were the days when he could romp and play with his siblings on the wooded highlands north of Route 161 and the city of Belleville. His ultimate destiny was seized from him—yanked—from his speckled paws. He must have been sure that his prior owner was fixing to take him on the hunt, maybe rabbits, squirrels, a raccoon or two. Whatever it was, Patches was sure he would be good at it; he was a Beagle, wasn't he?

What had he done to merit this abuse? He must have been a wicked dog to be cast away to a baldheaded old coot who threw him into a mound of rubbish, i.e., the back of my father's fifteen-year-old car, where Patches must have thought for a moment or two that he would perish by suffocation. The poor dog must have been jostled, thrown around among the mess of used insurance papers. Patches knew not where he was going; his best idea was a dump, where trash and bad little doggies go.

When my dad brought Patches home and introduced him to us, one might sympathize with the dog's trauma. One could also understand the disappointment Patches felt as he looked upon his new kingdom from our front porch and did not see more than a grouping of three or four trees together, and where the only rise in elevation was a puny three or four feet at the end of our street. It was clearly apparent that Patches was lonely the first few nights away from his siblings and the woodlands where he was born and missed. He howled those first few nights, wishing he were home again.

Yes, thought I, *he is sad now.* He has endured a lot today, but he'll adapt. My family will surely love him, and once again, he'll be a happy dog. My thoughts, rustic and shallow as they might have been, may have held some wisdom, had not certain incidents occurred over the next few days.

I do not know who invited the old four-footed chap to follow us home from Jones' Park. It could not have been me, so I have to cast the blame on Larry or John if the battered, old dog needed any inviting at all. A little pat on his flea encrusted, mangy-looking head might have been all that was needed for the dog to adopt us as his family. If my brothers and I were noble, we would have run through the forest on the way home to evade the old fellow. Were we noble that day? My remembrance of the good old days is mushy and hazy. Whether we possessed the great virtue that day and tried to evade the old dog really matters naught, as the mangy old thing was also a beagle, one who could run circles around us in his environment, the Jones' Park woods.

The dog's name was "Chester"—odd name, I thought, for a dog. I don't really know who named him, perhaps my father. Dad named my Teddy Bear Polonius and my brother Larry's bear, Gustav. Polonius was a good bear, so I'm not sure what he did to deserve a beheading by yours truly at age two, but that is another story. Perhaps the dog already had his moniker when he followed us home from the park. As I recall, he walked favoring one of his paws, so maybe he was named Chester after Matt Dillon's devoted leg-impaired deputy on TV's *Gunsmoke*. Who's to say? But his name was Chester.

One can imagine Patches' dismay when he saw this dirty, flea-bitten canine coming home with us that day. I wished that I could talk dog talk as we arrived from the park with Chester in the lead.

"You're our doggy, Patches, we love you and you will always be our dog." We patted Chester on the head in sympathy. We decided to wait and sort out the dog situation when our dad came home.

Dad didn't hesitate to take Chester by automobile back to Jones' Park and drop him off to go home where he surely must have been loved and missed. Dad arrived home from the dirty deed, and within five minutes, into our backyard trotted Chester with a quizzical expression on the old dog's face, which I am sure meant, "Hey, guys, you forgot me at the park."

My father asked us whether we'd been feeding the crusty old character. No one admitted to the offense. Surely, though, there would be more questions from my father, the famous prosecuting attorney, to which the answers would be mostly "I dunno," the *coups de gras* of all answers. My father tried one more time to send the dog home to his old stomping grounds. Somehow, we ascertained that he was kicking around at Thirty-First Street and Summit Avenue. We packed him into my father's back seat with the used insurance papers.

Going for a ride! the old dog must have thought. A few blocks away, an older sibling opened the door, lifted Chester out of the car, hopped in, and away went my dad toward the Mississippi River. The dog let out a forlorn cry and started racing after our beat-up old car. We turned right on Twenty-Eighth or Twenty-Ninth Street and onto Renshaw Avenue for a couple of blocks. Dad sped up to pull away from old Chester on Renshaw Avenue, with Chester continuously howling. "Wait, old man, you forgot me!"

The ride home was silent. Chester, the haggard old mongrel, had no place to go on Thirty-First Street. If he had been seen there, it was only after being dumped there by another person. "This person scratched my head, performed a kindness for an old dog like me," the old dog must have thought about the O'Connell family. "Maybe I can love them, and they will adopt me."

My father walked into our house, proceeded to his rocker, and sat, thinking the same thing. A couple minutes passed, and there was a familiar bellow our back door. My older sister, Anne, ran to the door, flung it open, and burst into tears. It was Chester, wheezing and panting, wanting everyone to know he found his way home. My father walked to the back porch, sat down, and pet old Chester, letting him know that here he would always have a home.

This might be the best of all worlds. Now Patches would have someone to keep him company, a friend and a beagle too, albeit an old, beat-up, flea-bitten rascal, but a dog. I guess that in most situations, Patches and Chester would have become friends after a brief time of getting to know each other. Unfortunately, the two dogs never could get to the bonding phase. At their dinner time, Chester had this nasty habit of growling at Patches, as if to say, "Back off, punk. If there's any left when I'm finished, you're more than welcome to it." Patches must have thought, *What the heck's going on here?* He stood his ground the first few meals. If the growling did not establish Chester as the alpha male, a few nips on Patches's hindquarters did the trick, as Patches scurried away from the food bowl. I intervened several times, which I am sure did not please Chester. At mealtime, Patches ate first those few times. I'm sure that a confrontation occurred at every meal. There were times that poor Patches got nary a morsel, as my chores did not include permanent guardianship of our dogs' food bowl.

Chester would chase Patches for no apparent reason. Perhaps, Patches was limping slightly, and Chester interpreted this act, however psychotic this thought might be, as a direct affront to his own old, beat-up leg. If Patches was receiving some well-earned petting from one of his owners, old Chester might have been riled with Chester attempting to say, "Get the heck away from this family! They're mine now!" I tried to protect poor little Patches by chasing Chester. I knew by the look on Patches' face he was saying, "Thank you for saving me this time, Tom, but where were you when he took a good bite out of me earlier today?"

I think the final straw, at least as far as Patches was concerned, happened over several evenings. My father came home from work at nine or ten most nights, exhausted. He was more than fifty years old, so most people would think that a man that age would still have quite a bit of spunk in him. Yes, although he was through with more than half of his life, he should still have had a lot of tread in those tires that people call legs and feet.

My dad was a chain-smoker of harsh cigarettes for thirty years as well as a chronic worrier about everything concerning his family. He was my father and I loved him, but if I were to be objective, he had a seventy-five-year-old body at age fifty. As he made his way to our front steps and started to climb the five or six steps, there was good old Chester wagging his beat-up old tail, ready to meet the man who had tried to get rid of him on more than one occasion. My dad had to reach down to pet the old mutt. Sometimes he sat and said kind words to old Chester, not knowing that he'd been a maniac all day, and had made life for Patches a living nightmare!

Patches, observing the relationship between the old man and Chester was highly indignant. "You took me away from my home, the forest where I was free, and from my siblings to a place where there was nary a group of trees and no hills where I could romp and play! I was willing to make a go of it, but then that psychotic dog, Chester, came into the picture and has made my life miserable. To top it all off, you pet and gently call out to this maniac of a dog the kind words of 'Good ole Chester,' you, you son of an ugly woman! I quit, Mr. O'Connell! Is there some type of paperwork in your back seat that I have to sign with my paw?"

Off poor Patches went on that night, never to be seen again on our premises.

About a month later, my younger brother Larry saw Patches with another family two long blocks away. He was happy with his newly adopted clan, although the environment, trees, and hills, appeared to be the same as ours. Larry was upset about the matter, Patches leaving home and getting adopted by another family. As for me, I am happy the whole situation worked the way it did for Patches because he sure was not happy with Chester and our family.

13

Ma

One of the benefits of the life insurance business is the number of people who cross your path. My dad was interested in the makeup of all people—their unique experiences, their paths in life, what made them tick, what contributed to their goodness.

He always wanted to know his own heritage and was eager to learn whenever his father talked about his life in Ireland as a boy. Unfortunately, Pop seldom told these stories, my dad knew little about his father. Pop thought it wasn't all that important for his children to know about him. This contributed to all the stories Dad told to me. He wanted his children to know about him and what constituted his character. I cherish the memories of my dad's stories. They were important to me. I'm so proud to be a son of William O'Connell.

As a life insurance agent with selling and monthly collecting duties, my dad had the good fortune to meet hundreds of people. A few of these people previously knew the O'Connell clan long before my dad took them on as clients. One of these women was Ma.

Uncle Laur was my dad's younger and closest brother. They were separated by only sixteen months and were extremely close as children. As told earlier, Uncle Laur decided, while attending Central Catholic High School in East St. Louis, to become a priest. Along with other duties, he became pastor at St. Regis parish in E. St. Louis. It was at this church where he met Ma, among a group of others who had stopped going to church. He convinced her to return to the church, to attend Mass and receive the sacraments. Ma thought the sun rose and set upon my father's younger brother while my father chuckled and mused about his brother pelting him with a BB gun while he was riding past on his bike when they were wee lads.

My father did not like calling any of his clients by their first names, preferring instead Mr. Brown or Ms. Whitney to keep things on a business level. He certainly did not like calling one of his clients Ma, but after she insisted five or six times that he should call her Ma, that was the name he used on subsequent visits.

She was a kindly old woman. Dad enjoyed their monthly visits and the stories she offered. She was several years a widow at that time, having given birth to ten children, all boys. The boys tended to be wild without a sister or two to tame them, unlike my well-mixed family of five girls and six boys. Ma tried her best to keep them in line, at least while they were in her home, but things could get out of control. I cannot be certain, mind you, and I do not want to be held to it by any means, but I think from the stories my father told me, at least half of Ma's boys spent some time in the big house; usually Menard Correctional Center in Chester, Illinois.

Menard Correctional Center is a prison that holds adult male maximum-security and high-medium security inmates—a place where I would not like to spend any of my days for doing something terribly wrong. Prison does not sit well with me in any form or fashion but going to a place where more than 50 percent of the inmates have been convicted of murder would cause me to soil my britches. I can only hope that if I'd been in a situation and was sent there, some noble inmates—seeing as though I'm a bald-headed old man who has trouble with his central processing unit—would have mercy on me.

Ma left her door open at all hours. Anyone was welcomed to come into her house. She had many sons and being no longer young might not hear a knock at the door and might miss visiting with one of her boys or friends like Bill O'Connell, her insurance agent. On one late afternoon, Ma heard quick footsteps on the same floor of the apartment where she dwelt. It appeared that the footsteps were coming closer, only briefly stopping at the doors of her neighbors, rattling the doorknobs to see if they were open, and then proceeding closer to her apartment. When he opened the door to Ma's place, he quietly closed the door, and there he stood eye to eye with Ma.

The man was scared, tired, and looked as though he had been running from the world.

"Ma'am, I'm not going to hurt you if you cooperate. I just need to hide out here for a while."

"Ma," she said, "just call me Ma, son. I know you're not going to hurt me. Why would you want to hurt an old woman like me?" she asked.

"If you start screaming, I might have to stop you, ma'am."

"It's Ma, son. Why would I scream when I know you're not going to hurt me? Sit down, son, you're all worn out. I'll let you rest here for a while. Do you want some coffee or water?"

The man looked puzzled as he asked for coffee. He did not follow her to the kitchen, which was puzzling in and of itself. "You should lock your door. There are bad people in this neighborhood," he said. "Take it from me, this used to be my old stomping ground."

"There's a little bit of good in all people," Ma said, explaining that she had several sons and would hate to miss one of their visits because she was lying down and did not hear the knock on the door. Ma said, "You said this is where you used to live, son. Where do you live now?"

The man chuckled and said with a big cockeyed grin, "Well, up to a couple of days ago, I resided at Menard Correctional Center in Chester, Illinois. You see, Ma, I'm an escaped convict running from the cops. I'm not a violent man, Ma, just a thief involved in a robbery where some people got hurt. That's why I was sent to Menard. There are some wicked people down at Menard and in this neck of the woods too. I'd seriously consider locking my door," he said a second time. "I just need to hide out for a while, Ma, and then I'll be on my way."

"A few of my boys have spent some time down there because of some, uh, altercations, which were blown way

Tom O'Connell

out of control," Ma said. "In fact, I have one of my younger sons down at Menard for twenty years because he tried his best to end two men's lives."

"Really?" the man asked. "What's his name? Maybe I know him." Hearing her son's name, the fugitive was flabbergasted.

"Him!" the man uttered in amazement. "He's a real nice guy. I know him well, Ma. He would be the last guy I'd ever imagine to be convicted for attempted murder."

"He is a nice boy," Ma said. "Hard worker too, and all he wanted was a few beers after work when these two men started bothering him. He has to work on that temper of his when he gets out of Menard."

The man talked to Ma for a few hours. While he was leaving, the last thing Ma said to him was to give her son her regards when he was captured and returned to Menard.

During the time my dad had Ma for a client, he saw most of her sons at one time or another. Once, when my father was there, in walked her son, Norm. My dad only saw him that one time. Norm was a giant of a man, must have been about six feet five inches weighing in at 275. When introduced to Norm, my dad could tell by his smile and the sway of his body that he was already three sheets to the wind and should be heading home.

"You been drinkin', son?" Ma said.

"Some, Ma," he answered.

"It looks like a little bit more than *some*, Norm," she retorted. "Ran out of drinking money, is that it, boy? Want some more money from your poor old mother?"

"I just came in to see you and the insurance man sitting over there, Ma," he said.

150

"When did you ever come over for a visit without your hand out for drinking money? You're drunk, and you know how mean you get when you're hammered. If I had a million dollars sitting right in my coin purse, I wouldn't give you a dime. Go home and sleep it off, son."

"Okay, okay, Ma, I know when I'm not wanted!" he said as he exited the apartment slamming the door.

"I have some boys who will never learn their lesson, Mr. O'Connell," Ma said. "Norm's been up the river three times now and the light doesn't ever seem to go on in that boy's brain. Mean, too, when he gets drunk, but I can handle him, Mr. O'Connell."

"Well, Ma, I would hate to meet him on a deserted street when he was feeling a bit testy. That man could tear off both of my arms on a sober day. Why, he's bigger than my younger brother, Father O'Connell, which is really saying something."

Ma could only smile. "I believe he's a tad bigger than your brother, Mr. O'Connell."

They talked for a few minutes longer. He liked visiting the old woman and hearing stories about her life and her boys. But since this was only a collection visit, he couldn't afford to while away an evening. As he headed to the door of the building, there stood Norm, blocking the hallway with his massive frame, no more than thirty feet from Ma's apartment.

"Hi, Norm, guess you're not taking your mother's advice and going home to sleep it off," my father said.

"Oh, what does she know?" he asked. "I've definitely had a few beers, Mr. O'Connell, but I'm certainly not drunk enough yet to call it a night."

"Well, I don't want to stick my nose into your business, Norm, but you are definitely pie-eyed. You're swaying at least 5 percent from side to side here in front of me. Your mother is just trying to help you stay out of trouble, but you are an adult, and you can do what you want. If you will just excuse me and let me by, Norm, I'll continue on my collecting run."

Norm continued to block the hall as if my father's last statement did not register. After a few seconds, he asked my dad if he had a few dollars to spare so he could get to the nearest tavern and continue to drink.

"No, I don't have any money on me," said Dad. "And I think even if I did have a few extra bucks, I'd be hesitant to give them to you. Why don't you just go home, Norm?"

"Sure, you have money, Mr. O'Connell," he said as he came a couple of steps closer.

"I just saw Ma give you more than enough for what I need. Be a sport, and I'll let you get on your way."

"The money that your mom gave me isn't mine," Dad said. "It's John Hancock money. I can't give you money that isn't mine."

For a moment, Norm seemed puzzled, as though the concept of the ownership of said property had him completely stymied. "I just saw Ma give it to you," Norm said in a louder and more demanding tone. "Now give me a couple of bucks or I'm gonna take it from you!" He moved two or three steps closer to Dad and said, "You know with a little effort, I can kick your ass, Mr. O'Connell, and take that money from you, don't you?"

"I don't think there would be too many men who'd have much of a chance with you, judging from your size," said my father in a louder voice. "But you're going to have to beat the tar out of me to get this money, Norm," as he wondered if he could take out one of his knees long enough to get past him. As Norm loomed closer, Ma's door opened and from within her apartment came a stern voice, "Norm, are you messing with Mr. O'Connell?"

Dad turned his head to see where the voice came from, and there was Ma with fiery eyes, and from the look of them, there'd be some harsh words from Ma tonight. Dad sure was glad his name was not Norm!

"I thought I told you to go home and sleep it off!" Ma exclaimed with those fiery eyes pointed directly at Norm.

"I was just fooling around, Ma, all I wanted was a couple more bucks from Mr. O'Connell."

"You don't need to go asking Mr. O'Connell for any money. You asked me for some, and I said no! You're drunk, son, and you get nasty when you're plastered. Do you want to go down to Menard for a few more years? Becoming drunker is the best way I know of to get another stay at Menard, compliments of the Illinois penal system. Furthermore, you were going to take Mr. O'Connell's money, were you not? That really makes me angry!"

As Norm took the stream of words from Ma, my dad felt sorry for him and embarrassed too, for being in the middle of it. As Dad let Ma verbally work her son over, he suddenly saw the scene as comical. Here Norm, a giant of a man, was being set straight by an old woman who was more than a foot shorter and half his weight. Dad knew he would have to take it too, if his mom were angry with him and needed to blow off some steam.

As Ma finished her tongue lashing, she said, "Now say you're sorry to Mr. O'Connell! And this better be the last time you say an unkind word to him!"

"Why should I say I'm sorry to Mr. O'Connell, Ma?" whined Norm. "I didn't do anything."

Norm, Norm, Norm, thought Dad, *you just had her calmed down and now you've riled her again.*

As my father slowly turned his head to look at Ma to see the damage to Norm's welfare that his last comment had made, Dad about bolted from the building. The seething anger now residing in Ma's eyes—she who heretofore had beckoned him to call her Ma—gave my father pause to reevaluate this gentle old woman. I do not ever want to see those eyes again, especially in a tangle, thought my dad.

"Did anything that I just said register in that head of yours, son? You are a big boy," said Ma, "and I have said my piece, you are going to do what you want anyway! I'm only going to say it one more time: Norm, say you're sorry to Mr. O'Connell and that it won't happen again." As Norm prepared to plead his case again with Ma, out popped a shotgun that she had concealed near the door. She aimed it right between Norm's eyes.

"I don't intend on saying it again," Ma said.

"Okay, okay, Ma. I'm sorry, Mr. O'Connell, and it won't happen again. Please get that shotgun away from my head, Ma, before it goes off!"

Ma slowly lowered the gun and said calmly, "That's a good boy, son, now take my advice and go sleep it off, or at least get the heck out of here."

"I will, Ma, I will," as he quickly scampered from Ma's door. She turned to Dad and asked him if he was okay. She asked because Dad had such an astonished look on his face: he was imagining Norm without a head!

"Ma, you wouldn't have pulled the trigger and ended your son's life, would you?" asked my father.

"Well, Bill, my husband is deceased now, so sometimes my sons need some rather strict guidance from their mother. I'm afraid had I not been present, my son would have taken all your John Hancock money, whether you liked it or not. Norm is mean. I don't think he would hurt me. He'd have to answer to my other sons if he did. If I felt threatened by him, Bill, and given the opportunity, sure I'd blow his head off."

"Ma, I just hope I never see those eyes leveled at me like they were at Norm."

"You're just a sweetheart, Mr. O'Connell. How could I ever be angry with you?"

Throughout high school and most of college, my relationships with women were purely platonic. By the time I entered college, I was no longer afraid of them, and I enjoyed many lady friends. I don't know how many of them were waiting for the question, "Do you want to go see a movie this weekend?" but there may have been a few. Some of the women I thought were friends would suddenly dry up and go on to hunt, I presume, in more fertile grounds. We suffered no disagreements. I hope each of them found what they were looking for in a relationship, which I was not able to offer.

It was not that I had not pondered the idea of a normal relationship with a woman, but women were clearly not for me at that time. I had worked a little bit at the paper route in the sixth grade, for a whopping $1.25 per week, but that small amount of money was long gone about the time I reached the eighth grade. I earned a little during my junior and senior years at the high school I attended, but when you got down to the take after my family's share, I netted only about $3 per week. I had an allowance, as did my younger brothers and sisters, paid on Sundays. "Sunday six cents" was what we called it. I cannot remember if I was cut from the take when I started earning my $3.

I could have pounded the pavement for work, but looking at my atrophied right hand and arm and the pronounced limp when I walked, I don't think I would have had much of a shot at any factory job. I'd be an accident waiting to happen.

If I met a special lady who was willing to spend a few of her hours with me, and I temporarily had the funds to use on an evening, I was stymied with transportation. No money, no car. I could have pleaded with my father to use his car occasionally. That would involve two or three days cleaning the used insurance sheets from his back seat but was doable. The only problem with this solution was Dad always had a manual transmission on his car, and I would have had one heck of a time operating one of those suckers with my right hand. That's a restriction on my current driver's license, the same as those who cannot drive without glasses.

I could have let the girl pay for the outing, but as I recall, there were not too many women who came rapping at the door on Alhambra Court with that proposal. I was not too ugly when I was young and had hair, although I had my fair share of ears and a more than adequate nose. I think it would have taken more than what I had to offer, though, to expect the fairer sex to pay the yeoman's share of the cost of the date.

I inherited Uncle Laur's car when he died in 1975, which was the year I graduated with a degree in accounting. When I started work after graduation, there were more-than-adequate funds to do what I wanted. I was living at home for a small room-and-board charge, but all the rest of my newfound wealth was available to spend or save as I wished. I was not in any special hurry to involve myself with one woman. I was past the age of enlightenment, where girls are special creatures to be admired and captured for a while, where they are exclusively yours, and likewise, you are exclusively theirs. They called it "going steady" in ancient times, although I never experienced the phenomena.

Now do not get me wrong, women are special, to be admired and respected as human beings, to be sure. There is not anything I would not do for any of my five sisters. The female sex is easily a far richer group of people than their male counterparts, and I say that the world would be a sight better if it were filled with them. However, I did not want to get too close to any of them yet, not close enough to have one of them throw a rope around me for good and I'd find myself wondering what happened when I was saying "I do."

I wondered if my dad forgot the fact that he was twenty-eight and a half years old when he took the plunge, and his older brother was more than thirty-five when he married. Did he forget the statistics when he'd periodically try to set me up with a lass he knew?

After a few "Thanks, Dad, but no thanks," I agreed to meet this girl who was the daughter of one of his insurance clients, who happened to be one of Ma's boys. Dad assured me that this guy was one of Ma's well-behaved ones who had become a good friend of his through the years. On occasion, Dad would encounter the man's daughter, who was always polite and always willing to talk a few minutes with old Mr. O'Connell.

"I tell you, Tom, this young lady is top-notch," said my father, "worth getting to know. If it doesn't work out, at least you gave it a chance, son."

"I don't even know this woman, nor does she know me, Dad."

"Well, Tom, she has medium-length blond hair, and she's pretty."

I did not like the situation, but my dad could be persistent, so I finally agreed. *What harm could it do to meet her?* I thought.

For some reason, my father brought along one of my older sisters, Maureen, for the visit to one of Ma's boys. I cannot really say that I spoke to the man much that evening. My dad was loquacious, and my sister filled in the empty places. I was mostly thinking of what was to come when I met this person. I was nervous, and I wondered if she was too. She loved her father as most children do, but she might feel that her dad went a bit too far in setting her up with his friend's unknown son.

We were talking for about forty-five minutes when in walked the woman I was to meet. After the introductions, my dad, his friend, and Maureen went into the living room to resume talking and left the man's daughter alone with me in the kitchen, where I presumed, we were supposed to get better acquainted. I said toward the beginning of our talk that it was awkward meeting this way. I followed up with a brief biography of the first twenty-two or twenty-three years of my life. After I spoke for a while, I listened to what she was doing at the current time. Frankly, I can't tell you much of what she said. All the time I was talking I stared at the table, trying to the best of my ability to talk in a succinct way and not to sound like a complete moron. I thought I did a decent job talking about myself, and when she began to speak, I looked at her for the first time.

I'm a large man, six feet five inches with coal-black hair and 230 pounds at that point. She was about five and a half feet tall, about a foot shorter than me. You could stack about two of her bodies together before she'd approach my body weight. She was, as my father said, a pretty blond woman.

As I cast my eyes to meet hers, there was Ma looking straight at me. I almost soiled my britches out of fear. Although she was smiling as she spoke, and I knew Ma was long dead, all I could see at that moment were the steely blue eyes of Ma, her grandmother. Trying not to whimper, I silently said to myself, "You can't fool me. I know all about you, Ma, from the stories I heard from my dad." I shivered a little as I finished my thought.

I know you're her granddaughter, and I know I'll be safe if'n I mind my Ps and Qs.

"I know you're almost a foot taller than me and weigh over a hundred pounds more," those eyes were telling me, "but you do have to sleep, don't you, buddy? You best be nice to me, or I'm going to take a baseball bat and work over those knees of yours when you go night, night. Then I'm gonna cut ya for a while!"

Let me tell you, she put the fear of God into me that evening. I surely did not want any part of a relationship with her. My guess is she was not too wild about me as a prospective suitor either.

Ma and I talked for about ten or fifteen more minutes while I tried to act like a real dud, loser type of guy which I was good at, if I do say so myself. I am not going to ask her for an additional meeting, if I can help it, I thought, but if she brings it up, I'll have to do what Ma says. I hope I don't start to bawl if she wants to get to know me better. We left the kitchen and joined the others in the living room while I escaped the unenviable question of "Do you want to see me again?" It was not too long before we were walking to the car and heading home.

My father unlocked his car, and I sunk to the bottom of all the used insurance papers on the back seat, feeling instant relief in not being in that young woman's home.

"Well, are you going to see her again, Tom?" my dad asked.

I looked at his face in the rearview mirror over the dashboard, wondering how I would answer this ridiculous question.

"Are you nuts, Dad? I'm so relieved we're in the safety of your car. Start her up and let's get the heck out of here before she races out of the house and asks me out!" I said.

One could understand the confusion of my father and Maureen. During the ten or fifteen minutes of conversation I had with the girl in the kitchen, nothing seemed awry.

"Tom, what's wrong?" Dad said. "You two seemed to be talking nicely and I *know* she's a nice young lady."

"Dad, everything you said about her was the truth. She did seem like a nice woman," I said.

"Well then, what's the problem, Tom? When we left the house, you looked like I just saved you from the guillotine."

"Did you ever take a good look at her eyes? Do they kind of remind you of someone else's, Dad?"

"I know they're blue, Tom, but that's the extent of my knowledge about her eyes."

"They're Ma's eyes!" I exclaimed. "Every time I looked at those eyes I shivered."

Dad had to laugh at that last comment. Once again, he assured me the young lady was pleasant, and that I should not worry.

"She is a nice young lady, Dad, just as I'm sure the young Ma was too, the first time she met her husband. Remember 'Ma's' eyes, Dad, as she was aiming the shotgun at her son's head? No, Dad. I'll pass on this one. I have enough problems without adding fear of my wife for the next fifty or sixty years."

14

The Last Journey

Shortly after Dad started work in life insurance there was talk of a union startup among the agents of John Hancock. My dad's father was a big proponent of all unions for negotiating contracts with various companies. There was not a union for any insurance company when my father started to work for John Hancock. The deal was cut-and-dried, my father thought. You made an amount for collecting the debit and an amount for commissions for any new business. He was hesitant to take a pro-union stand as soon as he started to work for the company.

However, when his fellow agents approached him on the matter, he said, "Guys, I'm still in training to learn the ropes of selling insurance. This is not going to sit well with John Hancock. It's the best way I know of for a trainee to get fired, but if you need just one swing vote for the union to be established, you can count on me."

This was how my father left it, not expecting the union to be accepted or fail, but to be notified if they needed his vote.

Dad's job required a weekly meeting at the Spivey Building, an East St. Louis skyscraper. It wasn't much of a skyscraper at twelve stories tall, but in 1927, it qualified as a tower. At that time, John Hancock occupied a chunk of the Spivey Building.

One day, as my father was riding the elevator to the office, two of his fellow agents were riding with him. One of them mentioned that he smelled an extremely vile odor. The other agent said, "Yeah, I can smell it too, Mac, it smells like an anti-union fink is in here!"

"Okay, guys, since there are only three people in this elevator who work at John Hancock, it looks like I'm the fink you're referring to. Now, when we get off the elevator, I'll take you apart one at a time, if that's how you want it, or you can tell me why you're calling me a fink."

"You're a company man through and through," one of them said. "Here we're placing our jobs on the line and you went and voted for the company."

"I didn't vote pro-company or pro-union," my father said, "this is the first time I've heard about any voting."

"That's not the way I heard it," said one of the men.

"Well, whoever told you is misinformed or a liar," my dad said. "I was just hired when this union talk started and was learning the ropes. I told the guys if they needed one more vote to carry the union, they could count on me for the swing vote. How in heck that could be misconstrued into 'Bill O'Connell's a company man,' I will never know, but that's the truth. Of course, I'll join the union, but I'm counting on the union to back me up in case John Hancock decides to fire me. I've only been here for a few months, guys, and I'd be angry if the union didn't stand up for one of their members."

My dad became active in the union, rising to president and consistently putting his job on the line when the company was unfair to any of the members. People knew you could always count on Bill O'Connell to stand with you until the matter was settled.

My father was drafted into the army in 1941, and when he returned from Europe after Germany surrendered in 1945, he was shattered. He saw many atrocities inside five battles, although he managed not to take a single life. As a supply sergeant, he was not active in the war, yet he supplied the troops with instruments of death, and that bothered him. Regardless of who tried to comfort him, he appreciated their efforts, but their efforts went for naught. All the people who were closest to him, people he loved, did not know what to do. Nor did he—how to cure what was aching deep within his soul.

He did not think he would be able to talk with people, something that was imperative if he elected to return to insurance. He delayed the return to his occupation until it became necessary, wondering whether this move would tip the scales of his sanity. Forcing himself to interact with the people he called his clients ended up saving his life, he told me.

He was loyal to his customers, and always kept in mind their best interests. Often, he talked a client into buying a $10,000 policy instead of a $20,000 one. These were young people who could see nothing but rainbows in their future, with no thought of the storms ahead, who commonly had three or four children under their wings. It would be easy to sell them more than they needed or could afford and never to think of what might happen to them later.

For five years, Dad received commissions on all new business. Selling high dollar policies would have made him more money but might have caused his clients to lose their policies twenty years later when the insurance money would be needed for food for their expanded families of six or seven children. Was my dad not meant to be an insurance agent? If you consider the amount he made for his family, perhaps not. However, if you ask the clients who put their trust in him, the answer would be a definite yes since there were storms to ride out in some of their futures.

When Dad gave his retirement speech, he talked for twenty to twenty-five minutes solely about his eleven children and his wife who raised them. I will tell you it was kind of embarrassing for me to have my laurels bandied about as well as my brothers' and sisters' accolades, which were far greater than mine. This was his day to shine. He could have mentioned his trustworthy service to his clients and the tremendous effort he put into organizing the union and helping his friends along the way. It was his opinion, I know, that these traits—honesty, trustworthiness, honor, and loyalty—were all part of the job at John Hancock, not to be mentioned. He spoke only of his treasures, his gold, what truly mattered to him, his family.

My dad started smoking when he was about twenty years old while handling freight. When he was fifty, he had been a chain-smoker of harsh cigarettes for about thirty years, three packs a day. He was a regular customer at the doctor's for many years, and I am sure his doctor mentioned at every appointment that the best thing he could do health-wise was to stop smoking.

He was skinny all his life, hovering at about 150 or 160 pounds at a little over six feet. He always had a fast heart rate. At one point, he was on twenty-four medications just to keep him out of the hospital. My mom said it was ridiculous that any person would need that many medications. She didn't seem to like Dad's doctor, while Dad trusted him, considering him a friend who knew a little bit more about medicine than his wife.

At fifty, my father had considerable trouble walking much more than a quarter mile. There were times when his vision was severely impaired. He also had instances of light-headedness to the point of passing out, and he had chronic balance problems. From discussions with his doctor, he knew about his arteriosclerosis, or hardening of the arteries like his father, which scared him.

At one doctor's appointment, my dad asked how long he had on this earth before being called home. If I were a doctor, I would not have liked this question. First, it's a negative question. If the patient did not have anything that would kill him soon, I as the doc would want to keep my patients positive.

"I don't know, Bill. You don't have anything that's going to kill you overnight. Just lay off those cigarettes, and you'll be amazed how much better you'll feel."

"Yeah, Doc, but that's not going to happen soon. Would you say I'll still be around here in a year's time?"

"I'm no fortune teller, Bill. You might be around five years from now. Just quit smoking those darn cigarettes!" the doctor said.

"So you'd say about five years max?" my dad asked.

The doctor threw up his hands. "You'll be pestering me with your silly questions until God wants you, Bill."

He retired from life insurance at sixty, intending to obtain his real estate license. Dad looked forward to selling something that was tangible, sales at which he knew he could be successful. Although he studied hard, taking the exam twice, he didn't pass either time. The first time, the test covered material not covered in the literature. The next time, he felt good about the exam and the questions were mostly those he had covered. Still, he did not pass.

Demoralized, Dad abandoned his dream. He reasoned that since he put in the time and felt good about the exam and still did not pass, he wasn't meant to be in real estate. Perhaps he should have tried again until he was successful. We should walk a mile or two in my father's shoes before we say what he should or should not have done.

Accepting what life gives us and attaining true peace is sometimes difficult. My father accepted this disappointment and continued with his life, doing what he deemed important and fruitful. He could no longer run a mile. He had to carry his trusty lawn chair if he intended to walk much more than a hundred yards.

He was a voracious reader who chose pastimes that meant something to him. Until I was thirty-three and acquired a house for my bride-to-be, I genuinely enjoyed staying with Mom and Dad. I talked for hours with my father and friend, often antagonizing him, pushing the buttons I knew would get him fired up, all in playful fun! He knew what I was doing, so generally, there was no harm done. When the words were meant to sting a little, we realized our friendship was far too great to be broken by a few hurtful words thrown at each other when one of us lost his temper.

There were times when I was not present, but I hoped he was whiling away the hours doing what he liked. One morning before I moved to my own place, I noticed he was having a tough time breathing, which concerned me before heading out to work. My dad assured me that it was only because he'd had a tough time sleeping the prior night, which calmed my worries. Still, I headed to work unconvinced that his problem was lack of sleep.

That afternoon, Mom called to say that Dad had been taken to the hospital about an hour after I left for work. My hunch was right. "Mom, is it serious?" I knew she was puzzled: it's always serious to any right-thinking human being if you have to be hospitalized. Truth be told, the hospital was my father's second home, and it was common for him to spend time in St. Elizabeth's two or three times per year.

"They think it might be his heart," Mom said, and knowing the hard breathing my dad was doing three hours ago, I told my boss I was leaving. I headed to St. Elizabeth's.

I felt guilty. I had known something was wrong. He gave me his flimsy excuse, but I wear big-boy pants now; I should have pressed him for more information. When I arrived at the waiting room, Mom was there with several of my siblings. They told me he was in stable condition and being evaluated. Old-man time was getting closer, ever closer to the day he would always win.

My dad was in the hospital for several days. I was living by then in my new house, awaiting my fiancé from Dallas, Texas, to fulfill her contract for a computer service company so that we could be married and settle down in Troy, Illinois.

My brothers, sisters, and I figured a system where each day, two of us would go to our parents' house to spend the evening with dad and give mom a few hours' break. Dad was in my former bedroom the first night I visited him after the hospital stay. For several years at that point, he had slept in his recliner, which eased his leg pain. In my former bedroom, I found my father in his recliner to the left of my old bed.

"How are you doing, Tom?" he asked.

"I'm doing okay. How are you doing in your new setup, Dad?"

"I'm doing fine," he said, and we talked about various things until my younger brother, John, came into the room.

My dad never again was in as good a shape as he had been that morning when I left him. He barely could stand; a catheter removed his urine. He was never hungry. There was always a cause of disagreement at mealtimes. Dad would say Mom was treating him like a child and giving him too much food. She was simply concerned about his weight loss and doing everything in her power to put a few more pounds on her husband. A drug now removed excess water from his body. His heart was in such bad a shape that it could not empty his chest cavity of water.

What was his quality of life? Yes, for sure he had a myriad of health problems in that last year of his life. But because a person is limited in what they can do does not equate to unhappiness. My dad was regularly visited by all his children during that last year. It was Mom and us kids who really counted to him. We all grew closer. We were able to clearly see the man's goodness and how much he loved us. That last year was one of the happier ones for my dad, I believe. He knew his life was winding down. His passing was only a matter of time. He had found true peace.

There were difficulties through that year. During many hospitalizations, I was sure he was being called home. At times he felt poorly, but when his children came to visit, he appeared miraculously to awaken from a deep sleep, not so ill. Once his older brother Dave came to spend some time with him. Dad was proud of his brothers and sisters. I remember pleasant dinners with his brothers, Laur, or Dave, his wife and boy. After dinner, Dad would ask his brother Dave to sing a few songs. Dave would say no a couple of times, but Dad would pester him until he sang. It was not the fact that my Uncle Dave was afraid or embarrassed to sing for a group of people. He sang solos at Mass on Sundays. It was that he was so humble that he didn't want to show off. He'd always include my favorite "Old Man River," which sent chills up and down my arms when he came to the last few lines. No wonder my dad liked to hear Dave sing: he was proud to call him a brother.

On one of those occasions when Dad was not feeling well and was answering my questions in truncated sentences, which was not like him, I asked Uncle Dave to sing a song for his brother again.

"What song do you want me to sing, Tom?"

"Do you know the 'Our Father'?" I asked.

"Yes, I do, Tom—at least one rendition—but why do you want that one sung? I don't think I ever sang it here before."

"I believe my dad would like his older brother to sing it for him," I answered.

So, Uncle Dave, a man more than seventy-seven years old, stood and began in such a magnificent voice that, once again, there were chills up and down my arms. I looked at my dad and his eyes were twinkling again, pumped up by pride for his older brother singing with such melodious charm a song that meant the world to him.

"You still got it, Dave," my father said.

We talked for the rest of the visit and it appeared that, prompted by his brother's songs, Dad improved. The music did not change the ultimate outcome, but it cheered him up that night. I do not know if I ever sufficiently thanked my uncle, except right after the song. I'm sure glad he was there that night to share the kindness of his voice in song.

Trivial things bothered Dad. However sick you are, those things remain with you. My oldest brother, Bill, arrived to take him to the doctor.

"Hi, Dad, are you about ready to go?

Bill likes to wear baseball caps, and he had one on that day.

"Oh, I'm just about ready, Bill. Sit down and take your hat off, and I'll be ready in a couple of minutes."

Bill sat down, intent on resuming their talk, but he left the hat on his head. Dad looked at him for a few seconds and said, "Well? Aren't you going to take off your hat, Bill?"

"No," Bill said, a little perturbed. "We're going out shortly, Dad, so I think I'll leave it on."

Dad looked at Bill. A few more seconds passed. "Bill, you know it's impolite for a man to wear his hat indoors." Bill began to steam, but he couldn't blow his top at such a silly rule as inappropriate indoor head gear! Bill did not respond to the question, but now he was going to wear his hat indoors as a matter of honor. After a few more seconds, my father said, "Well, it looks like you're not going to take your cap off, Bill."

"No, I'm not, Dad!"

Dad could tell Bill had had enough and said, "There's no reason to get all huffy about it, Bill. You're a man now and you can wear your hat indoors if you want. It makes you look like a jackass, but you have the right to look any way you want, son."

I laugh every time I hear that story from my brother. That was my dad through and through. Some of his antics embarrassed Mom to no end, as well as some of my more sensitive siblings, but not me. I took my father as he was: he added to the flavor of my world.

My fiancé Mary finished her three contracted years of work in early June, for a firm that did computer service for various companies. Her brother-in-law and a couple of his friends moved a few items from Dallas to our house. Our wedding was not scheduled until June 13, so Mary stayed at her mother's house until the wedding day. It took more than thirty-four years for me to be captured by a woman—or perhaps *more* than thirty-four years until a lady felt that my good points outweighed the bad. Suffice it to say, I was extremely relieved when I saw Mary Fox walking down the aisle of St. Boniface Catholic Church that Saturday. After the ceremony, there were several hours until the reception.

Sadly, Dad was not able to attend the nuptial Mass; he was too weak, and I did not want him to attempt it. Off to Fairview Heights we went, my new bride, Mary, and her fortunate husband, Tom. The wedding dress was large and flowing with its traditional style and train five or six feet long. Her mother had sewn it for her as she had done for Mary's sister, Alice. We were traveling to my parents house in her little compact car, and I wondered how she had tucked in the dress! Boy, I hoped not to slam the car door onto that train. It would be embarrassing to get to the reception and have the snot kicked out of me by her mother for ruining her dress.

Mary did thankfully stuff the voluminous train into the small car, and we arrived at my parents house to see my dad. He was surprised, as I suppose he didn't expect to see us that day. He complimented Mary on her beautiful dress, and we talked for about forty minutes until we needed to head to the reception. I don't think my new wife minded our little side trip. Dad was an important cogwheel of the good parts of me. He needed to be included, if only for a few minutes of talk and to see how beautiful my wife was on that special day.

It was Sunday, November 1, 1987, it was my turn to visit Dad in the evening. I arrived at my parents house about six o'clock. My sister, Maureen, was also arriving that day from Eastern Tennessee. Since my dad had become critically ill about a year prior, Maureen would routinely spend about ten days of each month in Fairview Heights, east of St. Louis. It was difficult for her to spend the time away from work, and I'm sure she appreciated the organization for allowing her precious time with her father.

Unknowingly to me, I was talking with my dad for the last time. He looked about the same as always in the last year. I knew it was just a matter of time until something profound happened and he would pass, but at least for this visit, nothing seemed different.

"How are things going, Dad?"

He always liked to tell you his life's story, health-wise that is, but this time he said, "Oh, about the same, Tom, status quo, son."

We talked a bit about sports and about the arguments he'd had with my mother that day over the copious amounts she put on his plate and how it angered him that she was still treating him like one of her children.

"Dad, you have to look at it from her point of view. You're extremely skinny, and all she's trying to do is fatten you up and give you a little more strength. You certainly look like you're under the magical 142 pounds where you physically break down."

"Yeah, yeah, yeah, you smart aleck. I'm just not hungry anymore, Tom, and she should know that after the dozens of arguments we've had on the subject."

"Dad, she's just trying to help you," I repeated and then jumped to another topic before the rebuttal I knew was coming if I didn't change the subject.

I looked at my watch eight or nine times before leaving that night. As an accountant for an industrial company, the first business day was always the busiest one for me. I told Dad I'd have to cut our visit short. I arrived at my house about nine, calmed down, and went to bed about ten. I was drifting off to sleep when the phone rang. It was Mom. Dad had taken a turn for the worse.

He had taken a lot of turns for the worse in the past year: I could not understand how he had become that much worse in an hour or two. "Mom, I just came home about an hour ago and he was fine then, well, not fine, but there seemed to be nothing life-threatening at that time." Was this just another one of those scenarios when he's down for the count, but up again in plenty of time to resume the fight?

"Tom, I don't know what his condition was the last time you saw him, but I think you'd better get over here to see your father."

As I hung up the phone, I thought, *I need to be at work early tomorrow.* Maybe Mom arrived home from bingo and thought that Dad looked worse for wear. I was battling my demons of going or not going over to my parents' house. I decided to go just in case. There were already five or six people at the house when I arrived. I did not go to his bedroom at first, but into the kitchen where most of my siblings were standing. I went to Maureen and asked what had happened in the two hours since I'd been there.

"He went down real fast, Tom. He's having a lot of trouble swallowing his medicine."

Having trouble swallowing his medicine, I thought, as I walked down the hall; what does that mean? He's had this happen before. As I opened the bedroom door, there was Ellen, my youngest sister, with her back turned to my dad.

There he lay—comatose, wheezing, and gasping for air for the last few times. I fell apart, weeping, unable to control myself. My father was dying before my eyes. My baby sister Ellen, a foot shorter and half my weight, came to me and held me like a baby child while I wept. Did I ever thank her for that?

I went to my father's chair, knelt, and took his right hand firmly in my left, and through my weeping and shattered voice, "I'm here, Dad, I love you, Dad."

I did not know what more to say but kept a hardy grip on his right hand. If he could hear me or feel my grip, he would know that someone was there for him at that hour, when he was afraid.

At the door, someone said, "You're going to heaven, Dad." Bill moved to my right and took his other hand. "I love you, Dad. We're all here."

As I knelt at my father's side, I remembered him saying to me more than once that at his time to go, I should not weep, but pray with him. I tried unsuccessfully not to weep. I couldn't help it. So I started to pray in my shattered voice the Act of Contrition:

> Oh my God, I am heartily sorry for hav-
> ing offended Thee,
> And I detest all my sins because of Thy
> just punishments.
> But most of all because they offend Thee,
> my God,
> Who art all good and deserving of all my
> love.

As I continued the prayer, all of my siblings recited it with me, so I am sure if my dad's hearing was intact, he heard us pray. We continued with the Lord's Prayer, and shortly thereafter, the paramedics arrived and took him to the hospital for the last time. My sister, Maureen, went with the paramedics in the ambulance. Dad expired before they reached St. Elizabeth's.

For two hours, we stayed in a room with my father. There was silence except for the sobs of my siblings who did not make it to the house before the ambulance left. My father requested a closed casket at the funeral home. He did not want people gawking at his bald head and saying how natural he looked.

Some of my siblings had a rough time for many years, missing the conversations with the colorful man who could make words dance for us. I'm grateful that I made that last trip to my father's house and did not chuck the idea. I'm not sure if Dad was too far gone for any of the prayers to help, but I hope he knew there were people who loved him standing near, waiting for God to call him home.

This man fought the good fight, always positive even in the last year when his body was failing him miserably. I feel fortunate to have known him, not only as my father, but as a friend. We all need to leave our mortal bodies at some point, and I know that father time is catching up with me. I've lost the instant recall of all the stories my father told. Yet at times an incident can trigger me to search the deep recesses of my mind for one of his stories of fifty years ago or more. I smile and say thanks, Dad, for spending time with me, unworthy as I might be. I love you, Dad!

15

The Kerthumper

It was August of 2008, and I had the beginnings of a raspy throat that precedes a head cold by one or two days. I hate these summer colds and I wonder why the darn things exist. I could understand the winter variety, especially as a child.

I didn't consider it necessary to wear a jacket until the temperature fell below forty degrees, so I endured more than my fair share of winter colds. The prevailing theory was that wintry weather sapped the energy from your body and made you more susceptible to the germs flying around. One might surmise that a chap who ran around in short-sleeve shirts until it was darn near freezing would catch three or four winter colds in any year. I cannot say that I wanted to get sick so I could miss school, but sometimes, I wondered if my parents thought that was my scheme.

This raspy throat was different from all my other summer colds. I should have gone to the doctor a day or two before I gave in and went to the after-hours clinic. It was a summer cold, I thought, and though they were a pain, I did not deem it a big deal. My wife and son had been diagnosed with strep throat a couple of days prior. It would not take a genius to conclude that my sore throat was strep. At the outset, it didn't hurt more than a normal sore throat preceding a cold. I thought, it will cost me at least $150 to go to the clinic. I think I'll just ride it out like a cowboy and if it gets worse, I'll go tomorrow.

It was Saturday, and my sore throat had not eased. I gargled and took lozenges, which relieved the pain a little, but I could tell this was going to be a doozy, coupled as it was with a bad summer cold. I should have seen the doctor today, I thought, but unfortunately the office had closed by the time I decided I no longer wanted to be a cowboy.

When I awoke on Sunday, I felt horrible. I'd never felt that much pain with any sore throat, and buddy, I had a lot of sore throats in my day. It felt like my throat was swollen and on fire, and I had a massive head cold. My wife had gone back to work a couple of days before that, and she was concerned about me. In my current condition, she felt it was not a bright idea for me to go anywhere alone.

"Tom, let me go to work and you rest today until I get home, and then I'll take you to the doctor," she said. I did not need too much convincing. So I rested in bed a bit, but mostly in my recliner. I did not eat much that day and it seemed to take forever for Mary's eight-hour shift to end.

I couldn't talk much by the time she arrived home. She helped me to the car, and we went to the late hours doctor's office, with Mary driving and our son Tom in the back seat. When we arrived, Tom raced to get a wheelchair, which seemed ridiculous to me, but Mary and Tom convinced me to ride. We signed in and waited for at least an hour.

The doctor peered into my mouth and administered a test for strep. I don't recall how long we waited until he returned with the results.

"You might have strep throat," the doctor said. I fail to remember what he said after that.

I might have strep throat! What type of diagnosis is this? I watched my 150 dollars smile and drift away. He wrote a prescription that would kill strep—if I had it! The checkout nurse was angry.

"He should have sent you to the hospital, Mr. O'Connell! Here you come into our office in a wheelchair, and not only does he not know what is wrong with you, he sends you away with some medicine that *may* cure you! Where did he get his medical training?" she asked.

Hey, hey, hey, I thought, *sending me to the hospital in an ambulance, I presume? How much would that cost me for a bad summer cold?*

My wife went to the drug store to get the medicine that might help. I was all worn out by the time we got home. I can't say I slept much that night. I was hoping the medicine might make me feel a little better by the next day. I had my wife call work for me and tell them I would not be in. My wish had not been granted during the night; I felt much worse. As Mary got ready for work, I laid in bed with a throat more swollen than the day before. Then I began having a tough time breathing. I was concerned. When Mary finished getting ready for work and walked down the stairs, I arose from my bed and staggered to the bathroom to take care of my necessaries and almost fell on my face. I was breathing as heavy as a quarter mile sprinter. Something is dead wrong here, I thought, as I barely made it to the safety of my bed. I called for Mary at the moment she was heading out the door. She heard me, thank goodness.

"Tom, what's wrong?"

"I've never felt this way before, Mary. I need to go to the hospital."

She called for an ambulance. Knowing from the preceding night's escapades, she did not think it wise to try helping me down the stairs to her car. I put on my clothes the best I could and waited in my bedroom for the ambulance.

The paramedics arrived in short order. Two guys came to my bedroom and asked me what was wrong.

"I've never felt this bad from a cold in my entire life, guys. In trying to reach the bathroom, I almost fell. I'm breathing heavy, and I can't stop. I think it best you get me to the hospital," I said.

"Do you think you can make it down the stairs, Mr. O'Connell?"

"Maybe," I said, "but I think I'd tumble down a few of them before I made it, mister."

One of them smiled and said, "Well then, we'll take you down."

While one of them left, I was thinking, *you'll* take me down? The two men were average-sized, which made me about one and a half the size of either of them after stuffing themselves with a hearty meal. *Good luck, boys*, I thought. Maybe I'd better try to descend myself.

A couple of minutes passed, and I heard a horrible mechanical sound coming up the steps. As a paramedic pushed the noisy contraption into my bedroom, it was a gigantic wheelchair, which made loud *kerthumps* as they brought it closer to my bed.

"What is *that* contraption?" I asked in amazement.

"Well, Mr. O'Connell, hopefully it's something we can use to get you down safely from the second floor and into the ambulance in one piece."

I rose from the bed and was helped into the kerthumper (my name for the contraption) by both people. They strapped me in good. I guess if the two guys had lost control of the kerthumper, I could have ridden it to the first floor, sticking out and locking my legs to stop the momentum as it approached the front door of my house.

"Are you ready now, Mr. O'Connell?"

"As ready as I'll ever be," and off we went—*kerthump… kerthump…kerthump.*

Man, was it this loud before? I wondered. And then I realized that there were 230 pounds of additional blubber on top of the poor kerthumper.

We had a little trouble passing through my door and aligning with the second-floor steps. There was a ninety-degree angle outside the bedroom that they had to negotiate to get to the stairs. I can't say whether there was a man on the top and one on the bottom of the kerthumper as we traversed the steps. But if I were the paramedic, I'd much rather be top man than bottom man.

"Okay, Mr. O'Connell, here we go," and I was tipped at a forty-five-degree angle, giving me a fantastic view of the ceiling down the steps from the second floor.

Each step down was an extremely loud kerthump as we descended the thirteen steps to the first floor.

At the hospital, I was immediately wheeled into the emergency room, I presume because I had come via ambulance. They might have considered my emergency a higher priority, due to the fact that they needed to determine whether I was having a heart attack. Although I experienced some new adventures that day, I would gladly have passed on that experience. I felt sicker and sicker as the day progressed.

It could not have been much more than two hours later when the doctor came into the makeshift little room.

"You have a severe case of epiglottitis, Mr. O'Connell. Your blood oxygen ratio is extremely low, and you're lucky you came to the hospital when you did. Another three or four hours and you would have expired. We need to get you into surgery for a tracheotomy so we can raise your blood-oxygen level. Can you sign this form so we can proceed with the surgery, Mr. O'Connell?"

"Is a tracheotomy what I think it is, Doctor?" I asked.

"I don't know what you think it is, Mr. O'Connell," he responded, "but a tracheotomy is where we open your throat so you can breathe and get oxygen to your blood."

That is what I thought it was, although seconds ago, I had not had the foggiest notion of where my epiglottis was.

"There's no other option, Doc?" I asked as I imagined a hole in my throat for the rest of my life.

"There's no other way, Mr. O'Connell."

I wish my wife were here, I thought, as I signed the appropriate paperwork so the doc could slit my throat—under medical supervision, of course. My mind was drifting. I thought it might have been better to have Mary sign the paperwork, so they had the signature of one who was competent.

I can't tell you much about the next three or four days. My sister Maureen came to Northern Kentucky from Eastern Tennessee soon after the surgery. I remember being flat on my back and trying to write on papers Maureen held about a foot from my face. Suffice it to say that I was reminded of the good, old fourth-grade days, as I attempted to write with a fountain pen for the first time after the stroke…with my left hand. When I was medically better, Maureen asked if I remembered what I had written those first few days after the surgery.

"I only remember attempting to write something once, but I was in and out of consciousness, so I don't recall, Maureen."

Maureen said she'd tried to communicate with me several times, and all I could write was "I wish I were dead." I could not believe I was capable of writing those five words, regardless of how terrible I felt. She proved it to me about a year later when she showed me my chicken scratching that read many times, "I wish I were dead."

The tracheotomy was a success, and I was in the ICU resting comfortably. Hopefully, the doctors told Mary I was going to be okay. A few hours later, this same doctor approached my poor wife: "Mrs. O'Connell, your husband's kidneys have gone dormant. We will have to put him on dialysis."

Mary came in from work the next day and met Maureen and they waited outside my room to hear the latest update. After checking me thoroughly, the doctor told them I was hanging in, although I had developed double pneumonia that day, and my kidneys were still dormant. I do not know what was in their minds that night, but my chances could not have looked too rosy to them.

The next day, Mary learned that I had had a heart incident, whatever that means, and that they were giving me more tests to see how much damage was done to the old ticker. Mary must have been hesitant to show up the next day. She might be informed that my head was hollow and that the doctors were left scratching their heads as to where the brain matter had gone. My son, Tommy, often has mentioned that this hospital trip was entirely my fault. "If you had just gone to the after-hours clinic a day earlier, Dad, you wouldn't have been in that predicament!" he always said.

Maureen must have stayed around ten days in Northern Kentucky with my wife and two children. I must have coughed thousands of times until I was completely healed from the epiglottitis episode. In the hospital, the tracheotomy hole in my throat needed to be cleaned often. It must not have been a complicated job (probably yucky) because they showed the procedure to Mary and Maureen. In my delirium, I thought my wife had screwed up the process, so I tried to fix it myself. (I am not too bright a person on morphine.)

I remember lying on my back, getting angrier and angrier with Mary. I knew she meant well: she has at least ten times the goodness I do. She just was not a good mucus-remover, or whatever the procedure entailed. Shortly thereafter, a nurse came in to look at me and saw the hatchet job I did to fix my throat. She roundly scolded me and told me never to do it again. The nurse did not ask who messed with my throat. It was apparent that only someone who could not see what they were doing attempted the foiled fix-up job.

I remember asking Maureen one night to stay with me until morning; I did not want to die alone. Maureen came over to my bed, gently hugged and kissed me and said, "Sure, Tom, I'll stay with you tonight. But you're not going to die."

I was in a bad place mentally; I had been through the wringer. The doctors put me on morphine for the pain. The morphine did its job but gave me horrible nightmares. In one of them, I was running around New York City from people who wanted to kill me. I ran down a wharf and jumped into some heavily churning water to get away, only to realize I did not know how to swim. As I struggled to get to the wharf so I wouldn't drown, the people who had been chasing me took long poles, pushed me under the water, and kept me away from the dock. Each time they were successful I could hear them laugh and jeer, as I prayed my head would emerge from the churning waters.

Maureen informed her employers that her brother who lived two hundred miles away was sick and needed her, as she did when our father was dying. Once again, they said no problem. Family comes first, which I really appreciated.

All four of my other sisters drove east about 350 miles as did my closest brother and his wife to let me know they were here and thinking of me. One of them brought a piece of my writing from about twenty years ago and read it aloud. Although I could not speak, tears rolled down my cheeks as I listened.

I was not allowed water for the first five or six days. I was so darn thirsty. I remember vividly those first few sips of water and how fresh and clear it tasted. The hospital gradually reduced the hole in my throat until it was closed. My kidneys resumed normal function and the heart incident proved to be nothing. I have a barely noticeable scar where my throat was slit but nothing more except memories of the incident, which seem to be fading. As the years pass, my mind sees them as lesser and lesser evils. One thing I will always remember is the concern of my wife for her husband and my brothers and sisters for their sibling and how they rallied at my bedside, giving me the insight and the knowledge that we are all here, buddy, and your life's worth living. Do not ever give up, Tom, do not ever give up. And when you go, go down swinging.

At around the age of sixteen, my elder sisters obtained work at Jimmy's Malt shop at Thirty-First and State Streets. It was a hard job making the ice cream, scooping the sometimes-rock-hard delicacy to the patrons, waiting on grouchy customers, and keeping the shop intact from all the guys wanting to show off their fierceness among their male cohorts. The job did not pay much but was far more than my sisters had ever seen. By then, there were ten of us kids, and Mom and Dad were having a tough time making ends meet. My sisters were glad to contribute 90 percent of what they made, to keep the wolf from the door. With their combined wages, my sisters figured they were contributing about half of what my dad made during the summer, and that gave them a good feeling. They were helping the family when Mom and Dad needed help in a dire way.

It was at Jimmy's malt shop that Kathie met her husband, Terry McCart. From their paltry take of seven cents an hour, my sisters would sometimes take their younger brothers and sisters to the movies at the Majestic Theatre at Twenty-Fifth and State. My older brothers dug graves for a year, worked for a bottling company, a nursery and for American Zinc for several years while they went to college, keeping only 10 percent of what they truly earned.

I do not know how many times I've thanked each of my siblings for all the work they did to support our family. I don't know if all the wages contributed to our family were done in the spirit of true altruism by my siblings, but that doesn't matter. They stepped up.

My parents are both gone now. Dad's been gone for more than thirty years. I am blessed to have ten spectacular human beings for siblings who are genuinely concerned about me. I want them to know I'd do anything for them, just as they have done for me. One would only need to capture a small portion of my life to know I'm a fortunate person with a close family. I yearn to be located 350 miles to the west to be closer to most of my family.

16

The Tree

About thirty years after the stroke, I had my first grand-mal seizure, which knocked me out for about an hour and a half. Strokes and seizures are happy bedfellows due to the scarring on the brain caused by a stroke. I have no idea whether the time span between the original stroke and the seizure was an aberration. Whether I am a unique fellow or an ordinary Joe, the fact is it was a seizure, which in Illinois is accompanied by the loss of all driving privileges for six months. Makes perfect sense; you do not want a person prone to uncontrolled seizures driving a car.

You do not realize what a convenience it is to drive until you lose the privilege, particularly when your workplace is thirty miles from home. As I was wondering how I'd solve the coordination of getting to and from work, my oldest brother's wife called and offered me a ride. I was moved by her kindness. She lived nearby and happened to be going in the general direction of my office. Still, she had to drive ten miles out of her way in St. Louis rush-hour traffic. She talked about it with her husband Bill before she made the offer, of course, and I tried to pay her, but she refused. She performed this kindness 117 times, and I do not know how often I thanked her. I hope she knows I will never forget each and every time she helped her husband's younger brother.

Likewise, my youngest brother, Mike, picked me up on the return trips. Mike worked at The Missouri School for the Blind as a job coach. I worked at a bottle-producing plant on the Hill about three miles away. When he was finished for the day, he would come walking into my front office at 5:30 p.m. promptly. One day, one of the employees who was hanging out after hours said to Mike, "You can sure tell you're Tom's brother; you two look exactly alike!"

As Mike and I left the plant, I could barely contain my belly laughs.

"Who was that clown?" Mike asked.

"Oh, he's a supervisor from the production floor, Mike."

"I really had to prevent myself from beating the tar out of that guy, Tom," he said. "If I look anything like you, then there's no hope for me!"

"I didn't like the comparison either, little brother," I said with a smile.

I will not say what my younger brother replied to that last comment. Suffice it to say it was not complimentary. I laughed all thirty miles home that day, which took a good deal more than a half hour in St. Louis traffic.

Doing the books for the manufacturing plant required me to work a few nights each month, so I had to rely on my wife to fetch me on those nights. My youngest brother did the kind service of taking me home on most evenings, a thirty-mile detour for him. The hours we spent talking on the way home were a big bonus. I offered to pay him for the mileage difference, but he, too, refused remuneration. I will always remember his kindness.

The medicine I was taking to control the seizures worked most of the time, but the times when it did not, some Good Samaritan always went out of their way to help me. On one eight-month hiatus from driving, I found a ride to work from Dennis, a worker in our plant. His old car reminded me of some of my dad's junkers. The car had a backrest for the front seat, which was an old-fashioned one-piece deal. On one trip, he stomped hard on the brakes to avoid hitting a car that had cut him off. As I braced myself for a collision, the poor old backrest must have said this is enough of this nonsense, and it collapsed, taking my back with it, resulting in an unobstructed view of the sky for me, only slightly obscured by the top of the car. Dennis stopped just in time, for there was no crash. I turned my head to see Dennis relaxing on his back as well, without a care in the world. Laughing uncontrollably, he regrouped quickly to face the rush-hour traffic. I took a bit more time to recover to a sitting position. Maybe I should have done a few more sit-ups in the past or was I laughing too hard to sit up? It was like I was quickly cast into a cartoon scenario, rather than the mundanity of simply driving to work with my friend, Dennis. Again, I offered him some remuneration for the time and effort, but like my family, he refused. A simple thank-you seems not enough: but here it is. I won't forget the generosity of Dennis and the many others who have helped me navigate the bumps and snares of my life.

I walk with a slight limp, and movement of my right hand and foot is severely limited. As recounted here, I toiled to learn how to walk and run again and have derived so much pleasure in the journey. I learned to write with my left hand and throw with my left arm, although at times I do not know precisely where the throw will land. The conversion of my left side to pseudo-dominant has been rewarding too. I thank God every day for giving me so much. When a sibling or friend wants to perform an act of charity for me, I let him or her do it without anger at my limitations or thinking that I'm autonomous and can do it alone. Instead, I'm deeply grateful for every kindness.

There is nothing I cannot do for myself, at least up to and including the present time. I might not function as well or quickly as the average Joe, but through struggle and repetition, I can succeed in any task set before me. I'm well aware that other people's perceptions of me are different from my own. Where someone else might see a bad break, I see a full and rich childhood and many ecstasies in accomplishing the smallest tasks. I fail to see any reason to be angry. If an act of kindness given to me helps a person feel good about themselves for a minute or two, why spoil the party? You know you can do it, Tom, but here is someone who wants to be kind to you. It impresses me every time I see it. There are many kind people in the world.

As mentioned earlier in this text, in 1953, I was the sixth child born into the O'Connell family. Less than a year later, my brother, Larry, was born, followed by John fewer than two years later in 1955. Thus, I was never lonely as a child. Even if I had trouble with a brother or two, there were always plenty more to hang with or to aggravate, if they happened to be my older brothers. Each Sunday evening, my parents went to visit my father's parents, brothers, and sisters, just a few blocks away. Mom must have cherished the few hours in the week when she could enjoy a peaceful respite from the hoards. Dad always remained close to his family, so I'm sure he, too, enjoyed the visits.

Kathie and Maureen were left in charge of the household when Mom and Dad were gone for those few hours. This did not set too well with me. I knew they were nine and ten years older, but they were my sisters,' and I did not want to be bossed around by the likes of them. There was still the dangling carrot they held at their discretion to giveth or taketh, which forced me to act like a halfway-civilized human being, rather than a wild man. If I was good enough, I might be rewarded with a treasured half-bottle of soda. Mom, with the Wisdom of Solomon, must have known that there would be little hope of controlling order in her kingdom for those few hours if she did not sweeten the deal. If we were deserving of the treat, Maureen or Kathie took charge of the distribution of the delightful nectar. The allotment of the soda was always a cause of disagreement. I do not know why we did not get out the old measuring cup and put an end to such foolishness. It might have been because that would have meant another dish to be washed by my older siblings. Kathie and Maureen did their best to distribute the soda fairly, but as soon as the distributor left the table, there were always grumblings about who had gotten the better deal.

I admired my older brothers. While they are five and six years older, and I was a pest to them, they still found time to give their little brothers some attention.

At the house on Thirty-First Street, the dreaded Mr. X would leave his signature inside our old garage, or sometimes high in the trees. The sign of Mr. X was always discovered by Bill or Dan and shown to Larry or me accompanied by the scary man's name uttered in a deep and serious voice by one of my older brothers. On one occasion, when it was twilight, Bill saw Mr. X.

"We are going to trap him once and for all," Bill said.

Bill pledged to stay as a lookout on one side of our house. If he needed our help, he would bang on a beat-up old washtub. As Dan struck out with Larry and me around our block in search of Mr. X, we heard desperate beating on the washtub. Bill's in trouble, I thought, and we raced to where he was on lookout. Poor Bill was lying on the ground, glad to see us returning to his aid. We never caught the wily rascal, but pursuing him was great sport.

I don't know how long it was after we moved to the house on Alhambra Court that the small Chinese elm trees grew near the street on our property. I do not recall their presence when we moved to the new address from Thirty-First Street. They grew at an astounding rate. In six months, they transformed from large weeds to trees approaching twenty feet. Their diameter was about three inches at the base so that a boy of eight or nine would be a nincompoop to try climbing one of them. On the other hand, a boy of five or six having little common sense might see the endeavor as a plausible challenge. My brother Larry and I enjoyed countless hours climbing those spindly trees.

The trees grew small branches that started at about two feet from the ground and were spaced intermittently on either side of the tree, manageable for my brother and me. Our feet could not have been much more than ten or twelve feet from the ground when the sway of the trees in the soft summer breezes started to scare us, causing us to cease climbing and to go no further toward the sky.

I clung to the tree like a cat, less the claws, and peered into the vastness far beyond the O'Connell property. Well, not too far, but far enough to see over the one story, box-shaped house across Summit Avenue, which always was decorated with outdoor Christmas lights outlining their roof over the front yard.

Another gust of wind was gathering, so I held tighter to the spindly little tree. You never knew whether it was just another soft breeze or if a storm was brewing. After the sound of the wind rustling through the leaves of the tree had abated, and the swaying of the skinny tree had ceased, I eased my grip and turned my head toward our house.

The roof on Alhambra Court was slightly below my eyes now, and I could see the three small windows of our attic. The only access to the attic was at the top of a closet about five or six feet past our front entrance. I figured it had to be a tight squeeze to gain access. First, you would have to fight all the coats of the ten or twelve people living at our house. This you would have to do while on a step-ladder or whatever you used to reach the nine-foot ceiling. The ladder would need to be well-grounded too. You would crash to the floor and, for sure, bruise your private area if proper precautions were not taken. Setting the ladder on even ground would be impossible, for there were stuffed into the closet two or three basketballs, roller skates, several bats, eight to ten baseballs, a number of softballs, a catcher's mitt and many baseball gloves, a couple of cork balls and a football for playing catch.

Of course, if one were industrious, he could remove the coats and the sports equipment from the closet with or without the intent to return them when the project was completed. That would not happen if I were in charge, I thought. If I happened to get to the entrance to the attic without landing in the hospital, it would be a tight squeeze. You'd have to negotiate the shelf where all the hats were stored and then bend over sharply to hit the entrance. It was feasible, I thought, although I never actually attempted it. First, I would have to go to the basement and find a stepladder, haul it upstairs past the kitchen, through the huge dining room and make a right-angle turn to the left in the front room before I could even see the closet. My mom would most definitely catch me and threaten me with a trip to the woodshed if I did not immediately take that ladder back to the basement.

I never learned whether there were boxes up there or whether it opened freely. But envisioning a secret room for myself helped me wile away some hours. The house was built in the 1920s. Surely there could be some boxes forgotten by former owners. Perhaps when President Roosevelt demanded that all the gold coins be redeemed, the owners might have said not my gold, buddy. Maybe the gold is still in the attic, probably not, but one could dream, couldn't he? Possibly it would not be gold, but a cache of Indian Head pennies. I would need to be sure not to spend them when funds in my pocket were a wee scarce. Then again, there could be photographs of the good old days, when you had to stand still for about thirty seconds straight, or the photo would be ruined.

I deduced the entrance to the attic was behind the three little windows and thus would give one ample purchase to crawl like a cat into the attic, where I was sure it would open nicely. What if you had to crawl like a snake on your belly for a few feet until you passed the little windows? That would be awesome, wouldn't it?

I turned my head slightly to the right to peer at the Hannigan's house, a two-story dwelling, so I couldn't quite see to the roof. *Wonder what makes Mr. Hannigan such a crabby old man*, I thought. I do not know who lived here before we did, but was Mr. Hannigan crabby to them also? I mean, my eight siblings and I were not playing in his yard *too* much and our junky cars were parked in our own driveway, weren't they? Mr. Hannigan and his mannerisms were a mystery to me.

I looked at the other side of the street and saw the giant trees lining Alhambra Court. I wondered whether I would ever be skilled enough to shinny up those trees to the first branches. At twilight, the trees were alive with locusts; I loved the noise they made. I cannot describe the songs of the locusts, but they broke forth in a pattern of singing that lasted for about five seconds. Then for a while there was silence from the giant trees, as the bugs caught their wind. Then their melodious songs would start again, after their short recess, from the trees across our street. The houses behind the trees looked like ours. I heard another gust of wind gather, I held on tightly until it passed.

I do not know whether I told my older brothers about my secret place among the spindly trees or if they came out and saw Larry and me roosting in them one day. Bill and Dan approached us, and Bill's grin was so wide I knew something was about to happen.

"How are you doing up there, Tommy?" Bill asked.

I answered tentatively, "Okay, Billy, just resting and looking out over the neighborhood is all."

"Keeping watch over the old homestead, eh, Tommy?" he asked.

I did not know exactly what that meant, but I answered quickly, "Yeah, Billy, that's what I'm doing!"

"Does the tree sway a little when the wind blows, little brother?" Bill asked.

"Yeah, it sure does, and its scary up here, Billy. I have to hold on tight to keep from falling out of the tree."

"Do you want a ride, Tommy?" Bill asked.

What kind of a ride could he give me up here? I wondered.

"Are you holding on real tight, Tommy?" Bill asked without giving me a chance to answer.

I grasped the tree as tightly as I could. "I'm holding on, Billy. Why do you want me to hold on tight, Billy?"

"You'll see," and Bill grasped the tree with both hands and started pushing it away in one action and then pulling it toward him in another. The procedure Bill used was slow and methodical. He pushed the Chinese elm tree as hard as he could, held it for a few seconds, and pulled it in his direction and held it for a few more seconds, repeating the process.

With the weight of my additional fifty pounds near the top, the sways of the tree were twenty degrees toward our house and then twenty degrees toward the street as it rocked. Unfortunately, I was positioned with my back toward the street. I can't describe my screams of holy terror, especially when it swayed toward the street. On the bend toward our house, I could see my older brothers laughing uncontrollably, with Billy trying to engineer a bigger sway. The rocking toward the street was scary, especially because my legs were not squarely fit around the trunk, so I had to clamp my feet on for dear life to complete the motions without falling. I do not know how many sways I completed before I exited the branches toward our house, plummeting about six feet.

The fall was an easy planned jump, and when I landed, I noticed that my older brothers were lost in peals of laughter. As soon as I landed, I exclaimed, "That was great, Billy!"

"It didn't sound like you were having too much fun while you were up there, little brother," Bill said.

"Well, it was scary, Billy, especially the swing back toward the street. I had to clamp my shoes around the tree to hang on," I said.

My older brothers enjoyed more belly laughs and guffaws after that last comment.

"Let me go up again, Billy, and this time, I'll hold onto the tree with my arms and legs!"

"Be my guest, little brother."

I climbed the poor little elm again, which was slightly worse for wear after what I could imagine was like surviving a gale, from the tree's point of view. I sandwiched my bottom between two of the branches and wrapped my arms and legs around the trunk. "I'm ready, Billy," and again, my older brother began his methodical push and pull on the thin tree. The tree did not seem to have the same elasticity as it did the first time. It was exciting, but not as scary as the first time. After about three or four swings, the tree came down to the ground, and I hopped off to spare the tree's back.

Bill and Dan had to help the tree stand up in a more or less vertical position after the second ride, and it took both of my older brothers standing on opposite sides of the poor tree to give the same effect as I felt on the original ride. It could not have been more than two more rides when I heard a sickening "crack" from deep within the tree, and I rode it as it plummeted to Earth, seriously compromising the area between my legs.

Of course, they laughed! What normal male human would not, except for the person who was racked?

After my older brothers had laughed themselves sick, they quickly entered an open basement window, retrieved Dad's saw, and sawed down the poor little tree, hauling the remnants to the garage for future bonfires, hoping Mom would not notice the destruction in our front yard.

I enjoyed the outing because it was something new to do, and more importantly, my older brothers had spent some time with me. Bill and Dan might have conceived the idea as just another chance to scare the pants off their little brothers, but it was spending some special time with them that keeps this memory vivid, even though it happened more than sixty years ago. My older brothers have always been a step or two above the norm, and I'm proud to be their younger brother. To me, their words bear more weight than others. I am sixty-nine now, so that makes Bill and Dan seventy-five and seventy-four respectively. We are all on the downward swing of life, but I cannot help believing that I'm still their little brother. I miss that little spindly tree and my time in his branches swaying.

17

The Parade

As the years pass and pile upon me, I realize that certain tasks become more difficult. I never was a world-class sprinter, but at one time, I could climb stairs two or three at a time. Now with my bigfoot-sized feet, I make sure I have a firm grip on the handrail and take it nice and easy as I descend our steps one at a time. I further realize that I am not alone in this problem. A couple of years ago, my extended family gathered at a sister's house. One of my sisters was sharing the complicated procedure she employed to get from a sitting position on the floor to standing. One of my brothers decided to try to rock backward on his back and stand up all in one motion, as the momentum propelled him forward onto his feet. It didn't work as he'd planned; he reminded me of a turtle on the back of his shell, struggling to get his shell turned upright again. I smiled but made sure not to say a word. I did not want to take a turn on *my* back.

It was not always this way; I'm sure all my brothers could accomplish this skill during their lives. Often, my older brothers would give us raise-ups when we were small kids. They would get on their backs and bring their feet parallel to the ground. I don't know how they accomplished this. Once I tried it with my older brother Bill sitting on my feet, and me saying uncle a few times to avoid my thighs being incorporated into my ribcage. I imagine it was a simpler process with Bill and Dan, raising their butts off the ground while grabbing their thighs and bringing them in as close as they could to their chests. Whichever manner they employed, it was successful, and Larry and I climbed onto their shoes, which were now pointing straight toward the sky. We held onto their shoes and were raised up and down by our brother's leg muscles. I know it could not have been more than a two-foot journey into the sky, but it was daunting due to lack of control by Larry or me.

Inevitably, there would appear a gleam of delight in Bill or Dan's eyes, followed by my propulsion from their mighty thighs. They called these expulsions "burrs," which as I ponder it now was a great name for the action. I do not know how high or far I was ejected from my brother's feet, but that was the first time I experienced the G-force effect. I tumbled when I hit the ground after the first burr but was a fast learner and landed safely on my feet most of the time thereafter.

My older brothers were cagey, so all future raise-ups did not end in a burr. They wanted to keep us guessing, I suppose. I don't know whether John received a burr, but I know if he did, his burrs were much more exciting. He would have been ejected higher and with much more distance, due to the weight difference between him and his older brothers. The raise-ups were done outdoors, spare one, and I do not know how long they lasted. It might have been just two or three days before our older brothers saw Larry, John, and me as snotty-nosed brats again, too young for cohorts.

One burr in the basement went terribly wrong. Just for kicks, I asked one of my older brothers for a raise-up. He laid down on his back on the floor of the red room and brought his feet parallel to the floor while I climbed aboard, expecting the raise-up. The ceiling was at most seven and a half feet high, with the top of my head approaching five feet from the floor. I certainly did not expect anything more than a few raise-ups. The first few times were raise-ups. Now I'm no psychic, nor have I ever claimed to be, but it might have been the slight cocking of my older brother's thighs that gave him away; or I had a glimpse at the gleam of delight in his eyes, which gave me the hint that a burr was coming. I lowered my head to my knees, and sure enough my brother gave me a burr on the last raise-up.

I'm not sure how close I came to the ceiling. I might have brushed it with the upper part of my back at the apex of the burr before I started reentry to earth. I was concerned about the wall of the red room, which I knew was fast-approaching. Somehow, I started to roll clockwise with my arms wrapped around my legs: I was proud of myself. God-given talent, I presumed. I was a cannonball now, and I made one complete revolution before I hit the red room wall about three feet off the ground and continued to crash through the aqua room wall, landing in the stinky room. My backside took a bit of a beating when it landed. My brother ran into the stinky room to see if I were still alive. When he was sure I was okay, he laughed his head off, and so did I until we realized there might be some explaining to do to our father. I do not remember more burrs after that. Was that my dad's edict, or did the big boys stop to avoid hurting one of us?

Although my older brothers were significantly older than me, they were generous with me. East St. Louis held a parade on Twenty-Fifth Street and into Jones' Park on Labor Day when I was a boy. I don't know where it originated, but I imagine it went along State Street for several blocks before it turned left on Twenty-Fifth, ten blocks from our house toward the Mississippi River. I was aware that my parents would never let anyone as young as I traipse as far as the place where the parade crossed Summit Avenue, at least not without someone older to supervise. I knew little of parades, as I was only five or six at the time.

Brother Dan was our chaperone. We walked north on Alhambra Court and turned left on Summit. We passed Wheeler's Confectionary and St. Patrick's Catholic Church and School and continued to walk up Summit Avenue. As we approached Thirty-First Street, I looked to the right and saw the old bakery where my dad often bought French bread, which some of my older siblings considered a treat. French bread's okay, just a little chewy for my liking. I enjoyed the doughnuts or the cherry, apple, or gooey-butter coffee cakes he brought home for us. On rare occasions, Dad brought home straws that magically changed plain milk into chocolate or strawberry variety. After several more steps, we crossed Thirty-First Street and passed another confectionary. Yep, that's where Mom slapped that older boy who took her pocketbook from me. I looked at our old house and remembered some of the good old times and wished I could relive a few of them. But we were on a quest to see a parade.

What would it be like? Would there be giant floats rolling down Twenty-Fifth Street? There would be bands complete with horns, trumpets, and drums marching along playing a tune, with young women twirling their batons and leading them to the park. There would be clowns performing their antics and causing me to burst into laughter.

We walked another two or three blocks and Dan said, "There's Slade School," pointing to the left as we passed this innocent-enough-looking building. It was at least three stories tall with a metal shoot winding its way down from the third story.

"If they have a fire and you happen to be on the third story, you have to slide down that metal shoot," Dan said.

"Boy, that would be scary, sliding down the shoot in the dark wouldn't it, Dan?" I asked.

"Especially if you got stuck about halfway down, Tommy."

The playground appeared to be covered in asphalt with some neat-looking swings and slides at its center. A fence about six feet tall surrounded the playground. It might have looked even taller to a boy my age.

"Look at that fence, Dan! I sure hope I don't go to *that* school," I said.

"That's to keep the bad boys from skipping school," Dan said. "Just don't get expelled from St. Patrick's or you'll be walking to Slade School every day."

"What is 'spelled' from St. Patrick's, Dan?" I inquired.

"It's *ex*pelled, Tommy, and it means that you get kicked out of going to school at St. Patrick's."

"How bad do you have to be, Dan, to be kicked out of St. Patrick's? I sure don't want to go to this Slade School."

"Real bad," Dan said. "If you broke one of the church windows on purpose or pulled the fire alarm at school you'd definitely get kicked out."

As we passed the public elementary school, I instructed myself not to throw rocks near St. Patrick's Church or go anywhere near the school fire alarm.

After walking a couple more blocks, I could see people lining the street on both sides in anticipation of the parade. We found a prime spot on Twenty-Fifth Street, and after standing around for two or three minutes, I sat on the curb, impatiently waiting for the parade to come my way. In the distance, I could hear something that sounded like instruments playing, and a muffled cheer.

"The parade, Dan! It's coming our way!" I stood up as high as I could to be the first one to see who or what was leading the parade. Soon I saw a marching band preceded by girls in sparkling outfits, tossing their batons high in the air. I saw police cars and fire engines with their sirens blaring and red roof lights flashing. Another couple of bands marched by, and then several miniature floats with people on top of them waving to me and the rest of the crowd. The floats were not gigantic like the ones I saw on television, but they were fabulous in person, rolling down Twenty-Fifth Street, no more than six or eight feet from my brothers and me.

Last, but surely not least, were the clowns. Some drove midget-sized cars, which they steered in circles. Some threw candy, and I was lucky that day to snag three cherished red suckers which I tucked into my pocket to be consumed later.

I don't remember if I said thank-you to Dan. This was more than sixty years ago, so it's amazing that I have any recall of the day. I want Dan to know that the kindness he showed his younger brother that day meant the world to me. If I was rude and did not express my appreciation, his thoughtfulness is written in my mind, never to be forgotten.

It was the second month of 1960, and my first-grade class was five weeks into the second semester. I had done well in the first semester. While I'd never experienced anything regarding the twenty-six symbols my teacher called "letters," I was intrigued by their sounds, which were made by combining the letters. I knew the concepts of arithmetic from the many puzzles my father had posed to me. I had made many friends in my first five and a half months. Then as time progressed, I lost a few of those friends and came to consider them enemies. During the first three grades, we enjoyed three recesses per day, which was cool—one morning recess and one in the afternoon that sandwiched the long lunch recess at noon. Since we lived about a block from church and our mother was still bearing children, we had to run home, eat as fast as we could and run back to school to preserve the maximum amount of playtime.

About three times a week, we had art class. Mom had bought us coloring books before we started school, and we especially enjoyed coloring in the assorted designs and animals in those books on rainy days when Mom wouldn't let us go outside. Art in school was different, and I looked forward to it.

At times, Sister Thomas Ann gave us some papers all of the same design. We attempted, like good little boys and girls, to stay inside the lines as we colored them in. At special times of the year, we were allowed to create our own designs. Early in the first grade, I drew mountains and fir trees scattered about a solitary cabin with smoke rising from the chimney. The mountains were three-dimensional and scattered, so some looked farther away than others. Sister Thomas Ann was impressed, although I messed up some of the fir trees, and the cabin left a little to be desired. It was the three-dimensional mountains that caught her eye.

We were making Valentine's Day cards in art class one day. Since this was my first card, I was full of excitement. Sister Thomas Ann constructed all the hearts before the project began. They all were symmetrical, and I could not imagine even the most-talented first-grade art student making such a beautiful heart. The hearts were cut out of red construction paper. I don't recall whether I made white semicircles outlining the heart or whether our teacher made those also. My recollection is that this was a paper and glue project, which gave her more than enough to worry about, what with spilled glue and devastated children with ripped-up hearts.

I put ample glue on my heart and while outlining, I drew additional smaller hearts on the front of my valentine.

What will I put inside? I wondered. The rest of the class must have been finished with the first page of their cards at the same time because Sister called all of us to order.

"In the middle, print something nice to whomever you're sending the card," she said.

"Who do we send the Valentine's Day card to, Sister?" asked one student.

"That's up to you, class," she said but then added, "It might be nice if you sent it to your mother."

I thought about this for a bit. My mom and I were not seeing eye to eye at that moment, and I would have to ponder long before I could write anything nice to her that did not stretch the truth. Now that I think about all the sacrifices she made for us kids, I'm ashamed that I didn't send my valentine to Mom.

I picked up my pencil and wrote:

Dear Billy and Danny,

Happy Valentine's Day Billy and Danny. I love you very much, even though you are mean to me sometimes.

Tommy

It was cute if I do say so myself. How do I remember my exact words of more than sixty years ago? Well, my mother died in 2007, twenty years after my father. My siblings worked hours and hours sorting through the stuff Mom and Dad had accumulated in more than forty-five years of marriage, plus the years my mother lived after my father's passing. I was already living out of town, in Northern Kentucky when my mom died, so I was spared the decision of what to keep and what to trash. There were three or four times when our extended family met to distribute these items.

I enjoyed the times we met and treasured the insightful words my siblings spoke of Mom and Dad. They had inherited Dad's good articulation, and although Mom was silent most of the time, if you could get her to talk about her true feelings, she, too, could express herself eloquently.

It was at one of these gatherings that each of us received a little package of what Mom and Dad considered important enough to save in the chest that sat beside Mom's bed. When I opened my packet, there were handwriting samples I had written with my right hand. One was completed the day before the stroke. I wonder who decided to save these papers and whether my parents' tears had fallen upon them. That evening, I gave one of these papers to my brother, John. I had given John a crude handmade giant airplane that I had constructed using both of my hands. Dad had purchased the plane from John for $1 after I had the stroke and lost the use of a side. John told me he did not want to sell the plane, but when you have your father begging you, you'd have to have a shriveled heart not to grant him his wish.

It was in this little packet that someone decided to save the Valentine's Day card—probably Mom. Certainly, if it had not been saved, I would not have remembered my words, which well summarized my feelings about Bill and Dan.

18

A Meaningful Comment

When I started school, my older brothers were about twice as old as me. I thought of them as men, although they were only eleven or twelve, and had a lot of growing to do before they could be classified as men either in stature or maturity. I was glad to be included in the group when they talked about their exploits, at least until I was shooed away.

Bill and Dan were good athletes. Bill played on the high school baseball and basketball teams and Dan on the basketball team. Dan went on to play some college ball as well. They did not make their living playing ball, mind you, but they had considerable skill. When I was in the sixth and seventh grades, my parents took me to all their basketball games, at home or away. I wondered why they didn't include my younger brothers on those trips. I had a suspicion, though, that it had to do with losing the use of my side. I should have told them I needed no special consideration. After my stroke, of course, my skill level in all sports took a considerable hit. But to me, the point of all sports is to have fun, and my enjoyment was enhanced, not lessened, after my life-changing event as a youth.

Admission price for me to the basketball games was only a quarter. I always thanked my parents for their generosity in allowing me to tag along and pay my way into the game. Sometimes Dad would give me an extra dime or fifteen cents for some popcorn. The bonus of a dime did not really matter. I was there to see my brothers play ball—those older brothers whom I admired and always knew would be there when I needed them.

Bill was quick, a guard who helped bring the ball onto Assumption's side of the court. Whenever Bill was open and scored from the top of the key, I thought, yes! That is my brother! At six feet, eight inches, Dan was the center. He took pride in patrolling the entire area, which he deemed a no-fly zone for anyone who dared to shoot. I loved to see him, and his squad warm up before the game. All of the Assumption patrons knew it was coming, just a matter of time. When it was his turn to shoot a layup, everyone wondered if this would be the moment. As Dan approached the basket, he sometimes went in hard, only to lay the ball gently off the backboard and into the basket. The Assumption fans sighed with regret and wondered if Dan would do it for them this game. Oh, he's toying with them, I thought, as I watched him rebound the next time. Sure enough, on the next two or three layups, Dan would turn on the speed the last few steps and slam dunk the ball with both hands as the crowd erupted with joy. *Yep*, I thought, *that's my brother they're cheering for!*

I enjoyed the challenge of converting myself to a one-armed basketball player. I've always had a large left hand. Had it not been for its size, the game would have been more of a struggle. It took me considerable time and practice shooting the ball with one hand and converting from my natural side to my less adept side. I spent hundreds of hours perfecting the balance of the ball in the one hand, always remembering to keep my left forearm at a ninety-degree angle to the rim. I also remembered the art of the shot versus throwing the ball at the rim, and again I imparted a clockwise spin on every attempt. Each hour I spent perfecting my abnormal shot was not an hour of frustration, but an hour of pure love for the sport. I knew that due to my father's constant worry about his third-born son, my participation would be relegated to our backyard, and that I could never compete with the boys my age.

After hours and hours of perfecting the one-armed shot, I knew that each shot I put up would be good. For those shots that found an errant way and were unsuccessful, I knew exactly why they missed. So I had merely to correct those miscalculations to make the next venture a true success. It did not matter whether I missed five or six consecutive times, the next shot was going in, buddy, and you could count on it. Sometimes I dribbled cross-court to the foul line and faded away as I jumped and shot the ball. There was no one who could block this shot I always thought.

One day, I'd been shooting baskets for an hour or so. I shot some foul shots, enjoying the fact that sometimes the ball bounced back to me if I hit it purely and imparted enough spin. I'm sure I drove cross-court to the foul line and tried my fade away jumper a few times. I practiced dribbling the ball toward the basket, sometimes with a successful layup off the backboard. The most important effort was to shoot and watch the ball head toward the rim and rip through the cords of the net. The ball would defy the laws of gravity for an instant, pausing and singing that wonderful note, which meant to me and to anyone who loved the sport, "Well done, master, well done."

I made my way up the back-porch stairs, carrying the trusty basketball, opened the back door, and walked into the house through the tiny hall that opened into our kitchen. I had planned to put the ball into its ring of honor along with the other sports equipment in our junky front-room closet when I heard my name, silently, not meaning to be heard, to the left and down the steps in my brothers' room. I paused, sat on the floor for a moment, and tried to be as attentive as I could to hear what they were saying about me.

They must have been watching me play ball for a while because it appeared this was their topic. Often, I'd see my father watching me from the back door as I attempted the cross-court fadeaway jumper or some other piece of the game. I tried hard to make more successes than failures if I knew Dad was watching, and I hope he knew how much enjoyment I received from his generosity in setting up the court that he offered his boys so long ago. I'm curious as to what he thought while he stood there and watched. I hope his musings were pleasant, at least as wonderful as my own thoughts while performing for him.

My older brothers were watching me do what I loved on the court:

"Can you believe our little brother?"

"I don't understand how he can balance the ball on one hand and make that many shots."

"It's not like he just stands there, tries to balance the ball, and then shoots it. He's actually dribbling the ball around the court before he attempts the shot. Somehow, he picks the ball up and by the time he's jumped, he's holding the ball in the palm of his hand and spins it with his fingers as he shoots."

"I'll tell you, brother, most of those shots look so pretty as they leave Tom's hand, whether they're successful or not. I can't imagine how he does it."

There was a pause for a few seconds, and I thought they caught me listening. After the moment passed, one of their voices broke the silence. "Can you imagine how good Tom would be at basketball, if he'd never had the stroke and could use both sides of his body?"

Another pause, followed by, "I can't imagine how good he'd be! Let me tell you, brother, it's scary to think about."

At that point, they must have sensed who was listening at the top of the stairs because they started hurling insults my way. They never tried to retract the compliments on my basketball skills, though. The beans had already been spilled, and there would be no do-overs of their prior conversation. Did they know how much their kind words meant to me? I knew the high degree of *their* skills, so their appraisal of my abilities came from people who knew the game, which meant a lot.

My brothers were looking at the finished product when they observed me shooting in our backyard that day. They didn't know about the hundreds of hours of love I spent on the court, both before and after I lost the side. Had they known. their comments might not have been so glowing. I don't dwell on the might-haves, though. Most successful athletes recognize the peak of their game as merely a segment of their life. The past. The times that surely are gone and need to be replaced by other ones, better ones. I, too, look forward to tomorrow and all the surprises it might bring. But I never shall forget the joy and the ecstasy God brought me by letting me recapture the gifts He gave to me. One should give thanks for their God-given gifts and know that He loves them regardless of the Rubicon they're currently crossing. He is always there to help us make it to the other side and never will abandon us.

19

The Pleasures of Fishing

My father enjoyed sports of all types when he was a lad, but fishing was not one of them. My grandfather, on the other hand, the one who ate burnt bacon for breakfast, was an avid angler. I don't know exactly when he introduced my older brothers to fishing, but I do know they were thrilled the first time the kind old man known as AC Palmer took Dan for a walk on St. Clair Avenue to a fruit stand where he bought two cane poles complete with line and hooks. He bought some bait at the fruit store and then followed Dan through the woods to Bill's softball practice. After practice, Bill and Dan led grandfather to a body of water known by all in East St. Louis as "the lagoon."

The lagoon was fifteen to twenty acres, and not much more than five or six feet deep. At about the midpoint, there was a bridge over the lagoon and a place we called "the dock" just west of the bridge. The dock area widened to about thirty feet by fifty feet long, built in a semicircle. One had to scratch his head as to why this concrete structure was called the dock. There was not any dock, *per se*, only a semicircular bend that followed the shape of the lagoon. A few years prior there had been rental boats at that precise location. I suppose you could call the embarking and disembarking place a dock. If they'd put in a wooden gangplank, it would have made a more authentic dock.

Was it the dock or the little grassy area, which helped support the bridge over the lagoon where my brothers first fished? All I recall is that they became fisherman for life when they proudly brought to our grandfather their diminutive catfish on a stringer and learned how to clean them from the man who liked blackened toast for breakfast. If it had not been for our grandfather, Bill and Dan never would have experienced the thousands of hours of enjoyment they derived from fishing.

My older brothers introduced all their younger brothers to fishing, making serious fishermen of John and Mike. Although I was not one of their converts, I enjoyed tagging along with them, listening to every word between them. I remember one day when the fish were not biting, Bill jumped into the lagoon and swam under the bridge several times. My younger brothers yelled at him to stop swimming and come to shore. I stood and laughed as I watched him swim under the bridge a few times. He hurried and jumped from the water, packed his fishing equipment and high-tailed it toward the woods, with his little brothers close behind him, as one of the park police yelled at us to stop running.

The man was old, I thought, and would never catch us with the head start we had on him. Soon he'd tire and end his pursuit, knowing he'd at least stopped one punk from swimming in his lagoon.

Bill and Dan graduated to rods and reels, as soon as they had enough disposable income, and they let their younger brothers use their cane poles once in a while. The City of East St. Louis stocked the lagoon, and my older brothers brought home a few good-sized catfish on some days. There was a wily old catfish named Old Hickory that they say was a hundred pounds abiding in the lagoon. Of course Old Hickory might have been a close relative of Mr. X, for all I knew. The biggest fish I ever caught there was a perch of about a pound.

My older brothers began fishing in Grand Marias Lake about the same time they started high school. I don't know why they took me along one day, but I was honored to be there. We rented a rowboat for the afternoon. A storm began to brew soon after we started fishing. The winds were hefty but refreshing in the dead heat of summer. Bill rowed into whitecaps that were two or three feet high. For a minute or two, I imagined I was Pop, fighting the storms off Ireland's coast that he and his two older brothers, Tom and Pat, encountered.

The skies opened shortly after the wind started to blow, and the boat was jostled about as Bill headed into the whitecaps. Bill rowed as hard as he could but was losing ground as the thunderstorm progressed. The coxswain, my brother Dan, like a seaworthy captain, gave Bill guidance to head the boat straight into the waves. I did not have the foggiest notion what they were talking about, but it was fun enjoying the bumps, rolls, and crashes whenever we crested a wave. I laughed outrageously for the few minutes of the downpour. The rainstorm and the wind that went with it traveled off toward the east. The whitecaps vanished and Bill rowed to the side of the lake, exhausted by the ordeal.

"Man, that was great," I exclaimed to my brothers. They looked at me with puzzled eyes.

"You know, Tom, we almost capsized this boat!"

As I was about to ask one of them what *capsized* meant, "What would you do in all that deep water?" Dan asked me.

"I don't know," I answered, "I'd try to swim to the shore."

"You don't know how to swim, Tom. You'd drown is what you'd do, unless one of us came to your rescue, and I'd have one heck of a time getting to the shore myself," said Bill.

"We wouldn't leave you out there, Tom. I hope you wouldn't become panicky and latch on to me so we'd both drown!"

Unfortunately, in a previous mishap in the same lake a boy had been in trouble and his brother tried to save him. In panic and distress, the boy clamped onto his brother like a cat, and they both drowned. I do not remember anything more about our conversation that summer day when the storm sneaked up. Still, I knew that if I ever needed help in my life, I could always count on my brothers.

Sometimes they explored other lakes around the area. One day, Bill caught a giant fish that must have weighed in at twenty or twenty-five pounds. I don't know what species it was, but one thing I can say for sure is that it was not a catfish. After he beheaded it, removed its fins, and disposed of its innards, the fish was still three feet long. He draped it over his left arm and began to chase our baby sister Ellen around the backyard. Ellen was sure he was going to touch her golden hair with the fish, so she demonstrated how loud and high-pitched she could scream. I was up in the giant maple, laughing to beat the band. If the positions had been reversed and I were running from Bill, hopefully, there wouldn't be any screaming.

Mom prepared the fish that evening with corn bread muffins and black-eyed peas. I never did like black-eyed peas, but I really savored the corn bread and fish combination. I had to be careful cutting the muffins in half and, of course, applying the butter or I'd be eating the crumbled corn bread slathered in uneven amounts of butter with my fish instead of muffin sandwiches.

After dinner, some fish was left over, and I snacked on corn bread during the evening. The corn bread muffins were reduced to pieces now, which did not bother me. I put the largest crumbles on my plate with two or three chunks of fish. Mom came to the kitchen and said that it looked like I was enjoying her corn bread and my brother Bill's fish.

"I sure do, Mom!"

As we were talking civilly for the moment, I looked at all the crumbles.

"Looks like we'll have to pitch all these crumbles, doesn't it, Mom?"

"There's not much corn bread left, is there?"

"There sure isn't, Mom, and it's a shame because I really like your corn bread."

"Your grandmother used to make cornpone for my dad from the leftover corn bread," Mom said.

"What's cornpone?" I asked, almost laughing aloud at the name.

"You take the leftover corn bread, add milk or water and bacon drippings, and mix it up. Then you put it into a skillet and bake it, Tom," she explained.

"Does it taste good, Mom?" I asked.

"My dad used to like it," she said.

Mom never did make any cornpone for me. Anytime she made corn bread, there was never enough left for the main ingredient. I often wanted to see how it tasted, anything with bacon drippings for an ingredient could not be bad. Maybe if you threw in some of my brother Bill's fish, the flavor would be further enhanced.

Dan majored in accounting at Northeast Missouri State and worked for a CPA firm for a few years, where he met friends who liked to fish. Along with those guys, Dan and Bill made an annual fishing excursion to Lake Taneycomo near Branson, Missouri, throughout the 1970s.

Lake Taneycomo is a cold-water manmade lake stocked with rainbow and brown trout. Fishing for these varieties was different for my brothers. They kept the tradition of going to southern Missouri at least once a year, regardless of whether it was only the two of them on the trip. My brother Mike joined them a couple of times before they asked me whether I'd be interested in going along to Branson.

I was not particularly interested in fishing beyond the first couple of times, when it was something different to do with my brothers on the lagoon in Jones' Park. To me, it was a boring sport on slow days when the fish weren't biting. I would throw my bait out there with my borrowed cane pole and if my bobber didn't disappear under the water within five or ten minutes, I would pull in the pole. That was enough fishing for me. There was plenty of other stuff to do at the lagoon, like listen to my brothers talk, play on the swing set and slides when I was small enough not to be embarrassed, or walk around the park.

It did not take me long to accept Bill's invitation to Branson. I paid my portion of the deposit, but the closer the time came for the trip, I worried about being bored sitting there for hours with a pole in my hands.

I was at least thirty years old on my first trip there, and I had never before owned a genuine rod and reel. Sometimes Bill would let me borrow a rod and reel on one of the rare times we fished together. I do remember breaking his rod to smithereens when I horsed it up on a presumed bite up at Pere Marquette. He was not too happy, as I recall, but did not make me pay restitution.

I did not want to destroy anyone's equipment except mine, so my first order of business was to buy a rod and reel. Now I do not know where I bought my first hopeful implement for reeling in a fish or two, but certainly I was not helped in the store by any kindly old man who knew about fishing. The truth be told, I went to a store as close to closing time as I could, snagged the cheapest rod and reel I could find, and hurried to the front. I was checked out by a clerk who didn't seem to have a clue about the equipment I was buying. I was thirty years old, for good-ness sake, and did not want any snickers thrown my way as some type of sissy who hasn't the foggiest notion about what he's doing.

When I arrived safe at my house, I opened the rod and reel set and looked at it for the first time. Hmmm, I always thought that the rod comes in two sections. As I peered down at a little one-piece rod that could not have been more than four and a half feet long I thought, I should have sought some assistance in acquiring this piece of machinery. I could have sucked up the little snickers at the store—so I'd have a genuine model instead of one that is made for a five- or six-year-old. Oh well, it's too late now. I had pushed off my purchase until the last day, and tomorrow I was due at Dan's first thing in the morning. Besides, I was not going to buy two sets. I had bought my life preserver several months ago, and let me tell you, it is a fine apparatus. I do not wish to be chastised again by Bill and Dan for not being prepared in case I should fall out of the boat.

We stop about halfway to Branson at this little place that serves loose-meat hamburgers. I always eat three of the burgers, plus fries and a drink, so I wouldn't be hungry on the way. They're tasty, although the price has increased significantly in thirty-five years from about five dollars to a little more than thirteen dollars. We arrive at our cabin about midafternoon, check in and pay for our Missouri Fishing License and our two-day trout stamp so we are legal. Then we unpack our fishing equipment, food, and clothes for the three-day stay. It seems as if my brothers always unload much more than their fair share of our stuff. I know they don't mind that the work is unequally distributed, and I've never really thanked them for it. It's one of those niceties that would somehow be lessened by a thank-you. They can see my atrophied right hand and arm and the fact that each year it becomes a little harder for me to walk. They also see the smiles and grins on my face as I wrestle the life preserver over my right arm, and at the same time, grab some of the food in a flimsy plastic bag with my right hand. I think if I walk into the cabin and let them handle the unloading, there might be an altercation. But as long as I'm giving it the good old college try, I won't get into too much trouble with the guys.

My brothers awaken before dawn on both days. I consider pitch dark the middle of the night. It takes me several minutes before I can shake the cobwebs from my mind. I stumble around, hitting the walls as I make my way into the bathroom. My four brothers have been awake for about half an hour, so I can't place the blame for my stumbling on lack of light. It takes me a while to get my sea legs. I take care of the necessities in the bathroom and then make my way to the sink to take my normal thirteen medications—for high blood pressure, diabetes, thyroid abnormality, seizure disorder, and multivitamins to take care of anything that might be going awry in my body. I do not usually eat breakfast, but I am going to partake of the offering of tasty little powdered-sugar donuts. They're not necessarily good for people with diabetes, but if the suckers are there, I'll eat 'em.

I dress and go to the front room to sit down. It is still dark outside, but it is interesting to see my brothers' faces at the second-story window, waiting to see the first patch of light illuminate Lake Taneycomo below.

"Do you think they'll be running much water from Table Rock?"

"I hope not," says another of my brothers as he turns to see the lake.

"We might not have too much luck 'still fishing' if they are," laments another.

I smile and think, *Yep, they're excited about fishing and the prospects of the day.*

"Do you think we'll catch a big trout this trip?"

"Could be, we haven't caught a good three or four-pounder on several trips."

I don't care if I tie into a big trout; I probably would lose it anyway, before it was landed. Bagging some trout is not the important thing for me; the hours spent listening and spending a few days with my brothers—that's the ticket. I've witnessed my brothers land a few big ones and I hope this would be their year.

The sun rises eventually. Usually, Bill and Mike are the first to head to the dock where our boat is waiting. Dan and John are close behind with me slowly but surely tagging along. During the last few years, I've carried only my fishing pole. I am the one to make sure that our cabin door is locked securely before I start my journey down to the dock. My gait is uneven as I swing the pole from side to side, making the right turn and starting the downhill swing to the lake. Since I do not have a trusty left hand to grip the railing, I have to slow to a creep as I approached the steps. I clutch my fishing pole, so I wouldn't damage it. I would need to think fast if I tripped—which is more valuable—my fishing pole or my noggin? It wouldn't matter much, I thought. My fishing pole would be destroyed, and my head seriously damaged if I fall.

Almost there, I make sure to pick up my right foot every time or I would surely stumble and have to run to catch my balance. In a run, if balance is not secured immediately, I could start picking up speed until I inevitably jump into the waters of Lake Taneycomo.

"Go jump in a lake" was my epithet to my brothers on dozens of occasions when we were young.

That's exactly what I would do if I were not careful. Finally, I make it to the dock. Only one more task: successful entry into the boat with my four brothers chomping at the bit to get to the water. Hold on, boys; this must be done carefully. If I fall in, I'd be in a world of hurt. Yes, falling into the lake was conceivable, not highly likely, mind you, but doable. What if I lose my balance and fall in the lake past John at the bow of the boat? I would knock myself out on the dock and it'd take all four of you to haul me in like a Marlin. My brothers are patient and try holding the boat as still as possible.

I always start entry with my right foot. It never fails to amaze me when I step down and my right foot lands securely inside the vessel, that I can't feel the sole of my foot on the bench of the boat. Maybe it's the diabetes or the back operation several years ago, but I only know that my right foot is secure because of my knowledge of gravity and the fact that the foot stopped sinking at the bench. I pull the left leg and foot into the boat while holding for dear life onto the iron railing of the dock and quickly sit down. Then we are off, with Bill as helmsman.

As we leave the dock, I clutch the fingertips of my left hand between crevasses of the dock, releasing my grip and grabbing the dock again a few feet farther toward the body of the lake, guiding the craft more or less from the stall to make sure it does not crash into the boat in the next slot. They gave me a couple of nicknames after the stroke— "Claw," because I used the left hand for everything, so it quickly became strong, and "Fang" because of my finger-nails, as I had trouble cutting the nails on my left hand. I'm glad that after grade school the nicknames didn't stick.

Usually, we venture to Cooper's Creek and cast off the two homemade anchors, tying them with enough slack to let the boat roll as other boats passed. John or Dan would fix me with a drift rig two or three feet long and ask me which color of power bait I want to use. I usually say orange, so they would take a glob of bait from a bottle and smash it around the treble hook.

"There you go, Tom!" and I always thanked them.

Bill or Mike would have extended the same courtesy had they been sitting next to me. For some reason, I screw up sometimes, releasing the mechanism on the reel either too early or too late, and the line would wrap around itself several dozen times. After John or Dan would either fix my line or throw up their hands and attach a new drift rig and bait again, I am successful with my cast this time. I've often wondered if I continued to screw up the next three or four times, whether Dan and John would toss me into the chilly waters of Lake Taneycomo. Neither one of them would have been strong enough to lift my heavy carcass and throw it overboard, especially with me fighting back. Hopefully, they'd simply yell at me and make me feel bad. The evil man inside me always says go for it and see how they react.

If I should catch a rainbow trout, John or Dan would examine the fish. If the hook were salvageable without doing irreparable damage to the inside components of the fish, they would do the surgery, retrieve the hook, and toss the fish into the lake to live for another day. If the fish had swallowed the hook, my brothers would cut the line and return the fish to the lake. In either instance, they would put more orange power bait on my hook or fix me with another hook or rig and bait it, so I could try my luck again. Thanks, I would say again before I cast. Nothing more needs to be said. I wonder if my brothers know how much I appreciate their efforts for more than thirty-five years. Maybe if the roles were reversed, I would do the same for them…maybe.

I could have tried to tie my drift rigs and attempted to bait my hook. As I look at my right hand, though, it would have been complicated. I don't know how long it would have taken me to lace the line into the tiny hole of the treble hook. I would have needed to hold the line with the atrophied right hand and the treble hook with my gigantic left. The chase would be on from there, with the treble hook's eye trying to catch the wandering line doing its best to remain stationary in the poor old right fist. I would have to ask my wife to remove the embedded treble hook from my left thumb or finger, trying my best not to use bad language on the third or fourth surgery. It appears that my success in hitting the bull's-eye with the fishing line does not increase, regardless of how tight I squeeze the treble hook. If I did the impossible and laced the line through the incredibly tiny hole on the hook, I would need lip surgery to remove the hook, due to the lip getting into the way while I attempted to double knot the fishing line with my teeth as a surrogate hand. If I were still willing to give drift rig tying a go, I would refer to the drift rig tying instructions supplied by my brothers; I haven't the foggiest idea of what you do next.

I could attempt to remove the hook from the fish's mouth. A colleague at work told me about an avid angler with only one arm. His method of removing the fish from the hook was to put the fish in his mouth and remove the hook with his one good hand.

"I don't know, Doug. Are you trying to get me to do another outlandish stunt?"

"Honest to God, I read it in a magazine, Tom!"

"I don't know, Doug, I'd have to clean the fish off really well. I wouldn't want any slimy fish in my mouth."

The more I thought about it, the more I deduced he was yanking my chain. Think about it: I would put the fish in my mouth, look down in a rather cockeyed fashion past my big nose, and attempt to extract the treble hook with a clumsy nine-inch paw. I don't think so. If my brothers elected not to fix me with a rig, bait it, and take care of the fish when I caught it, my fishing days would be over. This would not end my trips to the lake, though. It would only mean that the trip would cost me twenty-six dollars less, no fishing license or trout stamps. When I go to Southern Missouri with the boys, it's not for the trout fishing, but for the camaraderie and the pleasure of spending some quality time with them. Listening to their stories, some in which I played an integral part, others that I would have to rely on the telling for their veracity.

I lost my articulation with my right side. Yet I'm extremely fortunate that I've been able to hammer out a few words during the past sixty years, allowing me to communicate with the outside world. In the past twenty-five years or so, my speech has regressed. Most of the time it is imperceptible; other times I am mute for a while. The intricate skills that allow my thoughts to work their way to my vocal cords abandons me at times. This phenomenon usually lasts for about an hour, or at worst five or six hours. A mild aphasia occurrence might enable me to communicate slightly, a sentence every minute or two. One that lasts for hours is void of talking save some involuntary gibberish that I refer to as coming from "the old man in me."

A few years ago, I was meeting with Beth, the administrative manager for a plant where I was stationed, about the budget for the approaching year. I was having an episode of aphasia. Beth knew I was having trouble talking, so *she* talked, and I nodded. During our slightly one-sided conversation, occasionally I spoke gibberish. I tried to keep the old man in me silent, but since he never warned me when he was going to talk, it was difficult to contain the wily old rascal. Maybe I did a decent job wrestling the old fellow and only he and I knew of the battle. Perhaps the old man was silent about his mutterings, whispering the nonsensical words only to me so Beth did not hear them. After we finished our discussion for the day, I scribbled a note to her asking if she heard anything from me that she could not interpret as talking. "Yes," she said, "and it scared the heck out of me, Tom! I tried to ignore it, but if you got up and started coming at me with that unknown language, I'd bolt from my office screaming for my mommy!"

Poor Beth; she's an extraordinary woman, but I had to laugh. *I tried to stop the old man, Beth,* I thought. I guess the old bloke does not keep company with me alone and is audible to anyone near enough at hand.

Lucky for me, at least, the old man who speaks jabberwocky stays to himself and does not come out often anymore. Now that I can no longer work, the aphasia has lessened. The taxing work schedule, lack of sleep, stress, and the amount of talking I did, bore a direct relationship on the phenomenon of my muteness. It's all related to my central processing unit again, for the last twenty-five years, my CPU has screwed with my ability to talk.

If I were a windbag who wanted to expound his ideas on how the world should be run, one might understand my frustration. Even before I lost the treasured gift of articulation, I was always a thinker. I like listening to people and deriving the most I can from a conversation. I hope I've been able to help people with my limited few words.

As my brothers and I sit at Coopers Creek with our fishing lines in the water, waiting for the big trout, I listen to them talk about our past. Sometimes there'd be a lull in the conversation. Time to think, Tom, of how fortunate I have been to be blessed with five brothers and five sisters who mean so much to me. The fish are biting, and I watch my brothers' beaming faces as they haul in trout after trout. It makes me smile to see the wonderful times they have each year at Branson. Once in a while, a trout with very little common sense would hook himself on my line, so I'd flip over my pole and reel in the fish with my left hand. There must be a left-handed reel somewhere out there, I sometimes think. In my case, a right-handed reel does work well enough since I don't see myself as an expert angler. I am just trying to snag a few moments of my brothers' lives, opinions that I would gladly mull over and cherish long afterward. I always look forward to the middle of September when the five of us get together again.

20

A Summer Afternoon

The Terrible Trio is what we were called. My father coined the phrase, but it was a misnomer. We were not that bad, particularly after I lost most of the use of my one side. Some folks thought I'd lost the wind in my sails, had it not been for what I considered a minor setback, I might have been a psychotic maniac heading for Menard Correctional Center. Mom said, "If there was a single good thing about the stroke, Tom, it made you a kinder person to your younger brothers." I often wondered about that. I was a trifle nicer, but as I remember it, I was by no means an angel. The Terrible Trio nickname caught on, especially with Mom, but I never liked the idea of segregating Larry, John, and me and referring to us as the three Ts. Usually, Mom was looking straight at me when she uttered the phrase. I always thought they should have pitched the trio from the equation and called it Terrible Tom.

For some reason, the Terrible Trio never owned a BB gun. Each Christmas, I asked and asked our surrogate Santa to put a BB gun on his or her list for my younger cohorts and me, but my request never bore fruit. At about age sixteen, I threw up my hands and quit asking. My older brothers received their BB guns from Mom and Dad at age ten or twelve. My guess is that Dad noticed the same gleam in one of the Terrible Trio's eyes as his brother, Laur, did after he put a couple of BB shots into Dad's body.

There was the time we dug that six-by-six-foot trench in the side yard. It was about three feet deep when Mom caught us and made us refill it. I don't recall whose bright idea it was to dig the trench. I think one of Larry's friends was over that day. The friend of my younger brother, Larry, was big into army then, so I'll place the onus on him. Larry, John, and I were the only ones involved in filling the trench. I thought we did a skilled job with the cleanup detail, but as the days progressed to weeks, the trench began to show itself again. When the ground settled, there remained a rolling depression of about a foot. To this day, I don't understand where all the soil went. We were not yet pelting each other with clods of dirt, which might have explained the missing dirt. Mom caught us before any of that falderol could ensue.

It was not until I was eleven or twelve that I started going with Larry and John to Jones' Park to pursue our adventures. Sometimes we went fishing in the lagoon or caught crawdads close to shore. We never used the craw-dads as fish bait; nor was I too successful at catching the little guys. We picked them up just behind the two claws.

The quick little rascals would back up on me fast or turn ninety degrees and snap onto my thumb or index finger with those snappy little pinchers. I had one heck of a time getting them to release my fingers without wounding them. I had no spare hand available, and to be frank, we were messing with the crawdads' day while trying to catch them. It would have been egregious to hurt them further.

Occasionally, we just stood at the swimming pool fence, watching all the people splash in the cool, refreshing water while we sweltered under the midday July sun. For some reason, at those times there would be an increase in the frequency of disagreements between me and my brothers.

Sometimes we took a ball, bat, and our gloves and hit fly balls to one another. Often, I accompanied them to their softball practice at Jones' Park. If I were lucky, there wouldn't be enough players, and they'd invite me to play. I never asked, mind you, but there might just happen to be an opportunity, I thought.

The park was a little more than a half-mile from our house. We would start on our alley, cross Summit Avenue and walk Thirty-Fourth Street toward St. Clair Avenue. Depending on the traffic, we might need to run across St. Clair and then walk a path heading to the woods. The trees in the first section of the woods were not too high, but their abundance darkened the path. It always felt much cooler albeit more humid in those scruffy trees. We made some curves to the right and left, avoiding the trash heaps until we came to an old dirt road. As we proceeded north on the road, the trees abated slightly, and the temperature climbed a little. To the left of the dirt road stood an old foam-rubber factory that had burned to the ground in the midsixties. After a while, the terrain rose slightly, and we were delighted to come to two active railroad tracks.

Sometimes when a train was passing, you could see the locomotives and count the cars. On rare occasions, a train would stop at our crossing point. To cross the tracks, one had to go under the railcars or climb the ladder of a railcar and traverse the coupling to the other side. I only chose traversing the coupling if, in my estimation, the walk around the train was too far. My crawling skills were not good anymore, and I was sure if I tried to crawl under the train, I wouldn't make it. The loud and scary sound a train makes when it shudders and starts to move would surely happen exactly at the time I was bumbling along with my impaired right side, trying to get to the other side. The undercarriage of the train surely would catch me by the seat of my pants and carry me for a while until it cast me aside. If I cheated death, I'd have to think hard for an excuse to Mom about how my pants got ripped to shreds.

I often hitched a ride when the train was going slow enough for me to latch onto the ladder of a railcar. Once after softball practice, I hopped an eastbound train with a few friends. I hung onto a railcar behind my friend Pat. I'm sure Pat wished we had baseball signals privy only to us that day. He could have signaled me: "Jump off the train carefully, you idiot, or I'm going to beat the tar out of you next practice." I imagine, somehow, I would have gotten the message that Pat wanted to terminate the ride and I'd have jumped off first.

"I couldn't leave you hanging," Pat said to me. "I had to stay on my railcar until you exited."

We jumped off near Monk's Mound after about a mile and a half ride. I don't have the foggiest memory of it, but since Pat has such vivid recall of the event, it must have happened. It must not have taught me much of a lesson either because I remember hopping a train at Jones' Park that sped to about forty or fifty miles per hour and dropped me at a rail yard in Dupo, Illinois. It took me most of the day to walk back to Jones' Park.

Often, we explored a bit on our way to the park. There was a four-foot cylindrical brick structure about seventy-five yards to the right of the old dirt road toward the softball diamonds. The structure looked like a well without a wooden top or bucket. The hole, as you peered over the circular framework of bricks, fell twenty to twenty-five feet. At the bottom were two pathways about three feet wide on opposite sides of a waterway. A sewer, I thought, followed by a question of why anyone would make an opening to a sewer where there were no houses. I was tempted to somehow climb down to the floor of the opening and explore. Someone must have taken the plunge, I thought. Once I saw a large tree branch emerging from the bricks. I could envision a slight fellow making it to the floor of the sewer. While I never attempted this exploration, I sometimes pondered at the well for a while on my way to softball practice.

Farther to the southeast was a swamp. Tromping happily along the edges of the swamp, I wondered how deep it was in the middle. We only skirted the swamp on the way to Jones' Park, which gave our soaked shoes plenty of time to dry so Mom would never be the wiser. These forays did not enhance the life of the shoes, but they were great fun. The day I saw a five-foot-long snake squiggling past on my path ended any further splashing through the swamp.

I played catch with my older brother, Dan, as I broke in the baseball glove, I received for my First Communion in the second grade. Factory-signed by Roberto Clemente, I used it through the eighth grade for softball. The back strap of the glove was eventually torn away, which ironically was a significant help. Designed for a right-handed player, it was worn on the left hand so you could use your right hand to throw the ball after you caught it. When I lost the use of my right side, I still had to catch the ball with my left hand, as the fingers of my right hand never recovered much movement or dexterity.

After I caught the ball, I'd put the glove and ball between my chest and my right arm, pull the left hand from the glove and then grab and throw the ball. I'd hurry to place my left hand into the glove before the ball was returned by my brother, John, or whomever I was playing catch with that day. When I was new to this modified procedure, I would drop the glove frequently and reach to get it off the ground. There was little time before the ball would come back at me. I'm glad that my brother, John, showed me no quarter. If you can't put on a baseball glove in the time it takes to release a throw, the other person catch it, and then return it to you, then you deserve to catch it bare-handed or feel the ball zing off your knee, elbow, chest, or groin.

I tended to blame John when I didn't have time to put on my glove. I'm a human being with plenty of frailties. John assumed that my glove switch procedure would be successful: he was simply playing catch with his older brother.

Dad allowed me to play softball for the St. Patrick's team in the sixth grade. I was elated. Although I mostly sat on the bench, I enjoyed being part of the team. I had no problem with riding the bench if it gave us a better chance to win. I would have been more upset if we'd lost due to my poor playing, as I was well aware that other players were better than me. There were two practices during the week and a game on Saturday. I never missed a practice: I loved them all. Coach Johnston always put me in for a couple of innings or, at least let me bat if the score were close on game day. He would stick me out in right field and when the ball was hit my way, I always went through the same routine.

I'd field the ball, hopefully, then open my glove slightly and gently toss off the glove and the ball with a flip of my left wrist. The glove would go to the left side of my body and, if I pulled it off right, the ball would rise about a foot and a half before I'd snag it with my left hand and throw it to the infield as it fell. Sometimes the glove would get-hung up with the strap on the back of my left hand and the ball would squirt away. When the strap was ripped away from the glove, rarely was there a time when the glove clung to my wrist when using the "flipping the glove" procedure. There were not many balls hit my way to right field during the games Mr. Johnston coached. In games with my siblings, the missing strap came in handy.

It was late July of 1967, and I was about to play my last game for St. Patrick's Fast Pitch Softball Team. Our team was excellent; we had won every game. The final challenge was for the championship of East St. Louis. Our opponents were worthy. Their only losses were to St. Patrick's, in which both games were won by one run. I woke up on game day with a summer cold and a severe headache. I knew that I was running a fever but was afraid to take my temperature because my mom might keep me home from this last game. I held no dreams of playing a spectacular game and becoming the hero for St. Patrick's. I would sit on the bench and cheer for all of my teammates, hoping that they would come out on top again.

The game was close that day with the other team up by a single run. In the last inning, St. Patrick's had managed to get two people on base. There were two outs, one out remaining before the game would be decided. Mr. Johnston called time out and put me in as a pinch-hitter. There were about two hundred people cheering for our side; all my teammates rose from the bench, cheering for me. I took a bat, swung it a couple of times, and stepped to the plate.

The opposing pitcher had great control and could throw the ball hard. I surmised that I could not wait him out and hope for a walk. Determined to get my swings at the ball and not be called out with the bat on my shoulders, I suddenly knew what I was going to do—hit a frozen rope right down the right field line and win the game for my team. I may have missed the ball by a fraction of an inch on one of my swings. Unfortunately, after three swings and misses, the umpire had to do his duty and call me out. I immediately heard the opposing team's crowd erupt with joy.

I turned toward our bench with my head down and tossed the useless bat toward the other sticks of lumber. As I walked to the bench, I raised my eyes and saw at least half of our team get up from the benches and start to run toward me. My immediate thought was that these teammates were going to beat the tar out of me for losing the game. *I tried my best, guys,* I thought, *at least I wasn't called out on strikes. You know, there is a reason I sit on the bench most of the time, guys, and it is not because I tell Coach Johnston I don't wanna play.*

As the teammates reached me, there were smiles on their faces. They started slapping me on the back and acting like I'd just won the game for them. Most of the crowd for St. Patrick's started clapping, too, and I wondered if I'd been cast into *The Twilight Zone*. "Why are you so happy?" I asked. "I just lost the game for you!"

"We lost the game, not you. They were better than us today, Tom." A few of the members of the team said, "We see the effort you put into every play at our practices and games. You make us better players by just watching you play."

I appreciated their unwarranted compliments, as I *had* put forth the most that I could for the team.

Several years ago at a wedding reception, my brother, Larry, and I were talking about the good old times. Eventually, the topic of softball arose, and Larry remembered the differences I employed when catching the softball, and how impressed he was about my glove mechanics simply to catch a ball. This was the first time I'd thought about it, so many years later. I stuck up my right hand

and told Larry, "I didn't have much of a choice if I wanted to play catch with you, guys." I wonder how many other people noticed me in the field using my modified method of playing softball. Yes, I had a fervent desire to play. The truth is, I enjoyed sports of all types, and if I had to slightly modify the way I caught a ball, it was well worth the effort.

21

Laur

My dad was always close to his brother, Laur, separated from him by only sixteen months. I scratched my head as to why Laur was called Laur. His name was Laurence, so why in the heck he let his family call him Laur and not Larry has confused me to this day. My younger brother Larry has the same spelling of his formal name as our uncle. I'm sure that if I had ever tried calling him Laur when we were lads, a fight would have ensued.

We had a neighbor about ten years older than Larry and me whose name was Robert. Robert would talk to Sister Rose Brenden on occasion. They each had pronounced Irish brogues, and he sometimes kidded Larry that his name was Mary instead of Larry. My brother did not particularly like the substitution of "M" for "L," but for me, if I were Larry, it would be a toss up to be called either of those names— Laur or Mary. I'd have to wear dresses if being called Mary, but I would have the Wisdom of Solomon not to be called Laur, and thereby forego getting beaten up each recess.

Uncle Laur was no demure, sissified Little Lord Fauntleroy look alike. The guy was huge and without doubt the most competitive person I've ever known. At six feet five inches tall, he must have weighed at least 275. You would swear he'd have to turn sideways to fit through any doorway of average width, but I called him Uncle Laur, or Monsignor O'Connell if I addressed him outside our home.

My dad and his younger brother were close like me and my younger brother, John, three years younger than me. Often they thought and spoke in the same way, using some of the same language. It was as if they were reading each other's minds. They were not only brothers, but best friends, carrying their closeness forward until my uncle died of colon cancer shortly before his sixtieth birthday. Dad was proud and respectful that his younger brother had devoted all his magnificent mind, effort, and time as a priest to help others. Still, Dad saw Laur as a brother on Sunday nights as they debated whose nose or ears were bigger or who had less hair on the top of their heads. As they grew from boys to men, they had certain disagreements that were settled using boxing gloves in the basement.

Dad usually won those skirmishes, due to his edge in quickness and age, but Uncle Laur, because he was left-handed, occasionally laid my father on the seat of his pants. Dad often forgot that his brother was a southpaw and looked at his opponent's right hand expecting the next haymaker, only to have his bell rung by Laur's left hand. Sometimes

Dad worried. He would knock his brother down time after time, only to have Laur stand up, shake his head a little and motion to dad to resume. Sometimes after several of these knockdowns, Dad refused to box with Laur anymore. That was a win for me, my uncle thought, when Bill refused to leave his corner. That was fine with my dad; he didn't want to hurt his brother anymore.

Even though they argued, it incensed my father when anyone touched his younger brother with malice. If Dad saw anyone so much as push Laur, he immediately went on the offense. Before Laur could retaliate, his brother was on the boy, punching him: "Don't you *ever* touch my brother!" It didn't matter whether Laur was way off base in the argument that preceded the push; all my father could see was the boy had touched his younger brother.

When Dad was around age nine or ten, he and his brother took an interest in sports. Dad's favorite sport was soccer. He and Laur would kick the ball back and forth for hours. Dad refused to play in neighborhood pickup games unless he had Laur on his side. Sometimes the only way a game was played was with Bill and Laur on one side versus the entire neighborhood on the other side. My dad, with his quickness and agility, would always play offense, and my uncle with the aggressiveness of a lion would handle the defense. Shortly before Laur had the problem with his leg, he and my dad played in a men's soccer league. Laur at twelve years old played defense and gave no quarter to the men. He would take the ball away from the other team and feed it to Bill or another teammate. It infuriated these grown men to constantly have the ball taken away by a twelve-year-old punk.

In the spring and summer, they would play baseball. When they didn't have time to go to the park or play pickup games, Dad and his younger brother would play burnout. It didn't take long for my father to discover that he had the knack of throwing any spherical object incredibly fast and far. Regardless of how hard he threw the ball, his younger brother asked for no quarter. If Bill's arm didn't tire out, Laur was there to catch the ball.

I never saw a man hit a softball farther than my uncle did at the annual servers' picnic for St. Patrick. Each year, the altar servers were thanked for assisting the priest throughout the year. The servers' picnic was held in July, and the best part for me was that soda was limited only to the amount I could consume in a day. We got free admittance to a swimming pool plus hikes through wooded highlands, which I particularly enjoyed. There was, of course, the softball game in the early afternoon. Because of his messed-up leg, my uncle only batted. Since the age of twelve, he dared only to walk on it gingerly.

All the infield players moved back about fifty feet when Monsignor batted. If my uncle didn't accurately time his swing, it would be the luck of the draw if one of the infielders were not missing a few teeth when the game was over if the infielders didn't move back. The man was huge! After grinding the poor bat in his hands, he swung as hard as possible. When he timed it right, the old softball rocketed so far and high that I never saw it caught.

As my introduction to golf, he took me to the driving range a few times. I loved to watch him hit a golf ball. He would place it on the grass about six feet in front of the mat. He would take a Three Wood from his bag and swing the club as hard as he could to clobber the ball. Those of you who have an aptitude for golf know that brute force is not the way to succeed at the game.

Thus all my uncle's Three-Wood shots were not magnificent. Some were pushed or pulled at about a forty-five-degree angle and I'm sure that many a worm who happened to be in the way of my uncle's ball as he hit grounders must have lost their lives. But when he timed it correctly and the ball was clipped off the grass in the right way, it was spectacular. The ball sped away in what seemed like a line drive thirty or forty feet off the ground. As I watched the ball, knowing that eventually it would return to earth, it would take off about two hundred yards from the mat and skyrocket like the softballs at the Altar Boy picnic. I saw the ball land beyond a fence past the three-hundred-yard sign at the Grand Marias Driving Range. Due to the weeds, I could not see where it stopped rolling. This he accomplished with 1960s equipment.

I must have been twelve or thirteen when, in a conversation with my father, I first asked about my uncle's leg. I could tell it was a sore spot with my dad when he started recounting this chapter of Laur's life. After he turned twelve, a constant pain had developed in his upper-right leg bone, a pain that would not subside. After numerous tests, the doctors diagnosed Laur with acute osteomyelitis, an infection of the bone, which often occurs in the arms or legs of children. The doctors performed surgery on the infected part of the leg and shaved the bone down to about a pencil's width, in hopes that the bone would thicken as time passed. My dad's worry was as constant as his brother's pain, as one of the medical options had been amputation of the leg.

As Dad waited on the porch to greet his brother, he was warned by his parents to take it easy with Laur until the bone healed. A few days later, while Dad and Laur were messing around on the front porch, my uncle caught his foot beneath the banister and fell. Dad heard the dreadful sound of the leg snapping into two parts as Laur fell. As Dad's mother chewed him up one side and down the other, Laur, even in the excruciating pain caused by a compound fracture said, "Don't scream at Bill, Mom, it was my fault, Mom, it was my fault!"

As dad finished telling his story, he added, "When you see your uncle struggling to genuflect in front of the altar or limping as he walks, you'll know that I did that to him, I did that to my younger brother."

I said, "Dad, it was an accident. Surely you would never do anything to hurt your brother and friend. Still, my dad carried this guilt around with him for the rest of his days. I'm sure he apologized to his brother many times. I don't know the particulars of the next year of my uncle's recuperation, or how much of the three or four inches of his thighbone was left after it healed. I didn't want to press Dad anymore. I know my uncle needed complete bed rest and that he had to miss an entire year of school. When he graduated from Central Catholic in East St. Louis, he was over nineteen. For fear of doing more damage to the leg, he never could compete in mildly aggressive sports like baseball or soccer after the osteomyelitis set in.

As a staunch competitor, learning that he could never play these sports again had a profound impact on my uncle. It made him bitter for many months, as he lay in his bed and pondered his future. Laur crossed his first Rubicon in 1927, deciding finally that if sports were not possible for him, whatever he chose to do for the remainder of his life, he would devote all his competitive powers to becoming the best of the best.

He started Cathedral High School in Belleville and transferred to Central Catholic in East St. Louis for his junior year. He made the debating team at both schools and wrote for *The Pioneer Newspaper* at Central Catholic. Ironically, too, in his senior year because table tennis was mild enough, he became Central Catholic ping-pong champion. Then Laur began to think about his next step after graduation.

He thought about becoming a lawyer and defending falsely accused clients, making straight the legal way. Although this would be a laudable career, he surmised that if a guilty man needed his assistance, he would need to work just as hard to clear that person of their crimes as for one who was innocent. He kept this idea on the back burner as he considered other options.

What about a doctor who does groundbreaking research to cure the horrible diseases that plague humankind? This would save lives or at least give patients a better quality of life. This is a nobler option, my uncle thought, and potentially could save more lives without deference to the individuals involved. Yes, he thought, his occupation would be as a research scientist.

As he continued through high school, Laur delved further into what he could best do to serve. My uncle was brilliant; he had the mental capacity and the competitive drive to excel at any career. During high school, he made his final decision to become a priest, what he considered the highest and most worthwhile dedication of his life, to helping those in distress and leading them toward the greatest reward of heaven.

He only wanted to serve and help his parishioners. Although pastor for several parishes, he was also appointed superintendent of Catholic schools for the Diocese of Belleville, Illinois, for twenty-two years and served as the vocations director and the director of religious education for the diocese, among other duties.

Uncle Laur became pastor of St. Patrick Parish during my second-grade year. His duties included handing out first-term report cards to every St. Patrick student. He was a busy man, with scholastics high on his agenda. I don't know about the conversations between Monsignor and the people who did not do their best at schoolwork. All I know is that somehow the conversation between Uncle Laur and me was vastly different from a friendly, "Tom, try to do a little better next time."

Did my father and his brother talk about me on Sunday nights? Somehow, I think Dad might have casually worked into the discussions that the doctors said not to push the lad. After all, no one knew what had caused the rare occurrence of a stroke in someone so young. It was wishful thinking on my part, or these conversations went into my uncle's right ear and picked up speed before they exited his left.

At report card time, I don't remember any exchange of cordial niceties, as one would expect from an uncle who genuinely liked me. Instead, he'd begin gruffly: "Well, how do you think you did this term, Tom?"

Why those few words? He always knew the answer simply by looking at my report card. I sometimes thought about saying, "Spectacular, Monsignor, I think I did marvelously for my first term," but I never had the nerve.

That might've incensed him more and he might have added another fifteen or twenty minutes to the time he'd already allotted to discuss my scholastic performance.

The answer was always the same to his first question: "I don't know, Monsignor."

I was not about to answer yea or nay but would settle into my chair for a good tongue-lashing that I knew would last at least an hour. One by one, he would go through every subject on my report card. After each subject, he recited my grade with a sarcastic and mean-spirited tone, depending on how poor he deemed the grade. Now I know I received a couple of Bs on each report card and a straggling A here and there. He never danced around the desk in joy after reading my high marks; he just toned down his deep and disgusted voice. If I could have earned a string of those good grades, I might have left that room without enduring another tongue lashing. Alas, this was not to be, and if my grade were less than a B, his voice would rise loud and disdainfully.

After he was through with the grades, he would routinely ask what I had to say for myself. How in the heck does he expect me to answer that? I wondered.

"I'll try to do better next term, Monsignor," I would say.

"You always say that, Tom! But when I review your grades the following year, they're mediocre at best. Tom, you are limited in the ways you can make a living," he always said during these conversations when he was trying to appeal to my intelligence. "I know you're brilliant, and the competitive drive you've shown in recovery since the stroke is admirable. If you would just take a tiny bit of that drive and put it into your studies, I wouldn't have to lecture you. You do know that you can never achieve any of the professions you might have before the stroke, don't you, Tom? Quit feeling sorry for yourself and work to achieve whatever profession you desire. Go out there and be the best!"

As my uncle talked, I knew he didn't have a clue as to what was happening in my head. Couldn't he see the reason I didn't perform at optimum level was sheer laziness? There was no comparison between the enjoyment I received shooting a basketball versus diagramming a sentence. Of course, I knew I could not hold a factory job, and that it would be more ridiculous to think that I could earn my living at sports. But why would I feel sorry for myself because I lost the use of a side? Why would I be sorry when so much was given back to me, and that as I ran, I was able to feel the wind blowing through my hair again? Yes, Monsignor, I am sorry I'm lazy, but there is just not enough regret in the world to make me do homework, especially when I won't see you for another year. Give me a few more years to settle, and I'll buckle down and do what's necessary for success. But don't expect me to follow your path, Uncle, and be the best at one profession. There are far more important things in life than being the best at one thing and basing your self-worth on that one thing.

I did deserve to be scolded by my uncle, especially when I had an out with my parents after I had the stroke. Sure, there was merit in trying to make me a better student. I knew Uncle Laur had a genuine concern for my welfare. But what he wanted at this point was just not going to happen.

For some reason, he liked me. Maybe it was because we had similar instances in our childhood. It appeared to him that I had adjusted—that I had true inner peace. He still harbored high hopes for me though, like I was supposed to figure out how fusion worked or devise a fuel that would enable a craft to approach the speed of light.

Once I mentioned to my dad that I might like to invent things or design tall buildings when I became a man. This idea may have been spawned when I cleared some of the rocks on our basketball court to resemble a road, where my younger brothers and I could pretend we each had cars and could run along the makeshift road.

Dad must have told his brother about his budding young inventor during one of those Sunday-night conversations. If my father had switched names and used Larry's name in place of mine, Uncle Laur might have said, "That's great, Bill! I hope he's successful" and that would have been the end of the conversation. Laur could envision his nephew with analytical and invention skills. Yes, Tom would create an invention that would change the world.

My uncle bought for me a girder-panel building set, a crystal radio set, the makings of a static-electricity generator that would put out one hundred thousand volts if assembled correctly and a super ball, just to add interest. I have never forgotten these gifts intending to spur my interest in anything mechanical. I enjoyed the girder-panel building set and got immense joy in seeing how many times I could bounce the super ball off the ceiling to floor and ceiling to floor again on one bounce.

My dad helped me assemble the crystal radio set. The radio actually worked if you concentrated hard while the earphones were on your head. About two or three weeks later, I had finished my altar server duties with my uncle Monsignor O'Connell. Afterward, he asked how I was doing with his gifts.

"My dad and I worked on the crystal radio set a couple weeks ago and you can hear music coming from it, Monsignor."

"That's fine, that's fine, Tom," he said with enthusiasm. "How does it work, Tom?" was his next question.

How does it work? I thought this is an odd question.

"Well, you put on the headphones," I started to explain, and then was so rudely interrupted by his harsh tone of voice that sounded like the hour-long chat with him at the end of the first term of school.

"I know the mechanics of listening to a crystal radio set, Tom. What I want to know is how does sound from a radio station make its way into your crystal radio?" he asked again.

I thought, *How in heck am I supposed to know?* Dad mentioned something about radio waves, but I don't have the foggiest idea how those waves get captured in that radio set. It's a mystery to me too, how the waves are magically converted to music. Furthermore, I really don't give a darn how the radio or TV waves come into the house if there's a picture on my TV or the sound of a ballgame on the radio, I reasoned.

You know, my brother Larry would be a much better guy to quiz about matters such as these, Monsignor, I thought. He would know all about radio waves or any other types of waves. Frankly, I don't know how he can figure out all the stuff he does. He performs a bit better at school than me, but there is certainly room for improvement in his study habits. Too bad Larry isn't serving with me; I could use his help right now.

My answer was my patented "I don't know," which infuriated Uncle Laur.

The static-electricity generator was never assembled, and Monsignor never quizzed me about static electricity and how the contraption he gave me generated it. If I did not know the rudiments of radio waves, how could he expect me to know anything about electricity? I did give the old college try to assembling the generator, but I applied a little too much plastic cement in the process. Replacing most of the parts in their original container, I threw up my hands and said uncle. A few months later, Larry tried to assemble the static-electricity generator.

"There was only about half the pieces," Larry told me, which I had no reason to doubt.

When you are trying to glue two sections of a sphere together with a clumsy, giant hand and trying to hold it with another hand that always reminded me of a kangaroo's right boxing paw, one can surmise that it will not go well in most instances.

Perhaps Uncle Laur was disappointed in his efforts to spur my interest in matters intellectual. From my perspective, there was no change in our relationship. He was the same man to me—a little testy when it came to anything remotely competitive, but someone that I, as a nephew, could grow to like and love. I could always count on him, although our chats at report card time were never pleasant. He was trying to help me, I knew that, but I was not willing to be helped.

On the night of the stroke, he came to St. Mary's Hospital to give me the sacrament of Extreme Unction or Anointing of the Sick, as it's called now. The sacrament is given more frequently nowadays, but in 1962, was administered only to those who were gravely ill. After he said his Masses on Sunday morning, he arrived at St. Mary's only to see no progress on the diagnosis, treatment, or prognosis for me. He was furious. He informed the staff he was transferring his nephew to Cardinal Glennon where the medical staff worked on weekends.

"You don't have the authority to do that, Father," snapped one of the staff. "Only his parents can make that decision."

"You just watch me," said Uncle Laur. "His parents—my brother and his wife—are out of town and can't be reached! I'm making the decision for the family to transfer my nephew to a hospital equipped to make a decision about what exactly is wrong with him!"

Compared to his other nieces and nephews, Uncle Laur would always go the extra mile for me: trips to see St. Louis

Cardinals football games, inviting me to tag along on his vacations, or introducing me to the sport of golf. Although I appreciated and enjoyed these outings, I did not need them. I had lost nothing in the stroke, only gained which has most folks scratching their heads. On the other hand, I scratch my own head to think that anyone believes I lost a single thing.

My uncle died a mean death in 1975. In the summer of 1973, he began having problems, which warranted several tests. The diagnosis was colon cancer. He underwent surgery, and the surgeons were confident that they had removed all the cancerous growth. About a year later, he developed the same symptoms. The cancer had spread throughout his body.

"Terminal," Dad told the family—a horrible word, meaning death to one you have always known and loved as an uncle. Through many a night, Dad stayed with his brother through his last Rubicon until he died on March 19, 1975. The poor man weighed only 125 pounds when he breathed his last breath, a giant wasted to nothing but skin and bones.

I inherited my uncle's car, which I deeply appreciated. He knew I would need transportation after I finished my accounting degree later that year. While accounting is not particularly exciting, I know he was proud of my meager accomplishment, which ended up giving me gainful employment for thirty-seven years.

Many years later, I acquired his Breviary, from which he read sections each day. The Breviary is written in Latin, so I can't understand much of it, but I treasure it highly because it meant so much to him. Thanks for taking an interest in my life, Uncle Laur. It might not have seemed like I cared at the time, but you made a positive difference in my life.

22

A Trip to the Big City

Uncle Dave always was an aberration of the O'Connell boys. I knew from experience with my dad and his younger brother that they could be mean-spirited if you pushed them. I loved them, yes, and I could be counted on to be on their side if times were tough, but I'm just saying, objectively, that they were born with ample tempers. I'm a chip off the old block, mind you, with a temper that far exceeds my ancestors. I've been dealing with the problem for sixty-nine years, and while my temper's decreased, it still needs vast improvement.

Uncle Dave was an extraordinarily kind man. I could not imagine him ever saying a cross word. He was a quiet man, more than his father, always interested in what you had to say. After you spoke your piece, however brief it was, he would compliment you on the achievement. His son Dave might recall a few not-too-pleasant moments with his father, but I'll bet upon proper reflection that my cousin Dave would say he deserved every harsh word.

Uncle Dave and Aunt Helen lived with my grandparents in East St. Louis until Pop passed in 1957 and my grandmother in 1961. Dad's older brother and his wife inherited the house where my father spent his years growing up and kept the place for about ten more years until they moved to Fairview Heights.

My youngest brother, Mike, is about eleven years younger than me. He has accomplished many things in his life, and I was fortunate that he was working for the Missouri School for the Blind as a job coach after my first grand mal seizure.

Mike decided to relocate to Florida and live with his only child, David. We had the good fortune to have him stay at our house near Cincinnati, and I hope he enjoyed our time together as much as I did. In the course of his stay, I asked him why he had named his son Dave instead of Mike. I knew he liked the name Mike because his son's full name was David Michael. He said he named him after Uncle Dave, my father's older brother.

Dad visited Dave frequently after his move to Fairview Heights, particularly after he retired from John Hancock in 1974. Mike often accompanied him on those visits. It was during those times that Mike saw the gentle nature of my dad's older brother and realized the goodness of the man. I don't know what took place, but it must have been impressive for him to name his first boy after Dave. Mike's impressions of the man was only from a little boy's perspective. I do not know if he knew the courage, love, and loyalty the man possessed and demonstrated along with his wife, Helen, throughout their lives.

Dad was in bad shape both physically and mentally when he returned to the United States after World War II. He had been sure he never would see his wife and two daughters again as he crossed the Atlantic toward Europe. When he returned to St. Louis, he was so happy to see his wife and two babies, and to be in his childhood home. He was broken, shell-shocked, or burdened with PTSD. He waited until the last possible day John Hancock would continue to hold his job before he went back to work.

With Uncle Dave at his parents', along with Dad and Mom and their two girls, the house was crowded to say the least. To complicate matters further, Dad's mother and my mom did not always see eye to eye, which hurt Dad because he loved them. It put him in a bind as to whose side he should take. Dad's mom was feisty, and it didn't take much to set her off. My mom was no pushover either. Once I remember my mom telling me she was visiting her relatives in Louisiana with her parents. A heated discussion ensued with one of her aunts. Auntie made the mistake of slapping my mom across the face, which prompted my mom to beat the living daylights out of her. Nothing like that happened between my mom and grandmother, but I am guessing it was quickly and abundantly clear to Mom and Dad that they needed a house of their own.

The only problem was that my parents had no money for a down payment. Dad went to his older brother, Dave, and my uncle lent him enough money to buy their first house on Thirty-first Street. I know that Dad was anxious to repay the amount of the loan. As time passed and my parents were having a baby about every two years, Dad was unable to pay his brother. Dave never asked my dad about the loan, and Dad never needed to explain his dire circumstances. Many years later my father was able to make things square. He always remembered Dave's kindness. From Uncle Dave's perspective, all he needed to know was that they were brothers. He was proud of my dad and knew he was doing his best. He knew he did not need the money, but that Bill's family did at that time. I am sure if the situation were reversed, my dad would have extended the same courtesy to Dave. Family is what counts, not anything as meaningless as money.

I do not know why Aunt Helen was fond of me as a nephew, particularly after that two-week stint with me when I was about a year old while my mother was giving birth to Larry. Perhaps she wanted to see if I were in fact the true Prince of Darkness and whether the horns were protruded from my head. A little later, I assume, she might have been proud of me due to my developing a true peace and happiness following the loss of my side. Most people see cheerfulness and persistence as virtues rather than vices, don't they—when there's an obstacle to overcome?

In those days, I was suspicious of all people past the age of eleven. Someone my mom's age enticing me with a trip to the big City of St. Louis would give me reason to pause and think: is someone trying to trick me? My mom liked Aunt Helen too, which scared the pants off me. Maybe they'd arranged a little deal. Aunt Helen would take me to one of those gigantic stores in St. Louis, abandon me in the huge toy department and high tail it across the river, leaving me to my own devices. Well, regardless of how much money changed hands, I didn't *really* believe my aunt would do that to me. Aunt Helen was my friend, albeit an ancient one, but a friend. Somehow, I knew that I was well protected when I was in her hands, although she could not have weighed more than a hundred pounds.

My mom and I arrived at 625 N. Thirty-Second Street in the morning and were greeted by Aunt Helen on her front porch. She invited us in, where I saw my grand-mother sitting in a room which they called the parlor. The three women talked an inordinately long time. I wondered why they called this room the parlor. It looked like a plain old living room to me, although fancier than the one in our house. The longer I sat in the room with the three women talking, the more anxious I became. I did not want to be transformed into some kind of sissy. Finally, with a quick goodbye to her third-born son, Mom hopped into her car. Guess she was in a hurry before Helen changed her mind and sent us both packing on the short trip to Alhambra Court.

Aunt Helen took my hand, and we walked up toward State Street. It did not take us long until we were waiting for the bus to St. Louis. I did not have much to say to my aunt. As I had learned a long time ago, it was best to be silent and answer with as few words as possible to any question asked by any adult. While we waited for the bus, I was puzzled. Why don't we drive to St. Louis? Doesn't she know how to operate a car? I reasoned that cars might not have been invented when she was a young lady. I was on the verge of asking her that very question when common sense kicked in. I thought it might offend her, and she might take me to her own woodshed and give me a good walloping.

Buses arrived regularly in those days; I climbed the few steps, and she paid the fare of a couple of nickels and a dime. We spotted a couple of empty seats, sat down, and the bus lurched forward with a growling sound that increased in intensity as the seconds passed. As we headed toward downtown at about Twenty-First Street, the road dipped a little beneath an active railroad track. Hey, that's not fair! What if a train was passing? I wanted to count the cars! Around Tenth Street, we saw the Sears-Roebuck store on the right—two stories tall and impressive to a five-year-old.

We turned left after a couple of blocks where the right side of the road was lined with stores of every type. Can St. Louis be much grander than this, I wondered? There were red lights on every corner. I hoped we were stopped by each one of them so I could peer into the store windows to see what I could see.

"We're about to go over the Eads Bridge, Tommy," Aunt Helen said.

"A bridge!" I said. "An honest-to-goodness bridge?"

"Yes, Tommy," she said, "we wouldn't be able to drive over the Mississippi River without the bridge."

At one of the stoplights, the bus turned right and started to ascend. The grade was steep, and our ascension was by means of a narrow one-lane road with girders on the left. The height on my right grew at such an astounding rate that I was scared. I moved closer to my aunt, and her nearness calmed me. As we were about to level off, there she was: the mighty Mississippi River in the distance sepa-rated from the bridge by a mere handrail, or that's what it looked like to a five-year-old. When we crested the height of the Eads Bridge, the road spread out to four lanes of traffic. The bus tires hummed—a constant hum that gave me the sickening feeling the bus driver wasn't in control of where we were headed. Oh, we were heading west, okay, but sometimes, the bus would hit a bump, and whatever caused the tires to hum would redirect us toward the hand-rail of the bridge, giving us an all too unobstructed view of the Mississippi River far below. Imagine the terror of a wee child suddenly seeing the world from much higher than a normal car, with only his aunt to depend upon for safety. I was hoping she qualified for the Olympic swim team so she could save me from an uncertain fate in the Mississippi River—just in case the bus crashed through the handrail.

We hit the busy streets of St. Louis unscathed, and I could not believe the number of cars and people busily traversing the streets and sidewalks. There were streetcars on the streets. I remembered my dad saying Pop worked on a streetcar when he was a boy. Sweet job, I thought—riding the streets of East St. Louis and getting paid for it to boot. We did not stay long in the bus once we arrived in St. Louis. Aunt Helen treated me to gigantic department stores—Famous-Barr Company and Stix Baer and Fuller. As I recall, these stores had about eight or nine floors. We rode escalators to and from the floors at each of the stores. It took me three or four rides to get accustomed to the escalators, due to the oddly disappearing steps at the top and bottom.

My aunt must have let me ride the same escalator six or eight times, until we finally moved on to other departments. I was anxious and bored at the departments filled with clothes for sale. It seemed as though we always ended up in the women's section, which gave me the willies. In her favor I'll say that Aunt Helen did take me to the toy sections of both stores. Despite how many letters I wrote to the old man, I knew that Santa Claus was too stingy to bring me the presents I saw and wanted at the stores that day.

We ate lunch at Woolworth's between visits to the stores. My aunt ordered a sandwich served with potato chips for each of us and I had an RC Cola, which was a major treat.

After we finished shopping, we stopped at a park, sat on a bench for a while, and watched the people and cars go by. *What are they thinking about?* I wondered as the people scurried past. *Are they as lucky as I, sitting by my aunt, with eight siblings at home, who I can always count on to help me?*

Shortly after we returned to my aunt's house, Mom arrived in her car to drive me home. She talked to my aunt and grandmother for a spell in the parlor again. She asked Aunt Helen if I'd been a good boy.

"Yes, Evelyn," she said, "Tommy was a peach," which pleased Mom. I remembered to thank Aunt Helen as I gave her a little hug, which was the most I could do seeing that she was a grown-up girl. All the way home, I wondered why did she do this kindness for me? Did Mom say to her one Sunday that with her third-born son she was about ready to pull out all her remaining hair? It could be that my aunt just decided to give Evelyn a few hours break that day. I know Mom surely liked it and thanked her repeatedly.

As I saw it, Aunt Helen was a lion, and she had to prove it every day. At the end of the day, she was filled with radiant goodness and love that few people ever feel. She thanked God for giving her His innocence for another day.

23

Bobby

On occasional Sunday evenings, Mom and Dad took me and one or two of my younger brothers to Mom and Pop's house on Thirty-Second Street. My parents never took all the children weekly. Imagine the chaos that would ensue with eight of my siblings running around the place, tearing up my grandparents' home.

The evening started peacefully enough, with my mom threatening everyone from my age down with a long trip to the woodshed if we were not quiet. We knocked on their door and exchanged pleasantries. As we walked in, I tried to stay clear of the parlor since I knew I'd spend much of the night in there, due to some disagreement with one of my brothers that would be deemed entirely my fault.

At first, I would stay in the hall, and then mosey into the kitchen. If the sun were shining, I'd open the back door, descend the few steps, and make my way to their crusty old garage which seemed to be more of a barn than a garage. Sometimes I'd slide open the door just to have the fascination of seeing it close as soon as I released it. I don't remember taking a good tour of the garage, for good reason. If my mom caught me investigating their stuff, I'd be cooling my heels in the parlor for most of the night.

There were a few roses sprinkled through the backyard, along with other flowers, as well as pepper and tomato plants. There were no chickens in the yard as there'd been when my father was a boy. I can't swear by it, mind you, but I spied an old building that might once have been a chicken coop.

It was never long before my brothers and I were called into the house for the evening. Slowly, I'd climb the backporch stairs trying to absorb the last few rays of sunshine before being trapped in the house again. I would creep back into the kitchen and into the hallway near the parlor. My grandparents' house was two stories with ceilings about nine or ten feet high. I walked toward the front door and turned left. The staircase was before me, and I climbed no more than two or three steps before I'd make another left turn. The main staircase seemed huge to me at the age of five. I climbed it gingerly the first time or two, holding onto the heavy wooden banister.

It must have taken much courage, or lack of common sense, to jump out one of the second-story windows as my father had done when he was young. Each time I was at Mom and Pop's, I'd immediately head to the first door on the right to see if that special toy were there. Sometimes I had to hunt for it, but I always found it if I looked hard enough.

The toy was a good-sized top that spun on its base for a long time—multicolored with a plunger in the top that reached about six inches toward the sky. It was easy to spin. I took the plunger and thrust it toward the floor four or five times and boy, did it spin, singing a pleasant note for a long time. When the top started to slow, the music dissipated. Again, I would thrust the plunger down toward the floor three or four times to hear it sing once more. I wondered whether I would ever merit a top so grand from Santa Claus.

Which room were my dad and Uncle Laur quartered in when they were growing up? Certainly, it was on the second floor. I wondered what they'd talked about. What were their aspirations and how did they adapt when things didn't exactly go as planned? I could have looked at my life when I was older, but I never thought on it for a long spell when my road shifted a bit. The past was the past and I always looked forward to the next day and the challenges and expectations it would bring. Mind you, the future was not always peaches and cream, and sometimes you had to ride it out like a storm at sea. But I always found that if you had the moxy and the persistence to ride them through, good times would come for sure.

My mother would call me to the "parlor of woe" to sit and contemplate about whichever transgression had occurred with my siblings. It was brutal, sitting in the parlor listening to old people talk. I'd slink down to the floor, trying to remain still and unnoticed so none of the old folks would grill me.

While sitting in the parlor, serving my sentence for upstairs boisterousness, I'd sometimes hear a hefty cry from one of the nearby rooms. Aunt Helen would excuse herself the minute she heard the cry. I didn't know at first who the child was in that room, but I could tell by my aunt's tender voice of consolation that she would do anything to give him comfort and love.

Since I was not paying attention to any of the grown-up talk, all my focus was on the one who cried incessantly. Aunt Helen was feisty at times and did not give my father any quarter, which was amazing if you knew him. Her manner with the child she was trying to sooth was of a much different nature. When she carried her son into the parlor, I thought of my mother's favorite saying to me when I was whiney: "Quit crying, or I'll give you something to cry about."

She placed the boy near me. He was not as tall as I, and two or three years younger: "Here, Bobby, why don't you sit by your cousin Tommy for a while?" He continued to cry but said nothing more to his mother except through tears.

Then I saw a huge welt on his back. *This is why he's crying*, I thought. Someone must have had a fight with him and kept punching him in the same spot on his back. It incensed me that anyone could be so cruel as to punch a defenseless boy enough times to raise such a welt.

"Mom," I said, "who beat up my cousin, Bobby, and gave him that big welt on his back? I'm going to beat him up!" I exclaimed. "Who did this to Bobby?"

Mom quickly took my hand and hastily led me to the kitchen to explain about Bobby.

Was I in trouble? She sat down in the kitchen, turned me around to face her and said with a calm and gentle voice,

"Bobby is sick, Tommy, very sick. No one beat him up," she said. "No one is at fault for the big lump on his back; it is all part of his sickness. Pray for him and his mother and father too, Tommy."

My mother's explanation didn't make much sense to me, but I was glad I was not sick in the same way as Bobby. I guess with a five-year-old's concept of prayer, mine was a prayer of gratitude.

Uncle Dave and Aunt Helen met, fell in love, and were married late in life. After a couple of years, when Aunt Helen was a little over thirty-six years old, and Uncle Dave was thirty-nine, they had their first child. It was a hard pregnancy for her; she almost died giving birth to Davy. Her doctor told her in certain terms never to become pregnant again.

"You won't make it to full term if you do, Helen," her doctor told her. "You barely made it this time. Furthermore, if you are ever confronted by a pregnancy again, do not expect me to be your doctor. You'd die before the baby was born, and I am not going to tarnish my reputation by putting you under my care."

I would not like such harsh words to be spoken to my wife by a so-called doctor. I'd have given him a severe tongue lashing. I'd hope the man would have enough sense not to swing at me.

The pregnancy must have been hard on both my aunt and uncle. Her life was on the line, and my uncle must have felt helpless too. Although they did their best to avoid it, in five years, Aunt Helen was pregnant again.

My uncle and aunt were filled with happiness when they learned of her condition. Based on the doctor's warning, they were concerned. Yet they had faith that the second pregnancy would yield another beautiful baby. The doctor who oversaw the first pregnancy refused to be involved with the second birth. "You won't make it, Helen," he said and urged them to therapeutically abort the pregnancy.

They found another doctor to lead my aunt through her term, and in nine months, a beautiful baby boy was born without any of the problems they had experienced with Davy. They were overwhelmed with happiness with their two boys they could raise side by side as brothers and friends. Bobby was slower than Davy at learning. He slowly learned how to say momma and dada and took his first few steps. They repeatedly took him to the doctors and specialists for evaluation. Initially it was determined that Bobby was mentally impaired, which I'm sure made his parents sad. Bobby would never be able to reach out for the stars, grasp and hold onto his special one, and achieve what he desired.

Bobby was their beloved son, loved in a manner that only parents can love a child. Every day, Bobby seemed to be regressing instead of progressing. The first few steps he had taken began to evade him, so Dave and Helen put him through more tests, only to yield that he was impaired physically as well. My relatives were beside themselves; the first few words that he had grasped vanished from him. My uncle and aunt held onto Bobby with greater fervor and love, determined to do everything in their power to help him. At the suggestion of one of their specialists in St. Louis, they took him to Chicago for evaluation and a final diagnosis. The analysis of Bobby's condition would take two weeks. My uncle and aunt were advised to return to St. Louis.

I cannot imagine what went through their minds during those two weeks. Surely, they hoped that through the analysis, Bobby would be helped in some manner. They must have been scared and unable to raise one bit of sunshine on their heartbreaking problem with Bobby. They must have felt guilty leaving their son alone to endure test after test in a completely sterile environment. What did he think when he cried out for his mommy or daddy and did not hear the quick patter of feet and the gentle voices that always soothed him? They must have shed many tears.

My father broke down and wept uncontrollably when he returned from Texas to learn that I was deathly ill. I never saw him cry in the thirty-five years that I knew him, but I know he wept when I was in trouble. I know there were many prayers said for Bobby in that two-week span.

As Dave and Helen traveled back the three hundred miles to Chicago, one can only imagine their thoughts and hopes for Bobby and their desire to touch and hold him, vowing never to leave their boy again. The diagnosis was Hurler Syndrome, a mean disease that robs you every day of a little bit more of the talents given you at birth. Furthermore, the doctors said Bobby would never see his tenth birthday, as his organs would gradually break down and fail.

"I'm sorry to give you this report Mr. and Mrs. O'Connell. I know you were hoping for better news. Bobby will never stabilize. Hurler Syndrome is a horrible and rare disease that continuously ravages the body. This process for

Bobby will take years, Mr. and Mrs. O'Connell, and he will depend on you for a long time. One option for you is to leave him with us here at the hospital. He would have the best medical care available and would be looked after until the day he passes," the doctor said.

My uncle and aunt must have been shocked. Yes, they were prepared to hear that nothing more could be done and to take Bobby home and deal with whatever came their way. But they were unprepared to hear that their son would not live past ten. Abandon Bobby because he is going to be an inconvenience? Leave him in this sterile hospital until the day that God calls him home? They knew that in his limited mind, Bobby would be crying for his parents. If they abandoned him, no one except good meaning strangers would be there to comfort him in his times of distress.

I can imagine so vividly my aunt's next words.

"Don't you dare take my baby away! I don't care what obstacles lie before us. He's, our son! I will be here to soothe and comfort him as long as he lives."

My uncle and aunt gently took their beautiful little son home to East St. Louis. Dave had always been a quiet, meek, and humble man. His wife risked her life in the second pregnancy. He felt completely helpless and depressed to learn of the outcome for Bobby. They contemplated a trip to Lourdes, France, hoping for a miracle to make Bobby whole again. Surely with the deep faith they always had shown, God would show mercy to Bobby.

Uncle Laur, then a priest for twelve years, talked with his older brother and his wife. It was 1955. Laur knew of many miracles performed throughout the history of the church. He was also a pragmatist and knew about the horrors of Hurler Syndrome. No one knows the lengths to which a mother and father will go to protect their offspring or give them one last chance for a fruitful life for their desperately sick child. My father offered to change places with me when I was deathly ill. My uncle and aunt decided not to go to France, but to accept their role with Bobby. They always let him know he was safe and loved.

Since I'm a half-cup full type of person, I never thought of my stroke as a bad break. I do not know if that makes me mentally half a sandwich shy of a picnic, but to be honest, I don't sum the good breaks versus the bad or try to figure whether I was cheated by the Good Lord. One thing I know is I am still kicking at age sixty-nine—a mark to the good on the ledger. If my intuitiveness had been a little greater and I was a half-cup empty type, I might have considered it a bad break and shouted to God in anger why me, Lord, why me? In either case, all I would need to do is walk three short blocks west on Summit Avenue and then about two long blocks south on thirty-second Street and visit my cousin, Bobby. After visiting him for a minute or two, I would kneel and cry out for God's forgiveness. How could I be so selfish as to think that the mere loss of a side bares any comparison to my cousin's current state.

My uncle and aunt were filled with the goodness that only God can give. After her husband went to work, it was Helen's task to fill Bobby's day with all the safety, happiness, and love she could give. It was her task to dead lift him from his bed when the day began and to greet him each morning with a cheerful smile. Thousands upon thousands of times, she changed his soiled diapers without ever uttering a harsh word to him. She saw it as her honor and privilege to help her son. After feeding Bobby, she'd carry him to the couch to watch his favorite program on TV.

Close beside one another, the two of them would watch *Queen for a Day*, an old show where three or four women told heart-wrenching stories about their experiences. After each story, the audience would clap. Their clapping was registered on the "Applause-O-Meter," and after all the stories were told, the woman who received the loudest clapping on the "Applause-O-Meter" was deemed the winner, Queen for a Day. Bobby and his mother clapped after each story. The winner was adorned with a crown, robe, and roses. She was awarded household appliances, nights on the town with guests, and various other prizes. The cheers were the best part—Helen and Bobby clapping joyfully as the Queen was announced. I'd say Aunt Helen was *Queen for a Day* every time she watched that show with her son.

There were times when Bobby was crying and yet had no way to tell his mom or dad what was wrong. One of them would pick him up, caress him, and gently talk to him, letting him know he was safe and loved, never losing their patience. I imagine them using soothing words like sweetheart, darling, honey, or angel. My parents leveled some of these words at me on occasion when I needed them—words that made me sure everything was okay on the home front. The few times I was lucky enough to be included in the trips to Mom and Pop's on Sunday night and was sitting in the penalty box (the parlor), I often heard Aunt Helen call her youngest son one of those special words. Every time I think about those times, the scene brings shivers to my bones, and I realize the true meaning of love for a son or daughter.

"Precious… Precious… Precious" is what she called Bobby many times while she caressed and tried to comfort him. Precious. Not a hollow word, but a word with deep meaning for my uncle and aunt. I believe that in their hearts and minds, Bobby was a beautiful being who had nothing at the end of his life but was the most precious gift that God could have given them. I am sure when they knelt at the end of the day, they cried in ecstasy as they thanked their Maker for another day with their son.

Everyone who's old enough remembers the day John F. Kennedy was assassinated. I was eleven years old during that grim event, and I remember Sister Tarsella announcing the news to the fifth graders at about 1:30 p.m. and dismissing us for the weekend. But the assassination is not the key marker of my memory. For on the following day, my cousin, Bobby, died. On November 23, 1963, God called Bobby home to his everlasting reward with a shout of "Well done, Bobby!" as he, too, hugged him. A boy who was incapable of sin was welcomed into heaven that day. My uncle and aunt knew their son was with God forever. Although they knew their son was with God, their sense of loss was immeasurable.

My brother Larry was only six months older than Bobby. On each celebration of an event for Larry, Uncle Dave, and Aunt Helen were not present. They sent a card to Larry congratulating him, but mourned in silence for Bobby, who would have been celebrating the same event if he were alive and blessed with the talents few people give thanks for receiving. Time heals all wounds is how the saying goes, doesn't it? Well, when Larry graduated from college thirteen years after Bobby's death, there arrived that little card congratulating him on his achievement, but my uncle and aunt did not come to the party, even though they lived only four blocks from our house.

On November 22, 1997, one day short of thirty-four years since Bobby's death, my Aunt Helen took her last breath. When she was at God's house, ready to talk about her life with Him, there stood her husband, Dave, and Bobby, ready to meet her. Bobby, the boy who had little all his life, stood…a man in his full splendor…ready to greet his mother. As Aunt Helen ran to Bobby again, I'm sure she cried out to her son that special word—"Precious!"

As Bobby hugged his mother, surely, he answered, "No, Mom, you're the precious one. You're the precious one!"

24

Whatever It Takes

It was May of 1980, and I had worked for about a year in the tax department at a CPA firm (now defunct). I never particularly liked taxes, but since I attained my MBA degree after the summer quarter, all the jobs were gone from the audit department. Despite the distasteful work of hammering out taxes, I made some good friends during my two-year stint as a taxman.

The tax department formed a slow pitch-softball team with other firms in our specialty. Since I was in decent shape, I decided to join the team with my newfound friends. I held no grandiose ideas of being a spectacular man with the bat and glove, but this was slow-pitch softball. I figured with three whacks at a ball that was coming in as big as a beach ball, I ought to be able to hit at least a grounder. At twenty-seven years old, I was as fast a runner as I was in high school. One bobble by an infielder might be enough to beat the throw to first base if I hustled.

That evening, I looked hard for my old glove—the one I'd received for my First Communion as a wee chap of eight. The one imprinted with Roberto Clemente which I knew was well broken in from the thousands of throws it had caught. The one with the back strap torn off. Yes, they might make sport of me, these newfound friends of mine, but I would have the last laugh since this was the perfect glove for a man with a severely compromised right hand. Despite the position I was playing on any lazy summer afternoon, the glove would come off easily, if necessary, and there would be just a slight difference in the time it took for a normal ballplayer and me to field and throw the ball.

I must have emptied the closet three or four times, searching for that glove. Admittedly, it had been thirteen years since the beat-up old thing had seen much action. Maybe a brother sold it for retaliation purposes for one of those forgotten arguments, I thought. They could not have received much more than twenty-five cents for that chewed up old thing that I loved. Oh well, it was time to invest in a new glove.

I can't remember where I bought the new glove, but one thing I can say for sure it was not at a sports store. It was a glove for use with a team of friends, not to start the year playing for the St. Louis Cardinals. At home, I noticed the new glove had a pocket. It was stiff when I opened and closed it with my left hand. Probably needs scores of hours playing catch to be well broken-in for the first outing, I thought. Long past were the years when my siblings would be more than happy to help me with this predicament. But they have better things to do than play catch with their favorite brother and, as a result, land in the doghouse with their significant other. In the do-it-yourself department, I was stymied.

I could hold the ball in my right hand and toss it to my left. I would need to pry open the fingers to fit the ball for each throw, quite a feat. I dare say with as much certainty as the earth revolves around the sun, the ball would remain in the right hand after each attempt to throw it. If in some manner the ball was released, I'd be a serious gold-glove candidate, if I caught more than 50 percent of the softballs thrown by the right hand. One could only hope that the ball would fall harmlessly away. I could put the ball in my right hand, hold the glove in my left and try to clap my hands together, over my head mind you, so I could beat in a good pocket. Now that is silly, I thought, but at least I have a glove for our first practice.

For some reason, ball practice was scheduled at 6:30 p.m. I did not feel it was worthwhile after work to drive all the way home across the Mississippi River only to return to the city for practice. It never occurred to me to put in extra hours mastering the art of tax preparation or research. Not my idea of fun.

There was a Burger King on the way out to the park where I used to kill time until practice. I usually ate a light meal of two Whoppers, an order of fries and onion rings. I didn't want to get weighed down before practice.

We had a good turnout of a dozen or so tax accountants at our first practice, with three or four talented athletes who could have been starters on most any team. The rest of the guys were run of the mill softball players. Guys you could see had some experience tossing the spheroid around and a bit of expertise at the bat. These were men who never achieved the knack of becoming expert practitioners of the art, either by lack of practice or lack of talent. Average ballplayers, I thought. That's okay. People in glass houses shouldn't throw stones, should they, buddy boy?

I stood in the outfield with three or four other guys until it was my turn to bat as a converted left-hander. Since the stroke, the vision in my right eye has been poor— 20/200 the last time I had it checked. Since I would be watching the ball mostly with my right eye, this did not bode well for me. The first few swings were whiffs, which embarrassed me. Guess I was rusty. It had been thirteen years since I'd swung a bat. I slowed my swing a bit and after a couple more whiffs, started to hit the ball. While my swings yielded mostly grounders, I lined four or five balls over the infield.

"Last one, Tom! Run it out if you can," yelled one of the infielders. The last one was a grounder, so I started for first base, intent on beating the ball.

I was on the right side of the plate, a good step closer to first base than a right-handed batter. I always led with my left leg, then with the right reaching out as far as possible. I ran as fast as I could down the first-base line. Anything could happen, I thought, and if you dogged it down to first base, you might as well not play the game. The first few times I ran the bases I heard two or three of my teammates exclaim, "I didn't know he could run."

I smiled as I thought I'm not a fast sprinter, but to their astonishment, I could run as fast as my friends. At the end of our third practice, our first baseman tapped me on the shoulder and said "Please do not collide with me on first base, Tom. I hear the train a comin', and I'm waitin' for its whistle to blow! You scare the pants off me, Tom."

Here I was at 230 pounds and about as fast as I've ever been. My feet were digging in, so I'd reach optimum speed as I crossed first base. The first step was violent, with my left leg kicking out as far as it could toward first base. The next step slapped the ground, so I'd avoid falling on my face. The steps increased in frequency with the right foot continuing to slap the ground on every other step. *I do sound like a train*, I thought.

"Well," I said to Don, "you best stay out of the train's way. The track is straight, with the locomotive to follow it across first base and into the outfield. Please stay off the tracks!"

I never attempted to slide into a base to avoid a tag. To me, maneuvering my right leg to attempt a slide is downright foolishness and the best way I know of to cause a compound fracture of my leg. I never ran into a player. That'd be dirty baseball. So I'd try to run past the plate making sure to tap it with my foot to avoid the catcher at all costs. At 230 pounds, I found it not as easy to touch the plate gracefully as it was when I was fourteen and weighed 125. On three or four occasions, I had to veer to the catcher's left to avoid the tag at full speed. The train needed a little more distance to come to a complete stop when I was running at full tilt, so on several occasions I climbed the chain-link backstop. That maneuver must have been hilarious to the spectators. Oh, well, causing hilarity was worth it if I scored a run for our team.

I usually played first base. I would gladly sit on the bench if we had more than nine players. What really mattered to me was the friendship of my coworkers. It seemed we had barely enough players to field a team on most occasions, so I was positioned at first base. Mike was our shortstop both years. He was quiet, and one of the nicest guys you'd want to meet. He had vast range in fielding to his right or left, and he could throw hard to first base. I wanted him to barely miss the ball on one of those plays when he'd field the ball and zip it to the first baseman.

It seemed there was always at least one play per game, when Mike would be confronted with one of these situations. With grace, he would field the ball and fire it over to first. All the first baseman had to do was catch it. It didn't matter how hard he threw the ball: I'm no sissy, and the ball always seemed to land in the middle of my glove. Unfortunately, due to the lack of flexibility of the pocket of my new glove or my lack of skill at first base, the ball would pop out of the glove and fall harmlessly to the ground.

Mike was upset at the end of these plays. He had performed his part of the play, so he had a right to be angry as the ball lay on the ground no more than three feet from me. I could see him growing angrier and angrier as the fair-skinned Irishman's face turned beet-red. I was about to be chastised by my fellow countryman of many generations back. One could imagine the verbal beating I'd absorb. Well, I deserved it. Whatever harshness dealt me that day, it was well earned; I had ruined the play.

As Mike was about to speak, he must have thought, darn, the guy only has one good arm and hand. Oh, the mellow Irishman was still angry, but he internalized it and walked away, kicking up dust over the infield. I could hear him grumbling as he walked away. It was best I didn't hear what he said, or a rumble might have ensued. The only bit of comfort I could throw his way was, "Sorry, Mike, I'll try to catch the next one," which might have been, for any man with less character than Mike, the last straw.

After five or six of these unfortunate incidents, I was determined not to disappoint Mike again. There's only so much a man can bear, even one far greater in patience and goodness than most men. Yes, my plan might work, I thought. It has worked for me in other sports, although the balls were bigger.

I was at first base again and Mike was playing short-stop. I hoped that a ball was not hit toward him or that it was an easy one-hopper that would result in Mike lobbing the ball to me at first. As fate would have it, Mike fielded a ball that had to be fired to first. The ball was coming at me with good velocity as I centered my body directly in front of it. Luckily, the ball was headed toward the area slightly below my sternum. Had I been five foot five instead of a foot taller, or had the ball come in hard a foot below my beltline, I might have had to reconsider my plan.

I let the ball hit my upper stomach with a half-hearted attempt to make my body a cushion. My new glove captured the softball against my body before it escaped. The ball almost spun away from my glove before I clamped it down securely. All the players on both teams heard the ball make a loud thud against my body and I was amazed at the loudness of the sound. "You're out," said the umpire before he started laughing uncontrollably. Based on the chuckling and outright roar of laughter from my teammates, my play amused the whole team. As for me, the play was successful, although never repeated.

It smarted a bit. The Rawlings' emblem was emblazoned slightly below my sternum for about two weeks afterward. Mike came to me after the game with a smile that only an Irishman may have, and said, "Try fielding the normal way, Tom! It's only a game. It's only a game!"

25

The Joy of the Challenge

This is only a game, I often mused, as I worked my way through life; it is only a game. Whenever I chose a different pathway to proceed, as we all do, I imagine the challenges and am eager to set forth on any new adventure. Sometimes I wanted to pass on them at the outset, and sometimes I've had no choice. Life is wonderful. Every time a change comes my way, I've greeted it as an enhancement of the journey. It's the small triumphs that few people notice that make me grateful and fill me with life.

I was chasing my brother, John, around the furnace and chimney when I felt a horrible pain on the left side of my head. I ran over to the full-size bed I shared with John and laid down. *A headache*, I thought, and called to John "I have a headache, John, and it hurts bad. Could you please go upstairs and get some aspirin from Maureen?"

John immediately headed upstairs. I've often wondered why he addressed my needs so quickly that day. He was the one being chased and could have thought that my call for help was a ruse to take him by surprise and capture him when he returned with the aspirin. The stroke was occurring. John knew from the look on my face that this was serious and that I needed help.

Our bed was broken, with his side of the mattress lying on the floor. I had to lie still, or I would roll and crash into the gray clothes cabinets. I attempted to laugh at my predicament just as John came downstairs with an order to go upstairs so that Maureen could look at me. I might have given John a grunt or two, but I had lost the ability to talk while he was gone. "Maureen, Tom is sick! He can't come up the stairs! He needs help!"

I don't know much of what happened for the next few days. I do know that upon Maureen's insistence, Uncle Dave rushed me to St. Mary's hospital. Maureen cried that night, especially when Monsignor gave me the sacrament of Extreme Unction.

During the following few days, I don't know how my other siblings reacted. I imagine they were scared, although I never asked. As for me, March 10, 1962, was a gold mine. I was released immediately from the St. Patrick prison about three months before summer vacation, and there would be no homework for me. For five weeks, I was served breakfast, lunch and dinner in bed and the "warden" (my mom) was better able to deal with me during my hospital stay. She got feisty when she saw me eating canned spinach one evening at the hospital.

"Why are you eating this spinach, Tommy?" she asked. "You always throw it under Larry's chair when I serve it to you."

I don't know whether I answered the question with my patented, "I don't know, Mom." But she wouldn't want me to leave anything on my plate at the hospital, would she?

Three or four days after I was transferred to Cardinal Glennon Hospital, I must have received at least two hundred get-well cards. I did not have the foggiest notion who these people were, but a considerable number of them enclosed money with the card. I cannot say I read all of the cards but, thinking about it, the thought was nice, and it increased my net worth by about $150.

I was getting tired of lying in my hospital bed, especially when nature called, and I was relegated to do my business on a bedpan. If I had any sense, I would have asked the nurse to raise the bed to put me in a seated position, which might have helped. But since nearly all of the nurses were young women, I did not feel comfortable asking them to assist me.

One night when nature called, I decided to take matters into my own hands and jump off the bed, scurry over to my private bathroom and do my business. I was able to kick the sheets and blankets away, a protracted and monumental achievement. I realized at this point that the process of dangling my legs over the floor and attempting to stand would not be easy.

I inched my way over to the railing on the left-hand side of my bed.

I realized how difficult it was with only one good side to make one's body behave. It took a while to work my way to the railing, which was at least a foot high. I had not the foggiest notion of how to lower it.

I turned onto the left side of my body and was able to free up my left arm and hand. Since I had arms approaching the length of the legendary Sasquatch and a weight of no more than sixty-five pounds, I was able to put my right leg over the railing. I worked the impaired leg on the rail a bit and somehow managed to throw my left leg over and land on my feet, with my left hand firmly grasping the side of the bed. I do not want you to think it was a total success and that I am a distant relative of Superman. I was temporarily hung up on the way to the floor on the sensitive area that only men can fully appreciate.

I held the rail for a while to get my sea legs and to apologize to the body parts I hurt on the trip to the floor. Slowly I inched along the bed toward the bathroom until I reached the point of no return. When I learned to walk at nine months, it did not take me long before I took those few steps into no-man's land from the couch or a chair. I was eager to take the steps before I fell. There was no safety net, so I experienced bigtime the marvels of gravity. Here I was at nine years instead of nine months, learning how to walk again with one good leg and one helper leg. I did not know whether the right leg would be of much use. It was to time to decide.

I held out my left arm and hand, like a tight-wire artist to help maintain my balance and tried to do likewise with my right arm and hand. It was about five steps until I reached the wall on the other side of the room. I did not fall on the seat of my pants on the way to the wall, but I did lose my balance. Fortunately, my forehead crashed against the wall, which saved me from falling. I shook my head a little to remove the cobwebs and walked the remaining steps using the wall to the bathroom as an aid and…did my business in my personal restroom!

Instead of returning to my bed, I decided to go into the hall to investigate the remainder of the fifth floor of Cardinal Glennon. Walking was easier traversing the hall outside my room. I had to take only one or two steps when I came to an open doorway, rather than the eight or ten feet from my bed to the wall. I almost gave my dad a heart attack when he saw me walking along the walls outside my room. Luckily, he was talking to the neurologist about my prognosis when he spied me. The doctor calmed him, and they brought a wheelchair, asking if I wanted a tour of the place.

A stroke must be serious, I thought. They occur mostly to old folks and have a high mortality rate. My primary neurologist told my father, when asked direct, that I had a better than average chance of passing away than living for those first two weeks. I imagine this blunt point did not make my father feel rosy. Each day that passed gave me a better chance of living. I was in the hospital for five weeks.

"I don't know whether he'll be able to talk or walk, Bill, but he'll be able to think," said the neurologist. "The good point is that he's nine years old. Youngsters can recapture many of the things older people can't, or at least work around them," he said.

When I returned home, the house was all decorated for me. It made me feel special for a day, and then events reverted to the same old 783 Alhambra Court, where I was mean to my younger brothers and sisters. I did not like the fact that I was relegated to my sister's room. Now that I'm sixty-nine, I can see my parents' point. They did not want me tumbling down the basement stairs nightly, nor lose track of me a whole floor away. After all, no one knew what had caused the stroke. If I had my druthers, I would have camped in our backyard in mild weather, or in my dad's junky car all night in the winter, rather than sleep in the same room as my sisters.

It was around the middle of April when I was released from the hospital. I was not looking forward to the next six weeks of school. On the next school day, I was pleasantly surprised not to be awakened by my mom at 7:00 a.m. and told to get out of bed and ready for school. Maybe she forgot that she had another child to look after or had decided to give me a break. Neither of these two reasons seemed to make sense. My mom was brilliant. Certainly, she did not forget that I was home. Whatever the reason, I was not about to muddy the waters by asking why. I'm no dummy.

Three or four few weeks later, I asked my younger brothers why mom wasn't making me go to school. They had no idea either, but said I'd better quit asking stupid questions like that or I'd be waking up and going to school with them.

"Mr. and Mrs. O'Connell," the specialists had said, "we don't know why the stroke occurred to Tommy. It is extremely rare at his age. Do not put any pressure on the boy. Watch him closely. Our diagnosis is that he had a congenitally weak blood vessel in his head that clotted, but we do not know for sure. Expect depression. The boy has lost use of one side of his body. Be sensitive and let him know you'll always be here for him. Imagine how scared any parent would be. What if it happened again? I don't recall how long it took for me to stabilize enough to walk without stumbling. Can't say I was skipping or even had walking down pat in those early days.

My parents were hesitant to send me to St. Patrick where I would have to navigate the stairs with no supervision. What if I collided with a classmate during recess? Being a nine-year-old boy and a knucklehead was not exclusive to me. So were the other boys in my room. To add even more pressure and frustration, I'd have to learn to write with my left hand. This was why my parents as well as the school did not put Tommy O'Connell back in the mix with his third-grade classmates.

After four or five weeks of freedom, I was bored. All the kids were at school. Mom took me to physical therapy three days a week at Park Public Grade School near St. Teresa Academy, equipped with facilities for special-needs children. At times, I could talk her into stopping at Jimmy's Malt Shop for an ice cream cone or a malted. But usually, I made my mom angry during the day, which totally nixed the idea of any reward.

Ms. Hanes was my physical therapist. Ms. Hanes's first goal was to render me independent in the shoe-tying department. I hate to admit that I was becoming lazier and lazier about the necessities of life, and if my mom wanted to tie my shoes daily, then more power to her. Unfortunately, Velcro-type shoes had not yet been invented. Oh, I was going to walk and run by golly, come hell or high water. I wanted desperately to play with my siblings and the guys at school, but this shoe-tying thing was for the birds.

Ms. Hanes had two adept hands. I do not know whether she went to college, but I doubt that the fine art of tying one's shoes with a hand at 3 percent usage was in the curriculum.

She brought a boy to me to demonstrate how easy it is to tie one's shoes. The boy was about a year older than me. He had two able hands, so unless he was a magician or a good teacher, he was going to be worthless to me. He started by tying a conventional half-knot. The key process to learning how to tie a bowknot was in the offing, so I zeroed in on his hands. The boy performed a quite skillful additional half-knot and looked toward Ms. Hanes for her approval.

What, I thought, as I looked down at the knot he had made. I wanted to say, "Get out of here!" But before I could say a thing, Ms. Hanes thanked the boy for his kindness. As he was whisked away to his class, Ms. Hanes said with a beet-red face, "I'm sorry, Tommy. I thought a boy around your age would make you feel more comfortable."

"That's okay, Ms. Hanes. I'll figure it out by myself," I said. I wonder if my mom suggested to her that it would be nice if an expert had shown me the intricacies of the modified shoe-tying procedures for a person who had little use of one hand. If Mom had laid down the law and told me I would need to tie my shoes, that would have made things easier. Mom had been put through the wringer for the past eight or nine weeks. I was her son and although she did not fall apart like my father, she was deeply worried about my future.

As for as shoe-tying, it did not require much modification. I start with the left shoelace, wrap it around my right index finger two or three times and grip it tightly with the rest of the hand. I make the first half-knot using my left hand and pull it tight using both hands. I make the first loop with my left thumb and index finger, making sure I keep the laces taut with both hands. Then I start looping the left shoelace around the first loop with my right hand. About three quarters of the way around, I snag the shoelace in my right hand with my left middle finger and pull it taut with the first loop. I wrestle with the left lace for a while, trying to release the lace from my right hand. After some battle, the lace is released for the next step. I carefully bring the index finger of my right hand to the first loop, guiding the right index finger into the loop, sometimes having to use the last two fingers of my left hand to help. The left lace is now free and is poked by the middle finger through the second loop around the initial loop. The poked-through lace is now a proper loop that I grasp with my left hand. By moving both my hands in opposite directions, I pull the loops tight.

My modified shoe-tying is actually a straightforward process, although you might have to read the last paragraph a couple of times to grasp its simplicity. I admit it takes me a little more time than others to complete the process, and that I'm often not successful on the first go round. It's no trouble, though. If I'm playing basketball, I might miss a couple of plays if my shoelace comes untied, but no matter. If I magically recovered all the use of the right side of my body, I might be in trouble, as I've been tying my shoes this way for so long. I might need remedial classes in shoe-tying with two capable hands.

To regain usage, Ms. Hanes urged me to stretch out the fingers of my right hand, using the left. I must admit I did not stretch out the fingers as much as Ms. Hanes or any other reasonably thinking person would have done in my position. After hundreds of attempts yielding no results, I chucked the idea. If my right fingers were obstinate and returned to the same position, I was not going to waste my time prying them open again. I had another set on the left side. Sometimes I still pry my right fingers open, but my fingers always revert to something resembling a kangaroo's right paw.

Ms. Hanes used a machine that stimulated my right hand and fingers with electricity. The electricity was initiated in my left hand and exited through my right fingers. It escapes my mind as to how said electricity was safely introduced and processed without the possibility of electrocution. The machine had ten levels, each one introducing a higher voltage. Ms. Hanes used level three or four—nothing higher. *Surely if she turned it to level five, I would not be electrocuted. It'd give me a little zing of electricity, but surely nothing more*, I pondered.

My right hand sat on a pad covered with wire bristles and beaucoup amounts of saltwater. The electricity was given in pulses every five or six seconds. I heard a low hum when the light jolt was introduced into my body, and exited my right side, as my four fingers and thumb opened wide for as long as the current was exiting. My right fingers would snap back to resume their normal bent-over shape until the next pulse of electricity hit and they opened again. Fascinating! I did not have to tell the fingers to expand as

I did for the left side of my body. The electricity was in charge, buddy, not me.

Her jolt machine was Ms. Hanes's pride and joy. She looked at me for a response the first six or eight times I was connected. What did she expect me to say? Maybe if she knew what I was thinking, she would take her purse and smack me about the face to knock out my thoughts. We worked with that machine for all of my fourth-grade year, without my brain catching on. I was amazed each time I saw it in action. But I was not sad that my right fingers wouldn't work on their own. I was alive, living the good life and getting dismissed twenty-five minutes early from school for physical therapy.

I cooked up an idea and waited for the optimum time to execute it. Ms. Hanes was always present when the machine was operating. Did my mom give Ms. Hanes a heads-up that I could be sneaky? That she should always be aware? It was after Valentine's Day when the opportunity presented itself.

I was connected to the machine when Ms. Hanes received a call needing her immediate attention. "Tom," she said, "stay on the machine. I have to leave the room for a few minutes. I'll be back in plenty of time to take you off."

"Sure, Ms. Hanes," I said, "I like to watch my hand open up."

Ms. Hanes smiled as she left the room. I knew my comment would please her, as she likes the way her machine operates much more than I do. I waited a few minutes in case she was trying to pull a fast one by bursting back into the room. It was time.

I looked at the dial. *Let us be smart about this*, I thought. Set the dial to five instead of four. Four always zinged me slightly more than three. Certainly, five would not impart that much more of a zap than four, would it?

I set the dial to a five and eagerly awaited the first surge. As the pulses came and went, they were disappointing. I could barely discern a difference. While five did cause my right fingers and thumb to open again, there was no perceivable change. Is this thing broken? Or should I raise the level?

To truly know whether I alone was the master of this machine, I'd need another iteration. Should I bump it up slightly to six or should I push it to seven? I pondered. I cannot explain the thought process of my ten-year-old self in ascertaining the proper amount of electricity to be introduced into his body that day. Suffice it to say my left hand was near enough to the dial to switch it from a level seven to a level four, if the electricity generated from higher levels peaked at a geometric rate akin to the Richter Scale.

As the first pulse of level seven hit, I was delighted at the change of electricity flowing through my body. The change from a mere two levels was pronounced, although there was no pain. My right hand and fingers danced around the pad as long as the electricity exited my body. I don't recall how many pulses I enjoyed that day. My left hand moved away from the dial for a while as my fascination grew. I switched it to the normal level and watched as my fingers and thumb opened and closed. They did not dance as they had before, which saddened me a little.

I wish I could tell you the experiment was finished for the day. Unfortunately, that was not the case. The temptation was too great, and I had ample time before Ms. Hanes would return. It took courage, or maybe stupidity would be the better word, for me to test the machine's top measure of power. As I turned the level to ten, a last thought came into my mind for a brief second and was then dismissed: "Are you nuts, Tom?"

As I eagerly awaited the surge, I neglected to keep my left hand close to the level changer as I did when I had moved it up to seven. The pulse of electricity was vicious as it surged throughout my body. Its exit from my right side was decidedly unpleasant. Instead of watching my fingers waltz with no pain, they were rudely slammed onto the pad with a harsh sound, while the jolting pain in my five little guys was certainly undeserved. Shocked in many ways, I was trying to recover from the initial pulse of the level ten, when, because I did not return the dial to the safe number four, I was given a second dose of number ten. I am not stupid, although you readers might be pondering that very question. I quickly turned the dial so I wouldn't have to endure another number ten. Yep, that was the Richter scale if I ever experienced one! I might have gotten away with it, but when Ms. Hanes returned, she had a queer look on her face. Maybe my hair was standing on end, as when you grab a static-electricity generator at a science museum.

I don't remember how long it took me to become proficient at walking. Because I was nine years old when the stroke occurred, my age gave me a distinct advantage over someone older. I can't describe the modified methods in my gait; I learned them through trial and error as time passed. My parents forbade me to run, for fear I'd fall. That was like asking a bird to not fly. Mom screamed at me the first few dozen times I needed her services to patch my head after a fall. Gradually, my balance improved. Still, I drug my right foot a bit.

Scores of times I'd head into the alley and walk to Wheeler's, a confectionary on Summit Avenue between Vogel Place and Alhambra Court. On rare occasions when I had three or four cents in my pocket, I would stop for candy as I passed. I'd walk a few steps toward my street from Wheeler's and then break into a run as fast as I could. There was a nice-sized tree with big roots in the Hannigan's yard at the bend of Summit and Alhambra. As I made the bend onto our street, I purposely ran over those roots, trying to lift my right foot a little so I wouldn't catch it and fall.

At first, it was a rare event when I met my objective. Usually, I tripped on my right foot and often fell hard on my right side where I didn't have the ability to catch myself as I did on my left. Usually, I hit the right side of my head, and if bad enough, I'd go in and have my mom mend it. The times when I went in to have it fixed were rare; I did not want to be stuck in the house all day for disobeying my parents. One day, I remember counting thirty scabs on my head, but I was going to lift my leg a little to complete that bend on our street, by golly. No one, and I mean no one, was going to stop me!

When I was successful, it was meaningful to me, but I was not yet satisfied. I wanted to complete the bend every time, so I would know I was successfully lifting my right leg.

Words cannot express the joy and true ecstasy I felt as the wind blew through my hair again. It is only running, one might say—the art, like speaking—that all of us cannot remember mastering. But when it is completely taken away and you regain a small portion of it, how could you ever forget it? I am so grateful to God that He has let me attain the feeling of freedom again. Yes, I know I put in the necessary work to attain the ability to run, but I also remember the neurologist said I might never walk again.

I never stopped to think about losing the side, nor that people might think I'd had a bad break. It simply didn't matter.

As I sharpened my walking abilities and began to figure how to run and attempt to shoot a basketball solely with my left hand, my father must have often witnessed me cherishing the challenge. It appeared to him that I was happy and content with the way the world was treating me. He was proud of me because of my recovery from the blow he thought I had taken with the loss of a side. A number of months after the stroke, he told me, "I'm proud of the way you roll with the punches, Tom. I love you, son. You became a man at nine years old, when you accepted the stroke and didn't let the loss of a side keep you down."

I love my dad. But I had no idea which punches I had to roll with and why he was so proud of me. We're mandated to accept whatever happens to us in life, aren't we?

There's never been an instant when I've felt shortchanged. My life has been full. God has been so good to me. He gave me two stupendous parents who sacrificed their wants for their children. It was through my parents' love and teaching that each of their children has made a positive impact on the world. He has given me ten people I can count on when the chips are down, and I need help. It was He who showed me the true goodness of people. It was He who gave me enough intelligence to succeed, although at times I didn't seem to want it. It was He who gave me the never-look-back attitude so that I always look toward tomorrow and the possibilities the future holds.

Despite the hundreds of times I have hurt Him, He loves me with a love that is infinite, a love I cannot comprehend. He has always been there ready to help when I ask. I do not know which Rubicon crossing will be my last. Whatever the days ahead hold on my last road, there will surely be one who walks with me…who takes my hand and quells all fear, saying, "Come to me, my child. I will always protect you." Life is precious and worth pursuing down to the last measure. Seize the day!

ABOUT THE
AUTHOR

Tom O'Connell grew up in East Saint Louis, Illinois, in a family of eleven children. He was raised by parents who sacrificed their needs and wants for their children. He was never lonely. The author attended Southern Illinois University–Edwardsville and worked in various capacities as an accountant for thirty-seven years. He is married and has two children. The author and his wife currently live in the Northern Kentucky area.

CPSIA information can be obtained
at www.ICGtesting.com
Printed in the USA
BVHW042137100723
667055BV00003B/34